Health Care Systems in Liberal Democracies

Health Care Systems in Liberal Democracies looks at the way in which health care is organised and delivered in six countries: Australia, Italy, the Netherlands, Sweden, the United Kingdom and the United States. It examines the continuing quest for solutions to some of the seemingly intractable problems on the health care agenda.

The organisation of health care in each country is analysed within a common framework, the components of which are:

- the context of health care, including the demographic structure, epidemiological trends, cultural traditions and the governmental and political setting;
- the development of state involvement;
- the principal features of service delivery and administration;
- financing arrangements;
- contemporary issues in health policy.

Underlying the framework is the premise that there are similarities between the countries with respect to the challenges associated with providing health care in the developed world, as well as differences in the nature of response.

This book will be invaluable to students of social and public policy and to those involved as practitioners in health care provision. It is increasingly important for both groups to be able to draw on knowledge of other health care systems in order to inform an analysis of their own system.

Ann Wall is Senior Lecturer in Social Administration and Health Policy at Sheffield Hallam University, UK.

Health Care Systems in Liberal Democracies

Edited by Ann Wall

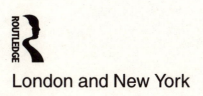

London and New York

First published 1996
by Routledge
11 New Fetter Lane, London EC4P 4EE

Simultaneously published in the USA and Canada
by Routledge
29 West 35th Street, New York, NY 10001

Routledge is an International Thomson Publishing company

Typeset in 10/12pt Monophoto Bembo by
Datix International Limited, Bungay, Suffolk
Printed by TJ Press (Padstow) Ltd, Padstow, Cornwall

British Library Cataloguing in Publication Data
A catalogue record for this book is available from the British Library

Library of Congress Cataloguing in Publication Data
Health care systems in liberal democracies / edited Ann Wall.
        p.   cm.
    Includes bibliographical references and index.
    1. Medical policy–Europe.   2. Medical policy–United States.
    I. Wall, Ann (Ann L.)
    RA394.H416   1996
    362.1–dc20   96–11329

ISBN 0–415–11806–9 (hbk)
ISBN 0–415–11807–7 (pbk)

Contents

List of figures   viii
List of tables   ix
List of contributors   xi
Preface   xii

1 Introduction   1
Ann Wall
The context of health care systems   2
The development of state involvement   7
The principal features of service delivery and administration   7
Financing arrangements   9
Contemporary issues in health policy   10
References and further reading   11

2 Australia   12
Ann Wall
The context of Australian health care   12
The development of state involvement   24
The principal features of service delivery and administration   27
Financing arrangements   38
Contemporary issues in health policy   43
Conclusion   45
References and further reading   46

3 Italy   47
Ralph Spence
The context of Italian health care   49
The development of state involvement   59
The principal features of service delivery and administration   64

Financing arrangements 69
Contemporary issues in health policy 71
References and further reading 74

4 The Netherlands 76
Roger Ottewill
The context of Dutch health care 77
The development of state involvement 82
The principal features of service delivery and administration 88
Financing arrangements 95
Contemporary issues in health policy 99
Conclusion 102
References and further reading 103

5 Sweden 104
Bernard Jones
The context of Swedish health care 105
The development of state involvement 109
The principal features of service delivery and administration 112
Financing arrangements 118
Contemporary issues in health policy 122
Conclusion 126
References and further reading 126

6 The United Kingdom 127
John Kingdom
The context of British health care 127
The development of state involvement 137
The principal features of service delivery and administration 144
Financing arrangements 151
Contemporary issues in health policy 154
References and further reading 161

7 The United States of America 163
Jim Chandler
The context of American health care 163
The development of state involvement 169
The principal features of service delivery and administration 172
Financing arrangements 177
Contemporary issues in health policy 179
References and further reading 182

8 Conclusion   183
  Ann Wall
  Socio-demographic context   185
  The necessity for state involvement in health care   186
  Escalating costs and limited sources of funding   187
  Cost containment   189
  Reassessing traditional approaches to service provision   194
  Values and health care systems   195
  References and further reading   199

  Index   200

Figures

1.1 The circular process of health care · 9
2.1 The structure of Australian government 19
2.2 Hospital patient status 30
2.3 Structure of the DHHCS 36
3.1 Age structure of population, 1989 50
3.2 Major causes of death, 1989 51
3.3 The organisation of health care 68
3.4 Health expenditure by category 69
3.5 Public/private mix in health care, 1984–94 73
5.1 The organisation of health and medical care services in Sweden: regional, county and local levels 113
5.2 The organisation of health and medical care services in Sweden: national level 117
5.3 Sources of health care funding 119
5.4 Health care expenditure, 1989 121

Tables

2.1 Selected measures of health status, 1960–90   15
2.2 Incidence of chronic conditions   16
2.3 Share of national resources devoted to health care, 1970–90   24
2.4 Organisation structures: state level   34
2.5 Funding arrangements   39
3.1 Population growth in the major cities, 1951–81   54
3.2 Death rates in Italy, 1981   55
4.1 Selected measures of health status, 1900–90   78
4.2 Share of national resources devoted to health care, 1960–90   82
4.3 Health care developments, 1983–88: selected statistics   88
4.4 The size of the health care labour force: selected professions   92
4.5 Interest groups within the Dutch health policy community   94
4.6 Funding arrangements   95
5.1 Beds in medical institutions, 1989   114
5.2 Average hospital stay, 1990   114
5.3 Categories of clinical personnel, 1990   114
5.4 Education and training periods for doctors   115
5.5 Distribution of health and medical care costs, 1989   121
6.1 Population size, 1951–2031   128
6.2 Elderly population, 1901–2021   128
6.3 Birth rate, 1901–90   129
6.4 Dependency ratio, 1951–2013   129
6.5 NHS spending, 1981–92   152
7.1 Percentage of GDP devoted to health care, 1960–91   169
8.1 Models of health care systems   183
8.2 Public expenditure as a percentage of total health expenditure, 1960–85   188

8.3 Expenditure on health care as a proportion of GDP, 1960–92   188
8.4 Public expenditure as a percentage of total health expenditure,
     1985 and 1995   190
8.5 Per capita health spending (public and private combined)   196

Contributors

Jim Chandler is senior lecturer and research leader in Political Science and Public Administration at Sheffield Hallam University.

Bernard Jones is principal lecturer in Public Administration and Public Sector Management at Sheffield Hallam University.

John Kingdom is reader in Political Science and Public Administration at Sheffield Hallam University.

Roger Ottewill is principal lecturer in Public Administration and Health Care Management at Sheffield Hallam University.

Ralph Spence is principal lecturer in International Business and Italian Area Studies at Sheffield Hallam University.

Ann Wall is senior lecturer in Social Administration and Health Policy at Sheffield Hallam University.

Preface

Comparative literature on health and health care has proliferated in recent years. This reflects both the sustained level of interest in health as an area of study and the continuing quest for solutions to seemingly intractable problems as those responsible for health care systems struggle to respond to the challenges associated with providing health care in the modern world.

Much of the material, however, is inaccessible to British students at sub-degree and undergraduate level not only in terms of its sheer quantity but also because of its analytical sophistication, which relies upon a good deal of basic knowledge about the systems involved. Many students are, therefore, restricted to a consideration of the British NHS and may well reach final year undergraduate level with little or no knowledge of other health care systems or even an awareness that the British NHS is but one example of a government's response to the health needs of a modern society.

As teachers of politics, public administration and health care management, we have become increasingly conscious of the need to ensure that students have a wider perspective and are able to draw upon knowledge of other health care systems in order to inform the analysis of their own. To this end, our intention is to present a concise and accessible examination of health care systems in six liberal democracies: Australia, Italy, the Netherlands, Sweden, the United Kingdom and the United States of America. These have been selected largely on the basis of the personal interests of the contributors.

Quite deliberately, our objectives are modest. We do not seek to apply a comparative methodology in the strict sense of presenting and testing general hypotheses. Instead, we have attempted to identify a number of salient features of health care systems and their contexts which, together, constitute a framework for analysis. Students will be offered the opportunity to acquire some rudimentary comparative skills and, more importantly, to gain insight into the ways in which other developed nations have tackled the task of promoting and maintaining the health of their people.

Chapter 1

Introduction

Ann Wall

Current interest in the health care systems of other countries has been stimulated in part by the increasing recognition that the problems they face have much in common. At the risk of over-simplifying a complex picture, these can be said to relate to three factors. First, the costs of health care have risen continuously as demand has been swelled by demographic trends, epidemiological changes, technological development, and higher public expectations. Second, broad economic and political trends have served to restrict the supply of resources which governments and individuals have felt able and willing to make available. Third, health care services have apparently failed to produce a real, overall improvement in the health status of populations. There is no more than a tenuous relationship between formal health services and the health status of the population, which is affected as much by individual and collective economic well-being, diet, housing and occupation as by access to the services of professional healers. In other words, there is a fundamental incompatibility between the supply of resources for modern health care and the demands made on them, and ambiguity surrounding the contribution of health services to social well-being.

It is this situation which has led policy-makers to search for new forms and sources of funding; to impose a variety of formal and informal rationing devices; and to engage in the policy shifts and structural changes which have characterised health care systems throughout the western world. Because these problems are common to a number of countries with reasonably well developed health care systems, comparison is tempting. Indeed, examining the experiences of other countries can enhance understanding and render evaluation more sound. Moreover, because health is one of the more self-contained aspects of welfare systems, it is relatively easy to construct a framework within which similarities and differences can be noted and discussed.

It is the intention in this book to do this. However, it is not proposed to use the framework as a means of drawing generalised conclusions of a comparative nature. Its purpose is the more modest one of providing the contributors with a common basis for undertaking descriptive analyses of the health care systems in Australia, Italy, the Netherlands, Sweden, the UK and the USA.

The approach adopted is premised on the belief that sound comparison must be preceded by systematic description, and in the chapters which follow a common set of headings is adopted for examining health care in each country. These are:

- the context of the health care system;
- the development of state involvement in health care;
- the principal features of service delivery and administration;
- financing arrangements; and
- contemporary issues in health policy.

It is felt that these are sufficiently robust to facilitate comparison and flexible enough to accommodate different national approaches to health care.

THE CONTEXT OF HEALTH CARE SYSTEMS

In seeking to understand the pattern of provision for the promotion and maintenance of health, it is important to take account of the socio-political context in which policies are made and services delivered. There is a dynamic and two-way relationship between health services and their wider context. Services are both shaped by their context and, in turn, help to determine the character of that context. The key components of the context of health care are: the demographic structure; epidemiological trends; cultural traditions; social factors; the governmental and political setting; and economic performance.

The demographic structure

The size, geographical distribution and the composition of the population in terms of age and gender affect the level and nature of demand for health services and the ability of service providers to respond effectively to that demand.

An important concept in this context is that of the 'dependency ratio', which is a measure of the relationship between the dependent groups, in particular the elderly and children, and the population of working age. A distinction is often made between the total dependency ratio (i.e. the number of persons under 15 years of age together with those over 64 years as a percentage of those aged 15 to 64 years), and the aged dependency ratio (i.e. those over the age of 64 years as a percentage of those aged 15 to 64 years).

Clearly any changes in this ratio will have implications for health care. For example, on the basis of demographic projections, most countries will face substantial ageing of their populations over the next few decades, with the result that health care systems will have to cope with growing demand for long term care. At the same time, where the number of young people is declining, issues concerning the staffing of services have to be resolved.

The geographic distribution of the population is another salient factor and one in which nations differ. For example, policy-makers and service providers in countries with large urban conurbations face different challenges from those confronting their colleagues in countries which are more rural.

Epidemiological trends

At the heart of this aspect of the context of health care is the so-called 'epidemiological transition'. This term refers to the move from a situation in which the major concern was infectious diseases associated with death in childhood (e.g. smallpox, diphtheria) and young adulthood (e.g. tuberculosis, complications of childbirth), to a very different one. The predominant health issues today include:

- chronic and degenerative conditions (e.g. arthritis, Alzheimer's disease), which are not life threatening;
- improved survival rates for those suffering heart attacks and strokes, both of which are principally associated with old age;
- new concerns surrounding AIDS, drug and alcohol abuse, child abuse, psychiatric disorders, and accidents;
- new environmental dangers; and
- a renaissance of interest in the relationship between the physical environment and health status.

A distinguishing feature of these is their stubborn resistance to conventional clinical intervention. The logic of current epidemiological imperatives appears to lead to a more preventive, educative approach to health care.

Cultural traditions

The size, structure and distribution of the population and the pattern of disease it displays have a self-evident relevance for health care. Culture, though less obviously related, is an important aspect of the context, and one which is all too easily overlooked.

Culture can be defined as deep-rooted, shared and fairly permanent ways of thinking and behaving, many of which come to embody a moral judgement and to reflect common values. Culture is learned in the home and school and reinforced by the media and commercial interests.

One of the most obvious ways in which culture affects health is through the medium of lifestyle. It is now known that lifestyle has a major impact on health. However, decisions relating to lifestyle are taken in the light of competing social, physical and emotional needs, and represent a synthesis of the attitudes, beliefs and values that hold sway in a community. There is no guarantee that the healthy choice will be given priority. Thus, behaviours harmful to health are deceptively difficult to change because they are deeply embedded in notions of social acceptability and may be reinforced by powerful commercial and political interests.

Culture also affects the way in which people respond to illness. Beliefs concerning the nature of health and illness; what can be expected in the way of treatment; what can be hoped for in the way of outcome; and the facility with which people can communicate with professionals and negotiate the system, all influence the individual response to an episode of illness. Class, gender and ethnic differences are likely to be evident in these areas.

Just as culture affects individual behaviour, so also it underpins the joint actions of those responsible for formulating and implementing health policies. In other words, the values which a nation shares will be reflected in its health care system. Western-style democracies tend, to a greater or lesser extent, to be professionalised and technocratised, so their health care systems are founded on a broadly biomedical model. With respect to the stance taken on other values, however, there is greater diversity. A society that holds its collective obligations in high regard is likely to have a health care system characterised by significant state intervention; a small private sector; a preference for tax rather than insurance funding; comprehensive coverage; and universal entitlement based on the notion of rights. By contrast, a society steeped in individualism will rely heavily on private enterprise and insurance funding; be selective in its coverage, and respond to consumer demand. Similarly, where equality is a valued goal, there will be explicit attempts to avoid discrimination and to facilitate participation, an approach conspicuous by its absence in other systems.

In some respects, developed nations share a common culture, though this should not be allowed to mask important cultural differences and the particularistic way in which nations respond to the same pressures.

Social factors

An equally important aspect of the context is the social structure. This refers to the way in which the population is organised and the individuals within it relate to one another. Patterns of employment, household composition and gender roles have an impact on health, particularly mental health, and also on the availability and willingness of people to undertake informal caring.

Social divisions along the lines of class, gender, race or religion affect both access to care and health status and may also be reflected in the way services are organised. If health care is to be effective, therefore, those responsible have to find ways of ensuring that services are accessible and acceptable to all citizens. This involves removing barriers, whether physical or psychological, and taking positive steps to ensure that services are meeting need in a sensitive and appropriate manner.

The governmental and political setting

It is a truism that the political setting is of central importance with regard to health care. The structure of government, the manner in which political decisions are made and the values that underpin those decisions, form the backcloth against which all policies relating to health are determined and implemented.

At the most general level these factors play a part in determining the degree of state involvement in the direct provision of health services. In this regard there is considerable variation between the countries studied, with the government in the USA having a minimum role, whilst in the UK, traditionally at least, the government has played a very large part.

More specifically, in seeking to understand the interplay of the health care system with its governmental and political setting, a number of factors emerge as significant. These include the party system; the way in which responsibility is divided between the centre and the localities; traditions with respect to accountability and citizen participation; the power of professional groups; and the methods by which professional advice is fed into the policy-making process. In all of these spheres there is scope for conflict.

Political parties may have profoundly different views regarding health care; the localities may vie with the centre for dominance; there is likely to be debate concerning the proper balance between democratic and managerial control; and the professions may demand (and even command) more power within the system than others are comfortable with. The chief battlegrounds will change over time and will vary between countries. Nevertheless, any one health care system will represent the temporary and, perhaps uncomfortable, resolution of these and other conflicts.

Economic performance

At one level the link between the health care system and its economic environment is self-evident: a flourishing economy means more resources for health services, and a good standard of health care will contribute to the nation's economic well-being. The reverse is also the case. A shrinking economy means fewer resources, and historical evidence suggests that a poor general standard of health has adverse consequences for economic growth.

At the same time, there is a relationship between economic performance and health status. It is now recognised that poverty, unemployment and the anxieties generated by economic insecurity contribute to ill health; and practical factors such as transport, time off work, and charges for health services all affect access. The sword is double-edged. As the resources available for health care (at both a societal and an individual level) contract, the demands made on them expand.

There is, however, a further point. Although poverty has a detrimental effect on health, continued improvements in economic well-being, beyond a certain point, do not yield commensurate improvements in health status. Once a society reaches a certain level of affluence, further rises in absolute income do not have much impact on health: what matters is the distribution of the income throughout society. The smaller the gap between the richest and poorest, the higher the overall standard of health. Moreover, as income differentials within a nation change, so does its health. 'Social justice is a crucial determinant of health standards throughout society' (R. Wilkinson, *Guardian*, 12 June 1991).

Wilkinson argues that income distribution may account for as much as three-quarters of the difference in life expectancy between developed countries. He is left to speculate as to why this should be. Perhaps income inequality actually damages the fabric of society and, because health is the outcome of a broad range of social, psychological and environmental, as well as physical, factors, this, in turn, damages health.

It should be clear that the interaction of the health care system and its context is both complex and subtle. The environment exerts a number of ambiguous and conflicting pressures on the system. The result is a constantly changing picture in which health services are subject to ongoing adjustment and modification in the attempt to achieve some kind of fit with the context. It is the way in which different countries respond to broadly similar environmental pressures and generate health care systems which reflect a particular pattern of adjustment which is of central concern here.

THE DEVELOPMENT OF STATE INVOLVEMENT

Although the chief purpose in this book is to set an agenda for horizontal comparison, that is, between countries, some reference to vertical comparison, that is, over time, is necessary. No system can be understood in isolation from its past: the present reflects past problems, conflicts and dilemmas and their resolution.

As with their context, the development of health care systems is also characterised by a mixture of shared and individual experiences, which helps to explain many of the similarities and differences between systems. Authors were asked to consider key developmental events as part of the process of explaining the present structures. Clearly, all health care systems are affected by wars and other conflicts; by urbanisation and industrialisation; by patterns of economic success and failure; by international initiatives such as the WHO's strategy of 'Health for All by the Year 2000'; by the growth of medical science and the medical profession; and by challenges to the hegemony of the biomedical model of health and illness. Moreover, for each nation, the timing of events is important in determining the unique pattern of legacies which every nation carries with it.

THE PRINCIPAL FEATURES OF SERVICE DELIVERY AND ADMINISTRATION

With respect to the analysis of the wide variety of related but distinct functions which constitute health care two principles are applied. First, since the focus is on the delivery and administration of services, in other words the 'sharp end' of health care, the starting point for the analysis of the structure is the lower rather than the higher levels of the health care system. Countries differ in their organisational structures, but in most cases it is possible to identify local, regional and national levels. Authors were asked to begin with an examination of the health encounter at the local level, and to address issues relating to providers and users; access and acceptability; professionals and managers; and staffing. It was anticipated that questions associated with planning and resource allocation would be more in evidence at the regional and national levels. In addition, at the national level, the policy agenda generates a number of themes worthy of discussion. These include:

- the degree of state involvement in health care and the proper role for the private sector;
- issues of eligibility and coverage;
- the impact on health policy of the party system;
- policy-making mechanisms and the methods by which professional advice is fed into the policy-making process;
- structural issues including the way in which responsibility is divided between the centre and the localities; and
- accountability and citizen participation.

Second, the activities subsumed under the heading of health care are conceived as a process rather than as a number of separate and discrete services. This process is illustrated in Figure 1.1.

Not all patients pass through every stage of this process. Nor is there necessarily an organisational link between one type of health care activity and the next. However, the figure does serve to illustrate the logical relationship between the stages and the continuous nature of health care. It also allows for the inclusion of health care measures directed at the population at large (public health) which might otherwise be overlooked. Furthermore, it offers a way of classifying services for the purpose of comparison.

There was no requirement that the approach be followed slavishly or that its use should preclude the use of other classification schemata. Another common way of categorising health care activities, for example, is in terms of different levels: primary, secondary and tertiary. There is no reason why a number of approaches cannot be used in order to produce a picture of the health care system's structure and administrative arrangements, the range of its functions and the balance between them.

What becomes clear from the investigation into the principal features of service delivery and administration is that these matters are not morally neutral. Decisions taken, conflicts resolved and compromises reached all reflect a value stance, a shared set of beliefs about what provisions should be made by a community for the promotion and maintenance of the health of its members.

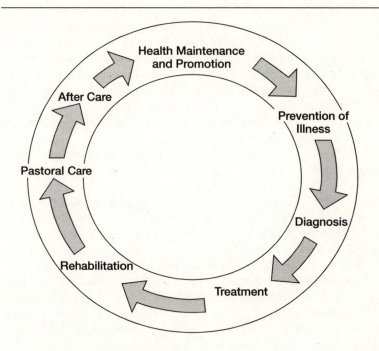

Figure 1.1 The circular process of health care
Source: Ottewill and Wall (1990)

FINANCING ARRANGEMENTS

Similarly, with respect to financing arrangements, decisions regarding how to raise the money for health care and how much to spend are value judgements not technical decisions.

> They reflect explicit policy decisions about the social as well as the medical objectives of the service, and they embody political aspirations about equality of access to health and medical care irrespective of people's ability to pay the economic cost of the service.
>
> (Butler and Vaile 1984: 65)

At a more practical level, policy-makers involved in making these de-cisions are constrained in two important ways. First, the total amount of money absorbed by health care services is substantial and growing. Moreover, there is an inherent incompatibility between those responsible for raising the money and those responsible for spending it, with the former group concerned to restrict spending, and the latter seeking to maintain or even increase it. This has given rise to attempts to control costs, restrict demand, seek alternative sources of finance, and make rationing decisions more explicit. There has also been a tendency to bring closer together those responsible for generating and allocating resources for health care and those who, in the exercise of their professional responsibilities, spend such resources. In this context the notion of 'purchasers' and 'providers' has become common.

Second, there is a limited number of ways in which the money can be raised. Broadly, these include some form of taxation or some form of insurance which may or may not be compulsory. Both have their merits and drawbacks. Taxation, for example, tends to be a highly sensitive issue for politicians and, in effect, to place health care in competition with other demands on the public purse. However, it affords governments considerable scope for raising money and allows for a progressive system of funding should this be considered desirable.

Insurance funding is inclined both to push the costs of health care up and to generate heavy administrative costs. It also makes co-ordinated planning more difficult and fosters the development of some types of health care at the expense of others. However, it is politically more acceptable in that it forges a link between payment and use.

All nations are subject to the same financial constraints and face the same difficult choices, but the way in which financing issues are addressed and resolved will reflect particular national circumstances and characteristics.

CONTEMPORARY ISSUES IN HEALTH POLICY

Issues may be said to arise in situations where there is no clear, unequivocal, or universally acceptable answer. In health care, the potential for such situations is enormous. Accordingly, authors were granted considerable freedom to highlight those issues which were of greatest salience in particular countries.

Despite much local variation, some general themes can be identified. First, conflicting contextual pressures can generate issues. How, for example, do policy-makers resolve the problems associated with demographic trends which swell the demand for long term care; technological progress which increases the demand for short term, curative intervention; and an economic climate which restricts resources?

Second, many issues arise in health care because of the seemingly intractable nature of the problems. For example, epidemiological trends suggest that the traditional approach to disease, based on a biomedical model of health and illness, is less appropriate than in the past. But how are the professionals and public to be re-educated, so that a more preventive approach, based on a social model, can be adopted?

Third, there will always be differences of view over values and questions of principle. For example, to what extent and how should governments intervene to ensure universal access to health care services? How far should the promotion of equality in health be given priority over other goals, such as efficiency?

It is the manner in which the issues and the questions underlying them are conceived and addressed in different national settings which constitutes the meat of this section of each chapter.

REFERENCES AND FURTHER READING

Butler, J. R. and Vaile, M. S. B. (1984) *Health and Health Services*, London: Routledge and Kegan Paul.

Field, M. (1989) *Success and Crisis in National Health Systems: A Comparative Approach*, London: Routledge.

Jones, C. (1985) *Patterns of Social Policy: An Introduction to Comparative Analysis*, London: Tavistock Publications.

Kingdom, J. (ed.) (1990) *The Civil Service in Liberal Democracies: An Introductory Survey*, London: Routledge.

O'Keefe, E., Ottewill, R. and Wall, A. (1992) *Community Health: Issues in Management*, Sunderland: Business Education Publishers.

Ottewill, R. and Wall, A. (1990) *The Growth and Development of the Community Health Services*, Sunderland: Business Education Publishers.

Chapter 2

Australia

Ann Wall

The Australian health care system is segmented according to the eight main geographic and political divisions of the country, namely the six states (New South Wales, Victoria, Queensland, South Australia, Western Australia and Tasmania) and two territories (Northern Territory and Australian Capital Territory) – hereafter referred to as 'the states'. Inevitably, a degree of structural fragmentation results and this is compounded by diverse and sometimes contradictory socio-political values underpinning health care. Consequently the health care system in Australia is complex and exhibits a high level of interweaving of the public and private sectors. Any attempt to describe and explain the nature of Australian health care provision must make reference both to the country's physical characteristics and to its socio-political culture.

THE CONTEXT OF AUSTRALIAN HEALTH CARE

The demographic structure

With a land area of 7.68 million square kilometres, Australia ranks as the sixth largest of the world's countries. Much of the country, however, is inhospitable desert, with the result that 80 per cent of the population lives in 1.65 per cent of the land area, mostly in large coastal cities. In 1989 the total population of Australia was 16.8 million; and it is projected to rise to between 19.5 and 19.8 million by the turn of the century, and to between 21.0 and 22.1 million by the year 2011. New South Wales is the most populous of the states, containing 34 per cent of the population. Victoria has 25 per cent of the population whilst Western Australia, although the largest in area, has only 9 per cent.

The annual growth rate of the population is 1.6 per cent. This is high compared with other developed countries, but represents a dramatic reduction compared with the period of rapid expansion following the second world war. Again, the states vary, with Queensland above the national average, and Tasmania below; this reflects not only natural increase (birth and death rates) but also both interstate migration and the pattern of settlement of overseas immigrants.

The slowing of the growth rate is the result of lower levels of both natural increase and immigration. With respect to the former, fertility levels (that is, the extent to which women exercise their ability to give birth) are declining; and although still higher than in many European countries, are lower than at any time in the past 200 years. Indeed Australia has a fertility rate below that required for the replacement of its population (i.e. 2.1 children per couple).

Several factors may account for this trend. The birth rate amongst women over the age of 30 years has continued to increase, but this has been outweighed by a declining rate amongst women under the age of 24 years. Moreover, while there has been an increase in births outside marriage, this has been counterbalanced by an increase in the number of childless couples and an overall decline in family size. The continued upward trend in the number of births is due to an increase in the number of women of child-bearing age; but this will, of course, level off as falling fertility reduces the number of women in the reproductive age group in the future. Australia's natural increase is projected to reach zero around the year 2030.

A marked decline in the rate of inward migration since the second world war has also contributed to the overall slowing of the growth rate. Of equal importance to sheer numbers, particularly from the point of view of those responsible for health care services, is changing trends with regard to the countries of origin. This is because the health of immigrants is influenced by the health status and morbidity patterns of their countries of origin. Asian migrants increased from 14.3 per cent of the total immigrant population in 1974 to 45.1 per cent in 1989. Since 1978 the immigration of family members has increased and now represents 50 per cent of all arrivals. By 1990 22.5 per cent of the population was born overseas, compared with 9.8 per cent in 1947 (Grant and Lapsley 1993).

The majority of immigrants settle in urban areas, regardless of where they come from. The high levels of urban density, to which this contributes, has important implications for the health care system. The health needs of those living in large cities, and the challenges they pose to those responsible for health care, are different from those of people living in more sparsely populated rural environments.

In common with most other developed countries, Australia's population is ageing, and this trend is accelerating. Over the last 100 years the median age has risen by ten years to 32.5 and it is projected to be 38.2 by the year 2011 and 41.5 by the year 2031. This change is due predominantly to the decline in fertility discussed above which has meant that, since 1976, the proportion of the population under the age of 15 years has gradually decreased. There has also been an increase in the number of people over the age of 65. These trends are, of course, similar to those apparent elsewhere in the developed world, but less advanced. Many European countries have an age structure which Australia will not reach for several decades.

The age structure of the population has great significance for those responsible for health care, since different age groups make different demands on services. The numerical relationship between those who are in paid employment and those who are not, such as children and the retired, can be expressed as the 'dependency ratio'. The demographic trends described above are contributing to changing dependency ratios. The child dependency ratio (that is, the number of children under the age of 15 years as a percentage of the number of people aged 15–64 years) fell from 45.5 per cent in 1971 to 33.4 per cent in 1989. The aged person dependency ratio (that is, the number of people of pensionable age as a percentage of people aged 15–64 years) rose from 13.25 per cent in 1971 to 17 per cent in 1989.

Not surprisingly, since it reflects biological rather than social factors, the gender distribution of the Australian population is unremarkable. As elsewhere, there are 105 males to 100 females at birth, with the proportion of men gradually falling as age increases, producing a ratio, for all ages in 1990, of 99.7 men to 100 women.

One of the most striking features of the Australian population is the existence of an indigenous, Aboriginal group. The Aboriginal population of Australia displays very different demographic characteristics from those of the rest of the population. It has higher fertility and age-weighted mortality rates, producing a sub-population in which over half are aged under 20 years. These differences are sufficiently marked to have an impact on the overall demographic profile of the states in which this population is concentrated. Most Aborigines are found in New South Wales and Queensland, where they represent 1 per cent and 2 per cent respectively of the populations. In Northern Territory there are fewer Aborigines but they represent 23.7 per cent of the population. Consequently, Northern Territory has a younger age profile than anywhere else.

Table 2.1 Selected measures of health status, 1960–90

Year	Infant mortality % of live births	Life expectancy at birth (M) Years	Life expectancy at birth (F) Years
1960	2.01	67.92	74.18
1970	1.79	68.10	74.80
1980	1.07	71.23	78.27
1990	0.82	73.81	79.94

Source: based on *ABS Deaths Australia* 1991 (3302.0); Australian Bureau Statistics, October 1992, p. 9, Table 7; *Health OECD Facts and Trends*, OECD, Paris, 1991; *OECD in Figures*, 1992, Supplement to *OECD Observer* June/July 1992, pp. 46–7

Epidemiological trends

On all health indicators Australia compares reasonably favourably with other developed countries and, as the figures in Table 2.1 indicate, infant mortality and life expectancy at birth have improved over the last thirty years.

However, with respect to infant mortality (which can be considered the barometer of a nation's health) the improvement has not been sustained over the last two years; the rate has remained constant, suggesting that there is little room for complacency.

Some of the major causes for concern in Australia are: the persistence of certain conditions, particularly those associated with lifestyle, which are either failing to improve or actually deteriorating; the increase in chronic sickness and disability associated with the ageing of the population; and new threats to health. In these respects Australia is not dissimilar from other developed countries. Each of these three concerns will now be examined briefly.

Taking persistent health problems, the incidence of cancer has shown no improvement since 1982 and is the leading cause of death for men and women, accounting for 26 per cent of all deaths. Ischaemic heart disease, although showing some decrease, still ranks second, accounting for 25 per cent of all deaths. However, it has to be noted that cancer and heart disease are associated with ageing and their incidence is affected by the age structure of the population. Of greater concern to those responsible for health care services are the persistent problems related to premature death and preventable ill health amongst young people. Deaths from suicide, for example, are increasing and, in 1991, overtook deaths from motor vehicle

Table 2.2 Incidence of chronic conditions

Condition	% of population affected
Arthritis	10.6
Hay fever	9.8
Back problems	8.1
Asthma	8.0
Hypertension	7.1

Source: based on Australian Bureau of Statistics, *National Health Survey 1989/90, Summary of Results Australia* (4364.0) ABS, August 1991, p. 3, Chart 2.

accidents (which are decreasing) as the chief cause of death amongst people aged between 15 and 24 years. Dental health continues to be a cause for concern, as does immunisation which is not at the level needed for complete protection of the population.

Turning to chronic conditions and disability, by 1988 15.6 per cent of the population of Australia was disabled compared with 13.2 per cent in 1981; and 66.1 per cent of the population suffered from one or more of the chronic conditions shown in Table 2.2. Again, some of these (such as arthritis) are linked to age and reflect demographic trends in this respect.

With respect to new threats to health, the significance of AIDS cannot be overlooked. In 1992 3,523 people in Australia had developed AIDS and 2,322 of these had died. The gender breakdown shows that 3,414 men had developed the disease, 2,256 of whom had died; 104 women had developed the disease, 63 of whom were dead.

More generally, Australians are becoming increasingly concerned with new threats to health posed by the environment. These tend to be exacerbated by the continued pursuit of economic growth in the context of technological development. Such a policy is known to carry heavy social costs. In describing Australian political trends in the 1990s, Emy and Hughes comment: 'It was recognised increasingly that modern technologies invariably created social costs . . . plus implications for the long term health and safety of the population which required continuous oversight and regulation by governments' (Emy and Hughes 1991: 94).

The health status of the Aborigine population is more akin to that of developing countries than the rest of Australia. Their life expectancy is twenty years less than that of the rest of the population, and their infant mortality rate three times higher. A particular issue is the high level of suicide. This is due in large part to the poor economic and physical conditions in which the Aborigines live. Improvement will come only with changes in the environment, housing, and conditions of employment, as well as specific health programmes appropriate to their needs and with which they can identify.

Cultural traditions

The development of health and other social policies has been shaped by a powerful individualist strand in Australian culture and a strong commitment to the 'work ethic'. The strategy of many Australian governments has been founded on the belief that working people should be equipped with the means to protect themselves. Thus they have directed their efforts at ensuring a 'living wage' through such mechanisms as tariff protection, compulsory government arbitration in labour disputes and immigration controls. As a result, adult male workers are assumed to be able to make their own provisions for ill health and other contingencies, and government measures have tended to concentrate on those who are not employed, such as children and old people. In other words Australian social policy has been selective rather than universal.

Despite rising unemployment and poverty in the 1980s, Australia remained wedded to selectivity based on income-tested subsistence benefits financed from taxation. Because these benefits were seen to be paid for by middle-class taxpayers and used by the 'needy subpopulation' (Heidenheimer et al. 1990: 263) they tended to generate resentment on the part of the majority of taxpayers. Indeed, it has been suggested that 'the tax-welfare backlash is strong and getting stronger' (Mishra 1990: 83). Australia can, therefore, be described as a 'welfare laggard' (Ife 1990: 84) with no more than a 'circumscribed' commitment to the values of social justice and welfare (Mishra 1990: 88). This set of values goes some way towards explaining why Australia has one of the lowest levels of social spending of all OECD countries and why the private sector has always played a large part in the delivery of health care services.

Some aspects of Australia's cultural heritage, however, contrast sharply with this picture. At the beginning of the twentieth century Australia was regarded as an innovator in social policy. Indeed, even today, evidence of a progressive approach is not hard to find. The values of equity, access, equality and participation underpin the design and administration of health programmes. This can be illustrated by reference to the mission statement for health policy in South Australia, which makes reference to:

- a consumer focus;
- access for people in greatest need;

- quality in service delivery;
- improving the potential for good health;
- community involvement in policy-making and service delivery; and
- co-ordination and co-operation between health agencies.

(Grant and Lapsley 1993: 81)

Australia's cultural traditions, therefore, can be said to constitute something of a paradox.

Social factors

Australians enjoy a good physical environment and a generally high level of prosperity. Indeed, by the 1960s Australia had achieved a standard of living virtually equivalent to that experienced in the USA and, although not universally the case, there was sufficient affluence to justify the nickname the 'Lucky Country'.

This picture did not apply to the Aborigine population, the position of which remains, without doubt, the starkest feature of the Australian social landscape. By the 1930s, over 90 per cent of the Aboriginal population had been destroyed in a manner which was close to genocide (Carson and Kerr 1988: 79) and their traditional tribal society had broken down. Nevertheless, they remain a distinctive group and most continue to live separately from the rest of the population. There are prodigious social differences between Aborigines and the rest of the Australian population. For example, their unemployment is six times the national average, their rate of imprisonment ten times higher, and the number of deaths in police custody a hundred times greater.

Apart from the Aboriginal population, there were no major ethnic or cultural cleavages in the first half of the twentieth century, largely because most of the early settlers had a common social background. This is now changing as a result of both the shifting patterns of immigration (mentioned earlier) and other social trends.

Given its importance for health, one of the most significant of these social trends is the increase in poverty amongst the elderly, children, and the unemployed. The growing number of claimants for low-level, means-tested benefits is testimony to the hardship which many Australians face.

But there are other social factors which should not be overlooked. Emy and Hughes suggest that 'Australian society has been moving further away from its relatively egalitarian past, and a small, though growing, upper class exists' (1991: 567). There are also gender differences in wages, and inequalities in health status between different occupational groups. Indeed,

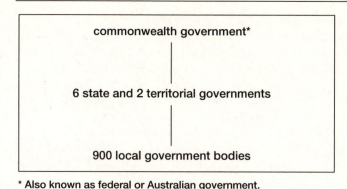

* Also known as federal or Australian government.

Figure 2.1 The structure of Australian government

Ife (1990) suggests that issues of class, race and gender have yet to be seriously addressed in Australia.

The governmental and political setting

As a polity, Australia dates back only to 1901 when a British Act of Parliament made the six separate British colonies (mostly penal in origin and each with its own capital city) one nation. Since that time, a three-tier governmental structure has operated. Its structure is shown in Figure 2.1. At the commonwealth level, parliament is based on the Westminster model of responsible government but constrained by a written constitution which has proved highly resistant to change. It consists of the Governor-General; an upper house, or Senate; and a lower house, or House of Representatives.

The Governor-General has considerable formal as well as informal influence, since his powers derive both from the constitution and from his status as the Queen's representative. The Senate is elected on the basis of proportional representation of the states and, since 1948, the government has not always had a majority in Senate. It operates as a house of review, working through committees and increasingly willing to reject government legislation, partly because party discipline is relatively loose. The House of Representatives comprises members representing the states on a quota basis. The party with the majority in this house forms the government.

In each of the states and Northern Territory (Australian Capital Territory contains the national capital, Canberra, and is administered directly by the national government) there is an elected parliament, and it is at this level that responsibility for the provision of services lies. However, since the commonwealth government is responsible for revenue raising, including most forms of taxation, the states are financially dependent on commonwealth government grants. Thus, commonwealth legislation tends to take precedence over that of the states.

Local government has responsibilities for environmental control, prevention of illness and promotion of health. In general there have been centralising moves which have reduced the powers of this tier of government.

Health policy is not, therefore, under the control and direction of a single national government. It is subject to the sometimes adversarial relationship between the upper and lower house and is vulnerable to the complex interplay of commonwealth and state governments where change has to be negotiated. A number of factors may be said to influence such negotiations. First, states may be fearful of compromising their autonomy. Second, in states which are perceived as outlying (i.e. Tasmania, Queensland and Western Australia), the governments can win political advantage by adopting a policy of non-co-operation with the commonwealth government and thus being seen as 'standing up to big brother' and protecting the rights of individuals locally. Last, the state government is often controlled by a different political party from that which governs at commonwealth level.

Taken together, these factors have given rise to administrative duplication and lack of co-ordination at commonwealth level; and, at state level, highly centralised services and large bureaucratic structures no closer to the people than the commonwealth government. As a result most aspects of health and welfare policy can be described as, at best, slow and cautious and, at worst, 'inadequate, complex, reactive, poorly planned, confusing and inefficient' (Ife 1990: 91).

Australia's political context is underpinned by a strong democratic tradition which pre-dates the establishment of Australia as a polity. Universal male suffrage, parliamentary government, and competitive political parties were achieved during the 1850s at state level. In practice, however, this democratic tradition has generated two interesting contradictions. First, there is a tradition of relatively high working-class mobilisation, with Australia being significantly ahead of Europe in the establishment of both trade unions and a socialist party representing workers, which, in principle, facilitated welfare developments. This high level of working-class mobilisation, however, has to be set against a much lower level of working-class control (measured by periods of left-wing government) which may explain, at least in part, the niggardly approach to public spending. The tension between high mobilisation and low control underpins Australia's somewhat equivocal stance with respect to the provision of health care.

Second, unlike most of their European counterparts, historically, Australian governments have been obliged to adopt an interventionist rather than a *laissez-faire* position, particularly in relation to controlling immigration and tackling the issues associated with settling the country. Moreover, the distrust of state power, often evident in other parts of the world, is not so apparent in Australia. Consequently, it has been natural for the Australian people to look to governments to protect and preserve the favourable economic conditions most wage-earners have enjoyed for much of the twentieth century.

Three parties dominate the political scene at all levels. The Liberal and Country Parties are on the right of the political spectrum, the former representing the interests of commerce and industry, the latter, the interests of agriculture. The Labour Party is centre/left and is supported by the trade unions. Labour also draws electoral support from the Roman Catholic community, which has had a significant impact on its health policy particularly in the fields of abortion and family planning.

The Labour Party has had three periods of office since the war and has adopted a strategy based on a form of social corporatism. At the heart of the strategy is the 'Accord', which is an agreement between the trade unions, employers and the state with respect to prices and incomes. The 'Accord' was seen by the Hawke government (1983–88) as the only way for the Labour Party to reconcile social justice with economic growth and may be said to have had a modest measure of success. However, the growing tension between the interests of welfare and capital led the Hawke government increasingly to side with the latter. This is of particular significance for health policy because the most vulnerable members of the community (e.g. old people, the unemployed, single parents) have become more marginalised in a system which focuses on the relations of production.

This tendency on the part of the Australian Labour Party is evidence of the growing legitimacy of 'new right' political ideas and a greater willingness to question welfare goals throughout the 1980s. However, during the 1990s, the social and environmental costs associated with the continued pursuit of economic growth were increasingly recognised, and what were once residual questions about the type of society which is desirable are coming more and more to the forefront of political debate.

Certainly until recently, Australia displayed most of the traits characteristic of a pluralist democracy. Not surprisingly, therefore, in the sphere of health care, medical pressure groups have wielded considerable power. Governments are obliged to consult with the Australian Medical Association (AMA) on every matter relating to medicine and health care. Over half of all doctors are members of the AMA and many of the colleges and societies representing each medical specialty are affiliated to it. The AMA tends to favour private practice and fee-for-service payments rather than state health insurance and free services. During the 1980s, however, it tried to present a more caring face, to demonstrate a genuine interest in health rather than simply representing the sectional interests of its members. Taking a cynical point of view, this was, to some extent, a response to declining membership of the association and a deteriorating public image of the profession.

Nurses also play a role in shaping health policy. However, despite the numerical size of the profession, its influence has been relatively slight. In part, this is due to the hospital-based, apprenticeship nature of nurse education and the slow growth of specialisms such as nurse-practitioner and nurse-anaesthetist. Even in the sphere of midwifery, although 40 per cent of registered nurses hold a midwifery certificate, a doctor nearly always attends a confinement and the midwife acts as assistant. Since 1985 there have been changes. These include: a systematic shift of nurse training from hospitals to the tertiary education sector; gradual up-grading of training (most basic nursing students are enrolled on diploma-level courses, and most post-basic students on degree-level courses); and the development of nurse specialisms, especially in the area of management. As a consequence, career structures are more attractive and more men are being drawn into the profession. It remains to be seen whether this will bear fruit in terms of the influence of nurses in the formulation and implementation of health policy.

Other practitioners include pharmacists, chiropractors, osteopaths, opticians, physiotherapists, chiropodists and social workers. Although there is some variation between states, in most cases registration is achieved on the basis of three-years' training. Most practitioners have their own associations and the larger ones also have a trade union which is involved in the determination of state and nationwide pay awards. Those without their own trade union tend to belong to a general one. Collectively, these professions represent a force which governments cannot ignore.

Economic performance

In the last thirty years of the nineteenth century Australia was the most economically developed and, in terms of GDP per capita, the richest country in the world. As industrialisation and urbanisation progressed, there was high demand for Australian goods and a shortage of labour, which, together, generated high wages and high rates of employment. However, from the late 1970s the recession, compounded by a period of drought, took unemployment and inflation up to 10 per cent and the growth rate to zero by 1983.

The expansionary monetary and fiscal policy of the Labour government in the mid-1980s retrieved the situation to some extent, and economic growth reached 6.7 per cent in 1984. At the same time the prices and incomes policies based on the 'Accord' brought inflation down to 3.9 per cent. Unemployment proved less manageable: it fell by only 1 per cent to 9 per cent in 1985 and remained stubbornly at 8.1 per cent in 1987. Moreover, the duration of unemployment was increasing. In 1976 the average had been 17.5 weeks; by 1985 it was 49.5 weeks. Although the commonwealth government took some steps to alleviate unemployment, these were, for the most part, based on the strategy of facilitating growth through macro-economic management. Job creation was left largely to the private sector.

This situation of sustained economic growth with high unemployment continued until the late 1980s, by which time there were more economic problems and the commonwealth government came to be preoccupied, in the closing years of the decade, with attempting to reduce the size of the budget deficit and the political imperative not to increase taxation. The desire to promote economic growth came to take precedence over measures to tackle unemployment. Indeed, arguably, 'Creating a more viable economy is *a*, if not *the*, major priority' (Emy and Hughes 1991: 83).

As elsewhere in the developed world, economic growth appeared to depend upon cutbacks in public expenditure and Australian governments adopted this strategy. Cutbacks in the order of 3 per cent were made between 1983/4 and 1987/8. Although health spending was affected by these, as the data in Table 2.3 indicate, Australia devotes a similar share of its GDP to health as most other OECD countries, and this has remained fairly constant at around 7.5 per cent over the last twenty years. In real terms, this represents a growth of, on average, 6.5 per cent per year over the last ten years, in both government and private sector spending. As such it is the second largest item of commonwealth government expenditure, exceeded only by social security.

Table 2.3 Share of national resources devoted to health care, 1970–90

Year	Total spending on health % of GDP	Public spending on health % of GDP
1970	7.4	5.4
1980	7.4	4.6
1990	7.7	5.3

Source: based on *Organisation for Economic Co-operation and Development Health Care Systems in Transition*, OECD, Paris, 1990, Table 1, p. 10; *OECD in Figures*, 1992 Supplement to *OECD Observer* June/July 1992, OECD, Paris, 1992

Nevertheless, in the context of declining manufacturing industry, the cost of new medical technology, changes in both the labour force and the age structure of the population, economic recession and a desire to remain a low tax nation, doubts arise as to whether the economy can sustain even the relatively modest levels of public expenditure achieved during the twentieth century.

THE DEVELOPMENT OF STATE INVOLVEMENT

The involvement of the Australian states in health care has its origins in the field of public health. It was the rapid growth of insanitary, overcrowded shanty towns in the 1850s, built to accommodate those joining the gold rush, which precipitated the passing of legislation to tackle pollution and other environmental hazards. The legislation created a central authority in each state, with responsibility for public health being shared between this agency and local health authorities. This administrative pattern for managing public health lasted until the early 1980s.

Early initiatives in the field of personal health care were undertaken by non-government bodies such as charitable organisations and friendly societies which pioneered infant welfare clinics and other measures in the nineteenth century. State involvement grew from collaborative ventures between charitable agencies and governmental institutions. One of the earliest recorded examples of such a partnership was that between the New South Wales government and a private charitable organisation in Sydney in 1820, to provide and maintain a nursing home for the poor, blind, aged and infirm.

Although state governments became involved more systematically with voluntary agencies in the provision of personal health care from the beginning of the twentieth century, it was not until the first world war that personal health was seen as a responsibility of the commonwealth government. The experience of the war, particularly the need to maintain the health of recruits, care for veterans and control the introduction and spread of infectious diseases, led to calls for a more vigorous national policy on health.

As a result of these exigencies, although the prime responsibility for health still lay with the states and non-government bodies, during the next two decades the commonwealth government took three initiatives: the introduction of a comprehensive service for veterans; the creation of a Commonwealth Department of Health (the main responsibility of which was, for many years, quarantine); and the establishment of several co-ordinating, consultative and resource agencies. In 1939 the Labour government increased the involvement of the commonwealth government and its agencies in health matters.

From 1950 to 1972, under Liberal governments, Australia remained one of the few industrialised nations to lack a mandatory social insurance scheme for personal health care. What it had was a complex system for subsidised voluntary insurance with little control over the private sector.

The Labour government led by Gough Whitlam (1972–75) rectified this to some extent by establishing a national health care system as part of a progressive programme aimed at replacing means-tested social benefits with those based on insurance. To this end, Medibank and the Australian Assistance Plan (AAP) were set up. Medibank was a compulsory health insurance scheme financed by a levy on taxable income and administered by a government agency, while the AAP involved commonwealth support for establishing social services in kind (rather than financial support) at local level. It also introduced controls over private health care insurance funds.

It was also during this period that the commonwealth government established a Community Health Programme which gave grants for the establishment or improvement of a wide range of community health services directed at health maintenance and education; illness prevention; rehabilitation; and the delivery of services in community rather than institutional settings. The programme resulted in the establishment of 300 community health centres offering a variety of services including: domiciliary nursing; counselling for drug abuse and mental health; health promotion; and primary medical care (in fewer than 100 of the centres).

Other notable achievements of the programme were the establishment of women's refuges; day care centres; and a family medicine programme for the training of GPs. At its height, the Community Health Programme represented 1.5 per cent of current health care expenditure.

The Whitlam administration also made progress in the field of dental health care. In 1973 a school dental service was set up jointly by commonwealth and state governments to provide free dental care to primary school children by dental therapists. In addition, in 1975 dentistry was included in the Medibank programme.

Perhaps because of a deep-seated hostility to social insurance and universal benefits on the part of Australians, these programmes were never well established, and proved vulnerable to attack. Under Fraser's right-wing coalition government (1975–83) there was a general retreat from publicly provided health care in favour of encouraging private provision. Medibank and AAP were dismantled and, after 1978, commonwealth funding for the Community Health Programme was reduced and the states curtailed their commitment. Indeed, in 1981 the programme virtually ceased to exist when separate funding was abolished altogether. However, it did not sink without trace as some of the services it generated have been absorbed into mainstream health care.

In 1983 a Labour government under Bob Hawke took office on the basis that it could rebuild the welfare state after eight years of attrition under Conservative governments. To this end, Medibank was restored in the form of a universal health insurance scheme known as Medicare. At state level, the separate structures responsible for public health, public hospitals and the care of mentally ill were unified on the grounds that the hospital sector had absorbed the lion's share of resources. But the objective of equalising the three sectors was not achieved. Indeed, the change resulted in an overall deterioration of publicly provided health care services.

By the 1980s, the role of the commonwealth government in health care had expanded significantly. It now provided more than half of all health funding and it was this financial nexus which caused the balance of power between the states and the commonwealth to shift. Nevertheless, the states retained responsibility for the regulation of health care activity and the provision and running of (public) facilities. Similarly, the commonwealth government held the whip hand with respect to private health insurance organisations, over which it exerted tight control.

Despite these changes and developments, there is still no universal state provision of health care in Australia. For this reason, the record of the Labour government was generally adjudged to be disappointing.

THE PRINCIPAL FEATURES OF SERVICE DELIVERY AND ADMINISTRATION

Primary health care

The first point of contact for most Australians entering the formal health care system is a general practitioner (GP) who thus plays a major role in the delivery of primary health care. GPs are self-employed and, although they usually work in partnerships for the purposes of sharing staff and accommodation, they undertake their clinical work as single-handed practitioners and patients identify with 'their' doctor. GPs have the power to refer patients to hospital, but in rural areas may undertake quite specialist work themselves. The personal, continuous nature of GP care has, however, been jeopardised by the steady decline in the number of home visits made and an increase in the use of deputising services.

Although traditionally it is a less popular area of medicine than specialist work, a growing number of new young graduates are now being attracted into general practice, for four main reasons. First, within medical schools there is increasing emphasis on 'family medicine'. Second, the commonwealth government sponsors training for general practice under its Family Medical Programme. Third, increasing use of deputising services by GPs has made the life of the GP less onerous and more appealing to newly qualified doctors. Finally, many young doctors undertake deputising work for GPs while they are doing their residencies, and this gives them an insight into an area of medical practice which otherwise they might not have considered.

Other important components of primary health care are:

* pharmacists, dispensing prescriptions and free advice and selling medicines and appliances from their retail pharmacies;
* dental services;
* dispensaries and clinics (especially baby health centres, providing antenatal, postnatal and infant care);
* domiciliary nurses: there are 200 non-profit home nursing services receiving public money;
* paramedical and speech therapy services for the elderly in their own homes, for which public money is available;
* community care for the mentally ill consequent upon attempts to de-institutionalise mental health care since the 1950s;
* health transport services, which have particular significance for a country as large as Australia;
* occupational health and safety; and

- environmental control and preventive medicine for which some responsibility rests with local government.

In addition there are certain social care services such as help with domestic work; meals on wheels; and community benefit for carers; which make an invaluable contribution to primary health care.

Secondary care

By and large, patients enter the secondary health care sector by means of a referral by a GP. Sometimes, however, they enter via the casualty department of a hospital, either as an emergency, or again by GP referral, since casualty departments sometimes serve as GP clinics as well. Many GPs hold hospital appointments of this kind and some hospitals rely heavily on GP employees. Direct access to specialist doctors is discouraged.

There are three types of institutional care in this sector: general acute hospitals; nursing homes for the elderly; and psychiatric hospitals for those with mental health problems. Additionally, there are some hostels, half-way houses and live-in rehabilitation centres.

The hospital service

The hospital service exhibits a characteristic mixture of public and private ownership, with 80 per cent of hospital beds being publicly owned. Public hospitals are mostly short-stay (that is, less than two weeks) and general; and exhibit great variation in size. They include:

- small rural hospitals with fewer than 50 beds;
- rural district hospitals with between 50 and 100 beds;
- rural regional, base and urban district hospitals with between 200 and 300 beds; and
- large teaching hospitals with more than 400 beds.

In addition to the great majority of general hospitals there are a few special hospitals including some for women, children, cancer, eye disease and tuberculosis. Australia has a high ratio of beds to population, and short waiting lists except for renal transplants where the shortage of donors creates delay.

Public hospitals are either the property of government or are vested, by government, in a statutorily constituted board of management and thus 'held in trust for the community' (Raffel 1984: 11). They are open to anyone in need of in-patient care of the kind provided in that hospital and thus admit both public and private patients. Teaching and research are also undertaken in public hospitals.

Very small public hospitals tend to be staffed exclusively by doctors employed by the hospital on a sessional basis. Larger ones also have some full-time medical staff who may have a limited right to practise privately. The large public teaching hospitals employ medical staff in an even wider variety of ways, including:

- full-time, medically qualified administrators;
- full-time salaried specialists;
- teaching clinicians holding appointments jointly with the hospital and with the associated university medical school;
- full-time, salaried house staff (interns, residents, registrars); and
- visiting staff working on a sessional basis.

Because of the presence of both public and private patients and the variety in medical employment status, the state government can achieve a measure of control over the specialists by paying them to treat public patients, and the specialists are content in that they can treat their paying patients in public hospitals.

Private hospitals are owned by religious or philanthropic bodies, individual investors (often doctors), business partnerships, registered companies and co-operatives. They have restrictive admissions policies and are not open to the public at large. Most operate on a profit-seeking basis, although some, especially those run by religious bodies, do not. These usually operate in compliance with the legislation covering public hospitals. According to Raffel, private hospitals concentrate on 'the rapid throughput of an uncomplicated caseload' (1984: 11).

It is unusual for private hospitals to have any full-time medical staff. Instead, doctors who own or have shares in the hospital can treat patients on a fee-for-service basis. Other doctors wishing to use the hospital to treat patients apply to the management for permission to do so.

A few hospitals, such as Repatriation Hospitals (which provide services primarily for ex-service people) fall outside this classification. There is a Repatriation General Hospital (RGH) in the capital city of each state except Tasmania where, in 1992, it was transferred to the state system. There is now a general acceptance that RGHs should be integrated into the system and a gradual process to achieve this has begun.

From the point of view of the patient, a number of possibilities exist with respect to hospital care, as Figure 2.2 illustrates.

The patient has, first of all, to decide between a public and private hospital. A patient entering a public hospital can opt for either a shared or a single ward. However, if the patient's condition requires, s/he may be treated in a single ward even though only a shared ward has been paid for.

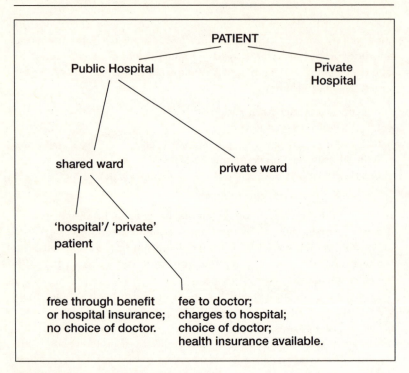

Figure 2.2 Hospital patient status

Patients accommodated in shared wards may be treated either as 'hospital patients' or as 'private patients'. The former are treated by doctors employed by the hospital and have no say over who these are. The latter, that is 'private patients', are admitted to the care of a doctor or group of doctors of their choice from amongst those on the hospital staff who have the right to engage in private practice.

Despite this diversity of patient status, the public hospital sector is reasonably coherent. However, it is not well integrated with the private sector, due, in the main, to funding barriers which inhibit patient movement. The situation has improved recently as a result of the growth in private hospital 'chains', which has made the sector less local and fragmented and has tended to facilitate communication and co-operative contractual arrangements with the public sector.

Poor integration also characterises the relationship between hospitals and other parts of the health care system. As Grant and Lapsley conclude, 'For historical and political reasons the hospital sector often has exhibited a lack of coherent integration with other sectors of the health industry'

(1993: 61). Discontinuities in planning and provision are apparent, and organisational barriers to access can be as great as financial or geographic ones. The desire to overcome the lack of integration in the interests of improving patient care and cutting costs has led most states to take steps to improve their administrative structures.

Mental health institutions

Most patients in mental health institutions are voluntary although there is some compulsory hospitalisation, particularly where a crime has been committed. However, the policy is 'admit reluctantly and discharge early' (Raffel 1984: 14). This, unfortunately, has fostered the growth of low-standard boarding houses for low-income social service beneficiaries with chronic mental health problems.

Nursing homes

The nursing home industry is heavily dependent on private profit-making providers, although commonwealth and state governments and philanthropic organisations also play a major part. There are 1,400 nursing homes providing 75,000 beds, which in 1982 represented 4.7 beds per 1,000 population. The commonwealth government controls the number of beds and fixes charges. The state government licenses nursing homes and as a result there is considerable variation in the amount and standard of such accommodation. Generally, state and commonwealth government standards are minimal, government fees are parsimonious and profit is low. The majority of nursing home residents are over the age of 65 (85 per cent) and female (70 per cent).

Service deliverers

In outlining primary and secondary health care, reference was made to medical staff. However, the part played by other service deliverers should not be overlooked. Nurses represent two-thirds of the health care workforce. There are three categories:

• professional (registered) and student (75 per cent);
• nursing aids and nursing aids in training (12.5 per cent); and
• nursing assistants (12.5 per cent).

In addition, there are a small number of mothercraft nurses who undertake an apprenticeship training and are allowed to work only with nursing mothers and babies.

The majority of nurses are employed in hospitals and nursing homes, working closely with doctors and involved with administration and teaching as well as nursing. Relatively small numbers are employed in community health centres or elsewhere in the community.

Other personnel, in the order of frequency with which they are consulted by the public, are as follows:

- pharmacist (provides free advice);
- chiropractor;
- osteopath;
- optician;
- physiotherapist (can only treat under doctor's orders);
- chiropodist (may be employed by a hospital but many are in private practice); and
- social worker (provides advice free of charge).

Administrative arrangements

The administrative arrangements which exist to facilitate the delivery of these health care services are complex and one of their distinguishing features is the extent to which functions are divided between the levels of government.

Local level

At local level, local authorities have limited responsibility for environmental control and for some personal preventive services.

State level

The major responsibility for health care lies at state level, where the main activities are:

- the determination of health policy;
- budgeting and finance for health;
- health care planning;
- determination and measurement of standards of performance in health services;
- health care programme and budget reviews;
- industrial and personnel matters in health services; and
- major capital works.

More specifically, the remit of state and territorial governments includes responsibility for public hospitals, mental health services, dental health services, systems of extended care, child, adolescent and family care, community health services, aged care services, services for people with disabilities, Aboriginal health programmes, women's health programmes, health promotion, rehabilitation, occupational health and safety programmes, and public health regulation.

Governments at state level are also responsible for the inspection, licensing and monitoring of privately owned health care premises. This includes setting minimum standards for accommodation, staffing, facilities and records. In practice, control over private hospitals is minimal.

The states and territories each have a statutory authority headed by a minister responsible for publicly provided health services and a civil service department with a permanent head responsible for implementing policy. There is also considerable commonality with respect to the organisational arrangements within the departments, which tend to be based on both functional and areal (regional) divisions. However, there are genuine differences, of which the greatest is probably the extent to which there is real devolution of power, both to regions and to individual institutions. In the case of the latter, until recently, the control which health authorities have over staffing, finance and operating policies has not been exercised very stringently in practice. Now there is much tighter control, especially over finance. The main features of these arrangements are summarised in Table 2.4.

These organisational arrangements have been subject to considerable change in recent years and it is likely that they will continue to be adapted in the future to meet the needs of a modern health care system.

National level

At national level, the role of the commonwealth government is to:

- ensure access to health care through funding arrangements;
- set standards for health care provision;
- develop health policy;
- support health research;
- support health promotion;
- provide the finances necessary for health services, which it does through the provision of conditional grants to states and territories especially for such things as health promotion, the reduction of drug and alcohol abuse and services associated with AIDS; and

Table 2.4 Organisation structures: state level

State/ territory	Statutory health service agency	Responsible minister[a]	Administrative head[b]	Organisation
New South Wales	Ministry of Health, Department of Health[c]	Minister for Health	Director General of Health	4 functional areas,[d] 6 country regional offices, 10 area health services
Victoria	Department of Health and Community Services	Minister for Health	8 Directors	programme and regional, 800 health agencies[e]
Queensland	Queensland Health	Minister for Health	Director-General, regional directors	4 functional divisions,[f] 1 central and 13 regional offices[g]
South Australia	Health Commision	Minister for Health	Chairperson of Commission	many specialist services organised state-wide, 16 regions
Western Australia	Health Department	Minister for Health	Commissioner for Health and 3 assistant commissioners	3 functional divisions,[h] 10 regions
Tasmania	Department of Community and Health Services	Minister	Secretary, 3 regional directors, 7 state programme co-ordinators	7 functional divisions, 3 regional divisions
Northern Territory	Department of Health and Community Services	Minister for Health	Secretary of Health and Community Services	4 functional divisions[i] incorporating 18 programmes, divisions[j]
Australian Capital Territory	Board of Health[k]	Minister for Health	Chair, and 10 members one of whom is the Chief Executive Officer	functional, regional

Source: based on Grant and Lapsley (1993: 61–90)
Notes:
a. Health tends to be a low-ranking portfolio.
b. Health department heads are not usually medically qualified.
c. There are several other bodies at this level in NSW, including the Health Advisory Council which advises the Minister on a variety of issues; the Mental Health Review Tribunal which reviews the treatment of mental health patients and makes recommendations to the Minister.
d. Public Health, Operations, Finance, and Administration and Information.
e. The relationship between the health agencies and the Department is based on negotiated Health Service Agreements intended to secure maximum management autonomy and responsibility at the same time as ensuring accountability of the

- directly administer armed services hospitals and Department of Veterans' Affairs hospitals.

With respect to the last of these, neither is integrated with the publicly provided hospital system although, since 1988, there have been moves to integrate Repatriation General Hospitals into the state system and there is slow but steady progress with this.

The commonwealth government fulfils its role through the operation of a number of departments and agencies, the structure and functions of which will now be outlined briefly.

The *Department of Health, Housing and Community Services (DHHCS)* has existed in its present form since 1991 when housing was added to its remit. (This is an interesting administrative arrangement in view of the growing recognition of the link between good health and an adequate standard of housing.) The department is responsible for planning and developing a range of national health and welfare policies including the universal health insurance scheme, Medicare. Its functions include:

- promoting health and preventing illness;
- funding services for the elderly and people with disabilities;
- ensuring that all Australians have access to services at reasonable cost either through direct provision or through health insurance;
- providing housing assistance including crisis and supported housing;
- providing housing industry assistance to facilitate the planning and development of cities; and
- providing child care facilities to remove impediments to community participation.

The structure of the DHHCS is shown in Figure 2.3.

Notes to Table 2.4 (*continued*)
system to the community. These agreements include: role statements; management objectives; plans and strategies; and the specification of the services to be provided and resources allocated.
f. Public Health Services, Corporate Services, Policy and Planning and Executive Support Services.
g. In Queensland it is intended that regional health authorities and regional directors should afford genuine local devolution of management.
h. Corporate Management, Health Policy, Public Health and State-wide Services, each the responsibility of an assistant commissioner.
i. Corporate Management, Hospital Services, Health Services and Community Services.
j. The organisational structure is an operational matrix linking programmes and districts.
k. ACT also has a Department of Health which is responsible for state-type functions such as liaison with commonwealth and state governments about policy. The chief executive of the board is also secretary of the department.

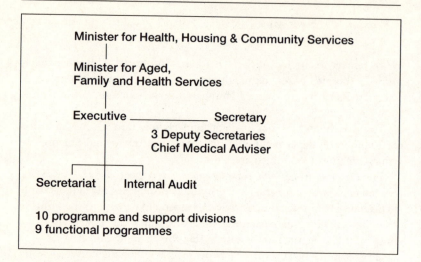

Minister for Health, Housing & Community Services

Minister for Aged,
Family and Health Services

Executive ——————— Secretary
3 Deputy Secretaries
Chief Medical Adviser

Secretariat | Internal Audit

10 programme and support divisions
9 functional programmes

Figure 2.3 Structure of the DHHCS
Source: based on Department of Health, Housing and Community Services *Annual Report* 1991–92, AGPS, 1992, pp. vi–vii

The Executive manages the Department and is responsible to the Minister. The ten programme and support divisions are:

- Health Advancement;
- Children's Services;
- Therapeutic Goods Administration;
- Housing and Urban Development;
- Health Care Access;
- Corporate Services;
- Aged and Community Care;
- Information Services;
- Disability Programmes; and
- Policy Development.

Each of these is responsible for advising the Minister on policy and developing programmes and administration to achieve objectives effectively and efficiently.

The nine functional programmes are:
- health advancement (e.g. drug abuse, environmental health);
- home and community care (e.g. home and community care allowances);
- residential care for older people (e.g. need assessment, quality control);

- assistance for people with disabilities (e.g. employment services, accommodation);
- therapeutic goods (e.g. drugs);
- health care access (e.g. financial support, provision);
- housing and urban development (e.g. housing access and affordability, housing for people in crisis);
- services for families with children (e.g. strategic planning of children's services); and
- corporate management (e.g. strategic policy analysis, corporate leadership, resource services).

In most cases there is an obvious link between the divisions and the programmes, but some programmes cut across more than one division. For example, the reduction of drug abuse is the responsibility of both the Health Advancement and the Information Services divisions.

The *Australian Institute of Health and Welfare* began as a small bureau within the Department of Health in 1984. It was made separate in 1987 but remained within the DHHCS's portfolio. Its mission is to improve the health and welfare of Australians by promoting debate and informing policy-making. Its activities include:

- collecting information;
- conducting and promoting research;
- assessing the provision, use, cost and effectiveness of health services and technologies; and
- making recommendations regarding the prevention and treatment of disease, the promotion of health and health awareness.

The Institute has four divisions (health services, health monitoring, health technology, welfare). It also funds four external units:

- The National Perinatal Statistics Unit (University of Sydney);
- The Dental Statistics and Research Unit (University of Adelaide);
- The National Injury Surveillance Unit (Adelaide); and
- The National Reference Centre for Classification in Health (Brisbane).

The results of its research appear in a series of publications, including the major biennial reference books, *Australia's Health* and *Australia's Welfare Services*.

In 1992 the *National Health and Medical Research Council* was established as a corporate body, separate from the Department, to provide advice; issue guidelines; and make recommendations for the improvement of health, health and medical research, public health, health care, and health and medical ethics.

The *Health Insurance Commission* was established during the Whitlam government by the Health Insurance Commission Act (1973). It is responsible to the Minister for Health, Housing and Community Services for the following functions:

- the operation of Medibank Private (Australia's only national private health insurance fund, in competition with other registered benefit organisations. It is open to all Australians and covers 2.3 million people);
- paying out Medicare benefits;
- servicing the processing of the Department of Veterans' Affairs treatment accounts;
- administering the commonwealth pharmaceutical benefits scheme which covers drugs supplied under the National Health Act (1953); and
- advising the government as required.

It performs its functions through a General Manager and Executive Support Unit, an Audit Committee, Divisions of Medicare, Medibank Private, Professional Review, Systems, Finance and Planning and Personnel Management. In this respect, it reflects the traditional corporatist approach which the Australians favour.

The Department of Veterans' Affairs *Repatriation Commission* is responsible to the Minister for Veterans' Affairs for the provision of medical and social care to ex-service persons and other beneficiaries.

FINANCING ARRANGEMENTS

The financing arrangements for the Australian health care system are complex. They incorporate social and private insurance as well as a considerable contribution from general taxation. Moreover, elements of compulsion are superimposed on a system which basically allows for free choice. There are also examples of both a universal and a selective approach to the allocation of public resources on the part of the commonwealth government. Table 2.5 summarises the main features of these arrangements. Of the $28.7 billion spent on health care in 1989–90, over half came from the commonwealth government, and, in total, $20 billion from state and commonwealth governments. This latter figure is made up of $2,385 million from Medicare contributions and the rest from general taxation. The remaining $8.7 billion came from private insurance premiums ($2.7 billion) and other out-of-pocket payments by individuals.

Medicare, which was established in 1984, is based on the principles of

Table 2.5 Funding arrangements

	Basis of funding	Type of care/service	Administrative agencies	% of pop. covered
a	compulsory insurance contributions (Medicare)	hospital and medical	registered health insurance funds	100
b	voluntary insurance premiums	all	health insurance funds	41
c	taxation	all	DHHCS	100

equity, universality, simplicity and ease of access. All Australians are entitled, under this scheme, to medical and hospital services free at the point of use. It is financed in part by a 1.25 per cent levy on taxable income and partly from general government revenue.

The main features of Medicare are:

- automatic entitlement to medical services at 85 per cent of the standard fee with a fixed maximum charge for any service;
- access to public hospitals without direct charge and treatment by doctors employed by those hospitals;
- reduced charges for private treatment in shared wards;
- funding of community health programmes; and
- subsidies to private hospitals.

Under Medicare legislation, all registered private health insurance organisations are required to offer a basic tariff of benefits equal to charges in public hospitals, and contribute towards the cost of private hospital accommodation. They also offer extensive supplementary benefits covering fees for items such as a single room, theatre, dentistry, physiotherapy, and home nursing.

Since 1984, various modifications to the scheme, undertaken in response to inflation and changes in the costs of services, have made it, according to Grant and Lapsley, more complex and less equitable than it was at its outset.

As well as universal coverage through Medicare, about 41 per cent of the population (mostly the middle aged and middle class) also have private health insurance. Interestingly, this is a declining proportion, having been 49 per cent in 1986. In 1991 there were fifty-two organisations operating seventy-one non-profit health insurance funds, and two organisations operating funds on a for-profit basis.

In 1989 the commonwealth government introduced community rating arrangements which meant that everyone was rated equally, for the purposes of social insurance, regardless of the degree of 'risk' they represented.

According to Grant and Lapsley, the main issues relating to private health insurance are:

- the increasing cost of private insurance;
- the complexity of the system;
- the characteristics of the insured population; and
- the effects on industry and on the private hospitals of fewer contributors.

Since 1981–82 the money raised through taxation for health care purposes by the commonwealth government has been allocated to the states in the form of identified health grants based on a per capita formula, determined by the Commonwealth Grants Commission. The formula is designed to achieve a distribution 'whereby each state would be able to provide comparably similar services to residents, provided that they make a comparable revenue effort' (i.e. raise a similar amount of money through taxation at state level) (Grant and Lapsley 1993: 117). The formula is based on a notional average, but states have the discretion to vary the actual level and pattern of revenue raising and spending. If, however, a state raises below-average revenue or incurs above-average costs, it would not be compensated through the grant. The grant system has a number of perverse effects, one of which is to favour the least populous states. Consequently, a government working party is currently looking at both the principle and the procedure for determining the level of grant to each state.

A small amount of commonwealth money goes directly to local authorities, some of which is health related.

State governments use their resources for health to provide:

- the bulk of capital money for public hospitals (individual hospitals may be allowed to raise loans, make public appeals, and inherit, although amounts are limited by law);
- recurrent funds for public hospitals (e.g. salaries, wages, running costs);
- a per-day payment to private hospitals for each patient insured through Medicare that they treat;
- baby health centres, providing antenatal, postnatal and infant care;
- capital and recurrent costs of mental health institutions;

- two-thirds of the recurrent costs of nursing homes;
- domiciliary nursing services; and
- paramedical and speech therapy services for the elderly in their own homes.

From the perspective of the service user, in most cases there is a direct charge levied at the point of use. Prescriptions, medicines and appliances are purchased from retail pharmacies (although advice is free). Patients visiting a GP are charged a fee which, in principle, can be determined by the GP, but in practice tends to relate to what patients, who are covered by social service security (i.e. people receiving government benefits for reasons of unemployment, age, etc.) or health insurance, will receive in the way of reimbursement.

Medicare does not cover nursing home costs; consequently the majority of residents in nursing homes are social service pensioners and they have to pay 90 per cent of their benefit towards the fee.

As indicated earlier, 'private patients' in public hospitals are subject to charges levied by the hospital for accommodation, nursing and ancillary services and are billed by the doctor for medical care. Insurance packages covering all or most of such charges and fees are available. 'Hospital patients' are subject to flat daily charges for accommodation and services imposed by the hospital. Cover for these charges can be obtained by taking out a hospital insurance package which is separate from Medicare and run by the hospital itself.

In private hospitals, charges for both care and accommodation are determined by the hospital. These are not regulated by government but are constrained by the rates paid through Medicare by registered health insurance funds. These rates are controlled by the commonwealth government and are, therefore, similar to those which pertain in public hospitals. However, private hospitals tend to levy additional charges, for example for the use of operating theatres or delivery rooms. Steps are now being taken, through peer review and hospital audit schemes, to scrutinise private hospitals with respect to length of stay and the necessity of certain procedures. Nevertheless, the patient in a private hospital is likely to be faced with a bill for a substantially larger amount than that of a similar patient in a public hospital.

The proportion of income spent on health is rising. Since 1984 there has been a 39 per cent increase in average weekly household spending, compared with increases of:

143 per cent in specialist doctors' fees;
100 per cent in hospital charges and proprietary pain relievers;

94 per cent in dental fees; and

35 per cent in hospital, medical and dental insurance.

Some service users are entitled to receive health care services free of charge. Those in receipt of social service benefits, for example, are entitled to hospital care in public hospitals and dental services free of charge under commonwealth or state health benefit arrangements. Veterans are entitled to nursing home services free of charge. In addition, certain people are entitled to 'fringe benefits' through a system of card-holding. Veterans, elderly and disabled people, widows, carers and sole parents below a certain income level have access to Pensioner Health Benefit cards. All those on sickness benefit, regardless of income, have access to Health Benefits cards. Card-holders receive: a range of subsidised pharmaceuticals; free supply and maintenance of hearing aids; free optometrical consultations; and other non-medical concessions.

Similarly, the unemployed, poor families, low earners, disabled people in work (available for the first twelve months), lone parents who have been on benefit for twelve months and are now taking up full-time employment, hold Health Care cards which provide them with government-listed medicines at concessional prices, and free dental treatment at public hospitals.

The income of those providing health care derives from a number of different sources and is influenced and constrained in various ways. Medical incomes are in the top 1 per cent of the national income distribution. All salaries of publicly employed doctors are fixed by commonwealth and state tribunals (which is true of most Australian employees). Thus the income of GPs, although deriving from health insurance arrangements and social service benefits, is also under the control of the commonwealth government and affords GPs an income similar to that of their hospital-based specialist colleagues.

Doctors employed in public hospitals (which may not seek to make a profit) whether as clinicians on a sessional or full-time basis, or as administrators and clinical heads of department, can earn income additional to their salaries through undertaking private work. In general, small public hospitals employ doctors only on a sessional basis; as the size of the hospital increases so too does the variety of employment statuses of its medical staff.

In the case of private hospitals, doctors treat patients on a fee-for-service basis. Those doctors who own or have shares in a hospital have an automatic right to do so; others have to secure permission from the management to use the hospital.

Other personnel, such as pharmacists, chiropractors, osteopaths, opticians, physiotherapists, chiropodists and social workers, all charge a fee for service which may be covered, in part at least, by insurance.

CONTEMPORARY ISSUES IN HEALTH POLICY

In 1984 Dewdney was able to conclude his study of the Australian health care system thus: 'the majority of Australians enjoy a high standard of health most of the time, and . . . when health services are required, for most people they are readily available and mostly of good standard' (1984: 36). Since then, the situation has changed and there is now serious doubt as to whether the level of funding is adequate to sustain good-quality health services for the whole population.

The dilemma is a familiar one. Numerous trends and pressures serve to swell demand, including:

- inflation;
- demographic trends;
- technological development;
- indexing of hospital funding grants;
- growing outlay on pharmaceutical benefits;
- higher levels of utilisation of Medicare services; and
- the trend towards more expensive services.

Against these, however, has to be set the concern of the commonwealth government to maintain low levels of taxation and thus the pressure to contain health care costs. Grant and Lapsley argue that it is the latter pressure which has dominated and the modest rate of growth in health care spending is a tribute to the effectiveness of the commonwealth government's cost-containment programme.

Nevertheless, there remains broad agreement that appropriate, accessible and equitable health care of a high standard should be available to the whole population. Hence the dilemma of how to achieve health care goals in the context of apparently insatiable demand and resource constraint.

In Australia, as elsewhere in the world, strategies designed to tackle this dilemma revolve around a radical reassessment of traditional approaches to health care; seeking new modes of delivery; rationing resources; and controlling the behaviour of health care practitioners.

Radical reassessment of traditional approaches

This has involved a number of themes. First, the health care system is too narrowly defined in terms of health care professionals and the specialist locations in which they deliver services. Such a definition will not be sufficiently robust for the achievement of health care goals in the future.

Second, and relatedly, there is a growing recognition that hospital-based curative approaches are unlikely to be as fruitful in the future as they have, at least, appeared to be in the past. The curative, biomedical approach has only a limited impact on the health status of the population at large and is particularly ineffective in dealing with preventable conditions, especially those associated with tobacco, alcohol and the ill effects of environmental factors, which continue to absorb resources; and the needs of the growing numbers of elderly people and people with disabilities and mental health problems, which are as much social as medical.

Finally, in the past, the social costs associated with the elderly and people with physical or mental disabilities tended to be shifted to the welfare sector, nursing homes, the voluntary sector, hostels and even prisons; and the personal costs tended to be borne by individuals and their families. In the future it is important that these agencies are adequately funded by the government; monitored for equity, access, quality and efficiency; and that the informal and voluntary sectors are not used by the government simply as a scapegoat for patchy, inadequate public services.

New modes of delivery

The key feature of new modes of delivery is, then, that they will take place outside the traditional narrow confines of the health care arena. Effective education and health promotion initiatives must be developed in a variety of community settings including schools, workplaces, shopping precincts and people's own homes. The challenge for the future is to formulate effective preventive strategies and these depend upon, amongst other things, addressing factors which lie 'outside the health care system' (Grant and Lapsley 1993: 39).

The mechanisms for achieving this change may well have to be examined. On the one hand, in the past, federal control has worked well to improve access and equity in provision and a strong commonwealth government will continue to be necessary to ensure that steps are taken to control the environment because these will be unpopular in view of their impact on manufacturing costs and levels of employment. On the other hand, in the future the traditional dominance of the commonwealth government over other participants may be inappropriate to more local, flexible modes of delivery.

More generally, the roles of the public and private sectors and the growing part played by the latter compounds the problems associated with ensuring comprehensive and high-quality care to the whole population.

Rationing resources

Regardless of how effectively new modes of delivery are implemented, rationing will continue to be a feature of the health care system and the likelihood is that it will become more explicit. Some states, for example, have adopted procedures for allocating resources based on population size and structure (age, ethnicity, patient flows, referral patterns). Explicit means of limiting demand may also be adopted as has been the case in the USA and the UK.

Controlling the behaviour of health care practitioners

Part of the process of restricting demand will, of necessity, be attempts to control health care practitioners who generate much of the demand. As elsewhere in the world, this is no easy task. Clinical professionals have strong traditions of autonomy and, in Australia, these have been endorsed by the adoption of the voluntary hospital insurance scheme imported from the USA.

CONCLUSION

Although Australia does not have a 'national health service' as such, it does have a health care system which aims to ensure that the health of the people is maintained and promoted and that no one is denied access to treatment for financial or any other reasons.

The same difficulties and dilemmas confront those responsible for health care in Australia as those facing other governments. These can be said to spring from the need to reconcile ever growing demands with limited resources. Given Australia's somewhat equivocal position with respect to the 'proper' division of responsibility between the public and private sectors, it will be interesting to see whether the system moves further towards marketisation and competition, in line with developments in Europe, or towards a larger role for the state, in line with likely developments in the USA.

REFERENCES AND FURTHER READING

Carson, E. and Kerr, H. (1988) 'Social welfare down under', *Critical Social Policy* 23 (Autumn): 70–82.

Dewdney, J. (1984) 'Health services in Australia', in M.W. Raffel (ed.) *Comparative Health Systems: Descriptive Analyses of Fourteen National Health Systems*, University Park and London: Pennsylvania State University Press.

Emy, H. V. and Hughes, O. E. (1991) *Australian Politics: Realities in Conflict*, 2nd edn. Melbourne: Macmillan.

Ginsberg, N. (1991) *Divisions of Welfare: A Critical Introduction to Comparative Social Policy*, London: Sage Publications.

Grant, C. and Lapsley, H. M. (1993) *The Australian Health Care System 1992*, University of New South Wales: School of Health Services Management.

Heidenheimer, A. J., Heclo, H. and Adams, C. T. (1990) *Comparative Public Policy: The Politics of Social Choice in America, Europe, and Japan*, 3rd edn. New York: St Martin's Press.

Ife, J. (1990) 'Australia – a limited commitment to state social services?', in B. Munday (ed.) *The Crisis in Welfare: An International Perspective on Social Services and Social Work*, London: Harvester Wheatsheaf.

Johnson, N. (1987) *The Welfare State in Transition: The Theory and Practice of Welfare Pluralism*, Brighton, Sussex: Wheatsheaf Books.

Kaim-Caudle, P. R. (1973) *Comparative Social Policy and Social Security*, Oxford: Martin Robertson.

Mishra, R. (1990) *The Welfare State in Capitalist Society: Policies of Retrenchment and Maintenance in Europe, North America and Australia*, London: Harvester Wheatsheaf.

Pilger, J. (1992) 'Pilger in Australia: perspective on social services and social work', *New Statesman/Society* 28 February.

Raffel, M. W. (ed.) (1984) *Comparative Health Systems: Descriptive Analyses of Fourteen National Health Systems*, University Park and London: Pennsylvania State University Press.

Thompson, N. (ed.) (1992) *Australia's Health 1992: The Third Biennial Report of the Australian Institute of Health and Welfare*, Canberra, Australian Government Publishing Service.

Chapter 3

Italy

Ralph Spence

The health care system in Italy is broadly similar to the health care systems elsewhere in Europe. The Italians spend approximately the same proportion of the GDP on health care as do the British. Life expectancy in Italy is slightly higher than in Britain for both women and men. Increasing life expectancy has presented Italy with exactly the same kind of problems that all the advanced industrial countries are having to address, that is, a growing demand for health care from an increasing elderly population. Italy also shares the problem of inflation in the cost of health care which is constantly several percentage points higher than general inflation. An increasingly elderly population is certainly one cause of this phenomenon. Another is the growing utilisation of high-tech medicine within large centralised hospitals at the expense of low-tech community-based medicine. Alongside these universal problems, Italy also has to suffer a number of problems which appear uniquely Italian.

The problem of cost containment in Italy is particularly pressing given the enormous size of the Italian public debt, which has reached over 110 per cent of GDP. Though the comparatively generous pensions system is seen as the most important single cause of the debt, this has not stopped policy-makers targeting the health system when cuts in public expenditure are planned. The problem of the health service in Italy, as numerous commentators have pointed out, is not that the system spends too much but that what it spends it spends badly. That the health service is inefficient there is little doubt. Since its creation in 1978, the National Health Service has been riddled with maladministration and corruption. The series of scandals unearthed by magistrates, which collectively have become known as *tangentopoli*, in American parlance 'bribesville', began as a routine enquiry into corruption in a Milan clinic and ended as an earthquake which has rocked the political system to its foundations. The old political parties which were blamed for the corruption, most notably the Christian Democrats (DC) and Socialists (PSI), simply disappeared in the elections which were held in March 1994. Several leading politicians have subsequently been placed under house arrest or put in gaol. Included amongst these were two former prime ministers, Giulio Andreotti and Bettino Craxi. The *tangentopoli* investigations within the health service led to the indictment of the Minister of Health, the director of the Higher Health Institute, the president of the Government Commission on Medicines, the president of the largest health authority in the south of Italy and the director of a clinic in Naples, to cite only the most notable. (The role of these organisations is discussed below.)

The destruction of the old parties led to the creation of a short-lived governing coalition centred around a party which hardly existed at all in 1993 and yet won 22 per cent of the popular vote in March 1994. The *Forza Italia* movement was founded by the media tycoon Silvio Berlusconi with the professed aim of ensuring that the Democratic Party of the Left (PDS), formed out of the old Communist Party (PCI), did not win the election as had seemed likely in late 1993. To this extent the movement was successful. For a brief period *Forza Italia* formed a governing coalition with the *Allianza Nazionale* (the old neo-Fascist party, MSI, under a new name) and, the other phenomenon of the 1990s, the Northern League.

The rhetoric of the new government was one of rolling back the frontiers of the state and providing the Italians with a Thatcher-style revolution in government. All the members of the coalition focused on the health service as a major target for privatisation. Before any serious policies could be implemented, the coalition collapsed. The fragility of Italian governments, of which the collapse of the Berlusconi government is only the most recent example, is yet another reason why the health service in Italy has proved so difficult to manage and control.

A reform aimed at confronting the problems of the health service was introduced in 1992 by the now disgraced Minister of Health. The reform has yet to be fully implemented. If and when it is, it promises to introduce a health service based on a quasi-market system similar to that discussed in Chapter 6 by Kingdom on Great Britain. This will be discussed in more detail below.

THE CONTEXT OF ITALIAN HEALTH CARE

The demographic structure

The population of Italy in 1990 was 57,576,429 of which 29,607,899 are females and 27,968,530 are males. These official figures underestimate the size of the population, since the Italian borders have been rather more open to foreign immigrants than the official figures would suggest. Estimates of the immigrant population not counted in the statistics are placed as high as one million. Uncontrolled immigration, especially from North Africa, has caused a number of problems for the Italian authorities, not least of which has been its impact on health care.

In common with all the advanced economies of the world, the average life expectancy of Italians has increased quite significantly during the course of the twentieth century. In 1900, the average life expectancy for both sexes was a little over 42 years. Half a century later life expectancy had risen to 66 years for men and 68 years for women. In 1995 the average life expectancy for men is 72.4 years and women can expect to live until they reach 79 years. Italians are, in this respect, slightly luckier than their partners in the European Union. Only men from the Low Countries live longer than the Italian male, and the life expectancy of the Italian female is surpassed only by her French sisters.

The problem of an ageing population is particularly acute in Italy, which has one of the 'oldest' populations in the world. Those over 60 years constitute over 20 per cent of the population. Those over 80 years total 2.9 per cent. In 1958 those in the population over 60 years numbered 6.4 million. It is estimated that by the year 2028 the figure will have risen to 17 million (Ministry of Labour 1990).

Perhaps the surprising feature of the demographic structure of the Italian population is the declining birth rate. Italy is the home of the Catholic Church and many Italians still claim to hold strong religious beliefs. Despite this, Italy has the lowest birth rate in Europe. In 1988 there were 9.6 live births for every thousand of the population. With 9.3 deaths per thousand, the Italian population is just managing to stay static. A number of people have tried to lay the blame for the falling birth rate on the liberal reform measures passed in the 1970s, most notably those legalising divorce and abortion. In reality the contributing factors are more diverse and much less obvious. Changes in the labour market (discussed below) have given women much more financial independence than they had in previous generations. This has enabled them to take control over their own lives in the form of later marriages and planned families. Whatever the reasons

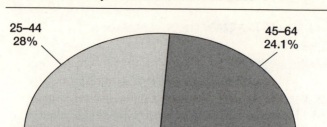

Figure 3.1 Age structure of population, 1989
Source: Ministry of Health (1990)

may be, the changing structure of the population will place increasing burdens on the health services in the future (see Figure 3.1).

Epidemiological trends

We have already briefly alluded to the improvements in life expectancy. Overall life expectancy is greatly increased when the battle against infant mortality has been won. It is only quite recently that the Italians have been able to bring down the rate of infant mortality to a figure broadly similar to that of their European partners. In 1950, when the Italians were still suffering from the economic and social effects of the war, the infant mortality rate was as high as 66.6 per thousand births. Each subsequent decade has produced a steady diminution from this extremely high figure. In 1960 the figure was 43.9, falling to 29.6 in 1970, to 14.4 in 1980 to 9.6 in 1995.

The major causes of death amongst the Italian population are broadly similar to those in other advanced industrial countries. Cardiovascular disease accounts for about 44 per cent of deaths. The next major cause of death, accounting for about 27 per cent of the total, is cancer in its various

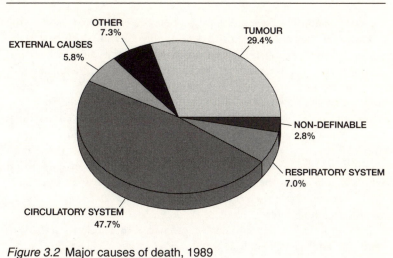

Figure 3.2 Major causes of death, 1989
Source: Ministry of Health (1990)

forms. Respiratory diseases account for 6.4 per cent. The next largest category are the various illnesses designated as degenerative diseases, which account for about 5.5 per cent (see Figure 3.2).

Some of the indices on disease show clear national differences. For instance, although the Italians have a similar rate for deaths caused by malignant neoplasms to that of the population of the UK, Italian women have about one-third less chance of suffering from breast cancer than do women in the UK. Moreover, Italians are less than half as likely to suffer ischaemic heart disease than are Britons. However, the Italians are almost four times as likely to suffer chronic liver disease than people in the UK. The now famous Mediterranean diet with its abundance of fresh fruit, vegetables and fish, and low consumption of animal fats, has been offered as an explanation of the first two phenomena. The downside of the Mediterranean culture is the high alcohol consumption. The Italians drink almost 50 per cent more than their British counterparts and this is reflected in a high incidence of liver disease.

Cultural traditions

During the 1960s it was popular amongst political scientists to seek to understand the way political and administrative systems functioned by identifying those aspects of a nation's culture which were politically relevant (Almond and Verba 1963). The term 'political culture' thus came to be used to identify values, attitudes and beliefs which were shared by the whole population and which had a determining effect on the nature of the political system. Distinctions were made between countries which had homogeneous cultures such as Britain and Holland and countries like Italy, where strong regional subcultures presented a picture of a highly fragmented political culture. The fragmentation was believed to be accompanied by an almost total disrespect amongst the Italians for anything that could not be eaten or was not very old. Italy was viewed as a collection of contrasts: a modern political and economic system based on a political culture hostile to order; an overwhelmingly Catholic population with Catholicism as the state religion and a subculture of rampant anticlericalism; and a predominantly industrial, commercial north and a backward, agricultural south.

Description of Italian culture has given rise to a rich vocabulary of terms. Individualism, familism, particularism, localism, clientelism and fatalism are but a few. To these can be added the lack of trust in others, in particular the major institutions of society, the lack of a sense of state and collective interests and the lack of a 'public ethic'. All these factors exist to some extent in the Italian culture and find expression in the way in which society functions, but it is easy to exaggerate their effects on modern Italy or their specificity to the Italians. The lack of a public ethic would appear to be confirmed by the *tangentopoli* scandals alluded to earlier. But Italy is not unique amongst its European partners in being engulfed by corruption scandals, as the inhabitants of France or Spain would testify. Many of the defining characteristics of Italian culture are, in fact, present in all the other countries in Europe. The problem for the Italians is one of interpretation of their meaning. As Vertone observes, individualism, when applied to the Italians, is not viewed as a tendency toward autonomy and independence, but rather as an obstacle to concerted action and cooperation or as a difficulty in putting themselves under any form of collective discipline (1994: 159).

From the point of view of the discussion of welfare in general and health care in particular, there is much evidence to suggest that despite the Italians' mistrust of public authority, there is a widespread commitment to the ideals of distributive justice and a belief that public welfare should act as an instrument of redistribution. Surveys of European opinion always demonstrate that the Italians are more willing to explain the existence of poverty as a product of the system rather than as individual failure. The extent to which there has been a fiscal backlash in Italy is due, in large measure, to the fact that tax avoidance by the rich has been seen as placing a higher tax burden on dependent workers. It has not been the fact of taxation which has caused the problem, but the unequal burden of taxes.

The concept of 'amoral familism' was coined by Banfield to account for the pathological effects that family-centredness had on southern Italian society. According to Banfield, the central precept was 'Maximise the material short run advantage of the nuclear family; assume all others do likewise' (1958: 85). The notion of 'amoral familism' combined with the Italian view of individualism, outlined above, created a climate in which the altruism and trust necessary for the formation of independent voluntary societies was markedly absent. The changes in Italian society which have taken place since the publication of Banfield's book in 1958 have removed many of the obstacles to the formation of such associations. Nevertheless, Italy is still some way behind many other countries in terms of voluntary activity. Some 21 per cent of Italians between the ages of 18 and 74 years belong to some kind of voluntary group, mostly within the realms of sporting activities. Of these about 21 per cent are active in the sphere of health and social care. Voluntary activity of this type is unevenly distributed throughout the peninsula. Most voluntary activity takes place in the north and centre of the country, with the south lagging some way behind (IREF 1986, 1988). Whether this is due to the persistence of 'amoral familism' in the southern culture or due to the continued economic backwardness of the south which leaves people with less money and free time, is open to conjecture.

One cannot conclude a discussion of the nature of Italian culture without making some reference to the role of religion in creating cultural demarcations in Italy. In many respects the fact that the Catholic Church has its headquarters in Italy does not appear to have hindered the progress of social developments which are in direct conflict with the Church's teaching. During the 1970s the women's movement was able to achieve important victories against the opposition of the Church in significant areas such as divorce, contraception and abortion. Nevertheless, the Church has played a key role in shaping the attitudes and morals of a vast number of Italians. In the area of social welfare for example, the Church has played a significant role in preventing the early development of a fully collectivist welfare state. The Church has always been jealous of its role in providing charity to the needy, and as a consequence suspicious of any state involvement which might hinder its ability to proselytise through Church-controlled welfare organisations. The Church's influence within the Christian Democratic Party and the latter's control of all Italian governments until the 1994 elections, enabled it to delay welfare legislation and, where delay was no longer tenable, to dilute its impact.

Table 3.1 Population growth in the major cities, 1951–81

City	1951	1961	1971	1981
Rome	100	132	168	172
Milan	100	124	136	126
Naples	100	117	121	120
Turin	100	143	162	155
Genoa	100	114	119	111

Source: based on King (1985)

Social factors

Italy has undergone a major social transformation since the end of the war. Urbanisation, which had more or less been completed in Britain by the turn of the last century, only really began in earnest in Italy during the 1950s. Mass migration from the predominantly agrarian south to the industrial north produced the present situation in which over 85 per cent of the population live in communes defined as being urban or semi-urban in nature. Taking the population of the major cities to stand at 100 in 1951, their growth during the subsequent thirty-year period can be seen from Table 3.1.

The growth in the population of the major cities placed enormous strains upon the structure of their services. The economic miracle which had created the migration to the cities was not matched by a social miracle in terms of the quality of life the people experienced (Serpellon 1983). The massive social unrest which occurred at the end of the 1960s, often referred to as the 'hot autumn' of 1969 when students and workers joined forces in quite violent demonstrations, was the product of dissatisfaction with the quality of health care, transport, housing and education in the large population centres. The system of welfare which had been created during the previous sixty years or so proved totally unable to cope with the demands placed upon it by the changing structure of the population.

No discussion of the context of health care would be complete without mention of the impact of social class on the distribution of health care. In Italy, as elsewhere in the developed world, a lively debate is taking place concerning the relationship between such factors as education, professional status, socio-economic conditions and geography on mortality and morbidity rates (see, for example, Fox 1989; Paci 1993). As the data in Table 3.2 demonstrate, life expectancy is greatly improved the higher the subject's level of educational attainment and occupational status.

Table 3.2 Death rates in Italy, 1981

	Men		Women	
Age	*18–25*	*55–74*	*18–25*	*55–74*
Education				
Elementary	114*	104	144	104
Lower middle	90	103	102	100
Upper middle	73	90	82	79
Degree	58	82	83	69
Professional Status				
Imprenditore (entrepreneur)	75	75	73	60
Manager	64	61	107	67
Administrative	69	63	73	40
Skilled manual	73	57	63	56
Unskilled manual	80	53	57	46
Unemployed/inactive	359	118	123	103

Source: ISTAT (1990)
* 100 = average for population

Hidden within these statistics are a number of trends common to many of the countries studied in the present work. There is, for instance, a growing body of evidence which links high rates of suicide with unemployment, especially amongst young males. The suicide rate in Italy per 100,000 of the population in 1984 was 6.5 amongst the employed and 25.7 amongst the unemployed.

The nature of the debate surrounding the above statistics expresses itself in a number of questions. Do people become ill because of the nature of their work or does prior illness dictate the type of employment the subject can choose? Is it the nature of the work or individual behaviour which exposes people to the risk of illness? Are people with low levels of educational attainment less likely to seek medical advice and therefore expose themselves to greater risk than their better-educated colleagues?

There is no doubt, for instance, that in Italy, as elsewhere, high alcohol consumption, smoking and poor diet are more likely to occur amongst those in the lower educational and income groups. It is equally true that semi-skilled and unskilled workers suffer a greater risk of industrial accidents and illness than do other occupation groups. A study in Turin showed that highly educated people were less likely to smoke and were five times more likely to indulge in physical exercise than were people with low levels of education (Costa and Pronta 1993). A study of the accident and emergency department of a Turin hospital showed that the lower the level of educational achievement of the patient the more likely he or she was to delay the request for treatment and by so doing increase the level of risk (Vineis and Capri 1994).

In Italy the weight of evidence points firmly in the direction of a strong link between life expectancy, morbidity and utilisation of health services on the one hand and socio-economic and cultural conditions on the other. It is difficult to see how the reforms to be discussed later in the chapter will address such issues.

The governmental and political setting

If one formed one's opinion of the Italian political system by reading a copy of the Italian Constitution, one would be left with the view that government in Italy is conducted on broadly similar lines to that of its close European neighbours. Any such conclusion would be gravely mistaken. Over the forty-eight years which have elapsed since the Constitution was ratified in 1947, the political system which has emerged in Italy is only a pale representation of the one which inspired the imagination of those who drafted the Constitution in the dark days following the end of the war.

In their desire to ensure that Italy was never again subjected to dictatorial rule of the kind imposed upon the country by the Fascists, the architects of the Constitution left the organs of the state with far too little, rather than too much, authority (see Hine 1993). A far too stringent system of checks and balances left a power void at the heart of the political system, which was rapidly filled by the political parties. Every aspect of political life in Italy became their preserve. The Italians use the term *partitocrazia* to denote a power system based upon rule by parties. In one sense it could be argued that all western democracies are based upon rule by political parties. The textbooks tell us that parties aggregate demands, put up candidates to fight elections and, if they win, they occupy the positions of power at national or local level. However, the term 'partitocracy' in the Italian lexicon implies a pathological process in which every nook and cranny of public life is controlled, or in some way influenced, by party considerations. Positions in any organisation which is in any way dependent upon state money are filled by party members or supporters in order to ensure that the maximum benefit accrues to their party of origin. The health service, as will be shown below, has been particularly vulnerable to the worst aspects of *partitocrazia*.

The pathological nature of the process is exacerbated even further, as the *tangentopoli* enquiries have revealed, when public money begins to be redirected from the purpose to which it was allocated and absorbed into the coffers of the political parties or the bank accounts of individual party officials. The *tangentopoli* uncovered corruption on a vast scale involving people in both the public and the private sectors as public officials sought back-handers for awarding contracts to the private sector for public works and services. The ex-Minister of Health is, as already observed, locked in a Naples gaol awaiting trial for taking money when awarding contracts for the publicity for the anti-AIDS campaign.

Leaving aside the illicit aspects of Italian politics, problems still remain with regard to the way the political system operates from the point of view of the democratic changeover of power. The Italian experience has been described variously as a 'blocked' or 'bargained' democracy. The main characteristic of the former is the failure to produce any semblance of alternating government. Though the Italian Communist Party (PCI) was by far the largest communist party outside the communist bloc and, at its height in the mid-1970s, challenged the supremacy of the Christian Democrats, it was permanently excluded from power at the national level. The PCI's exclusion left power in the hands of the Christian Democrats and their centre allies, the socialists, social democrats, liberals and republicans, to which there was literally no alternative.

The concept of bargained democracy denotes a situation in which weak and unstable coalitions respond to demands emanating from powerful groups in society in an *ad hoc* and haphazard fashion. Each separate demand is responded to with minute pieces of legislation which themselves produce new grievances and further demands for yet more legislation. The main victim of this kind of political behaviour is consistent and effective decision-making. The creation of the National Health Service (NHS) in 1978 is, in this respect, very untypical of the Italian political process and was the product of rather unusual circumstances. This will be discussed in more detail on p. 63.

As far as the organisational structure of government is concerned, power is distributed between governments at national, regional, provincial and communal levels. Despite the fact that the 1947 Constitution grants a good deal of autonomy to all the peripheral levels of government, successive governments at the national level have denied the sub-national units any real autonomy. Indeed, it took over twenty years for the central government to pass the legislation necessary for the establishment of the regional governments despite the key role allocated to them by the Constitution. The communal system of government has a history which pre-dates by centuries that of the unified Italian state. Despite their long history the role of the communes has been more one of decentralised administration than of devolved government. The provinces are even less units of devolved government than are the communes; their principal function is to provide a power base for the all-powerful prefect (Spence 1993).

Since 1990, however, the structure of sub-national government has been changing in a substantial way. New metropolitan governments have been created, based upon the large population centres, and the communes have been given a great deal of statutory autonomy, enabling them to adapt their structures and procedures to local requirements. The problem of local finance has still to be resolved, however. Despite recent changes, permitting greater local tax-raising powers, Italian government remains the most centralised when considered from the perspective of local fiscal autonomy.

The system of regional and local government has been critical in determining the nature of health reform since the creation of the NHS. Many of the reasons for the failure of the reforms to achieve their objectives have been laid at the door of the communal system of government. These issues will be discussed in more detail in the consideration of the administrative structure of the health system (pp. 64ff.).

Economic performance

Despite the many political problems which have beset Italy throughout much of the post-war period, the country has undergone rapid economic growth. Depending on how the GDP is measured, Italy has either overtaken Britain as the fifth-largest economy in the world, or is just behind Britain, in sixth place. Given Italy's low starting point in the devastation caused by the second world war, the process has been nothing short of an economic miracle. The term 'economic miracle' has been used to describe the years roughly coinciding with the thirteen-year period between 1950 and 1963. From 1950 to 1958, Italy underwent a period of economic growth based largely on the growth of the domestic economy through large-scale investments in infrastructure. The second period between 1958 and 1963, which was largely dominated by production for the export market, produced a rate of growth in the Italian economy matched only by the Japanese economy during the same period. Throughout the whole thirteen years, growth in the Italian GDP averaged around 6 per cent and in one year, 1961, reached 8.3 per cent.

One of the principal factors explaining the economic success during this time was a constant supply of cheap and unorganised labour from the south. When the southern workers became fully integrated into the trade union structures such rapid growth on the back of cheap labour was no longer a possibility. In the 1970s Italian wage levels began to approach those of the rest of Europe and Italy's competitive advantage started to disappear; growth rates came into line with those of its immediate trading partners in Europe.

Economic growth has had an enormous impact upon the nature of the labour market in the post-war period. In 1950 about 42 per cent of people were directly employed in agricultural occupations. By 1983 the numbers had declined to just over 12 per cent, falling still further to around 9.5 per cent in 1990. In 1951 just over 32 per cent of people were employed in manufacturing industry. After rising to over 44 per cent in 1970 the figure decreased to around its 1951 total before declining again to just under 30 per cent in 1990. The major area of growth has been in the service sector (private services and public administration). In 1951 this accounted for about a quarter of total employment. In 1980 it accounted for just over 53 per cent and had risen to just over 68 per cent in 1992.

The sectoral changes in the labour market have been matched by equally dramatic changes in its social composition. The movement towards a service economy has brought with it a rapid increase in the participation rate of women in the economy, to the extent that in 1990 female participation amounted to just under 49 per cent of the labour market. This is bound to clash with the role traditionally allocated to women as carers. This fact, along with the changing age structure of the population, is bound to place even greater demands on the health service in the not too distant future.

THE DEVELOPMENT OF STATE INVOLVEMENT

In Italy the first public initiative in the sphere of health was taken in 1865 when legislation was enacted making it obligatory for the provinces and communes to provide medical care for the poor, mentally ill and their dependants. This was followed by later legislation (1888) placing responsibility on the provinces and communes for maintaining sound hygiene and public health. The impact of the legislation can be judged by the fact that almost half of the 19,000 registered doctors were employed by the provincial and communal authorities (Piperno 1986: 154). Both these pieces of legislation were inspired more by the desire to maintain public order than by a humanitarian concern for protecting the vulnerable in society.

Despite the rapid development of social insurance legislation during the first two decades of the twentieth century, no major steps were taken towards greater involvement of the state in health care. Extensive discussions did take place within government concerning the extension of the social insurance system to cover health care in the immediate aftermath of the first world war (Cherubini 1977). Any government plans to bring this about were met with strong opposition from the medical profession and hospitals, which feared a loss of independence. There was also stiff opposition from employers, who were unwilling to contribute to the insurance funds. These debates were brought to an abrupt end when the Fascists took power in 1922.

With the advent of the Fascist regime, the question of social insurance was given the highest priority. The regime claimed social insurance to be the highest form of collaboration between the classes (Cherubini 1977: 272) and set about extending the existing social insurance schemes covering retirement, invalidity, industrial accidents, unemployment and maternity, to cover an increasing number of workers, mainly amongst the industrial working class.

Within the realm of health care, the government adopted the principle that no collective agreements between employers and workers would be considered legitimate unless they contained elements aimed at providing health care for the workforce. The result was the creation of a system of health insurance paid for by contributions from workers and employers without any contribution from the state. Linking health insurance to collective contracts in this way, the government created a system of health care which conformed to Titmuss's industrial achievement-performance model of welfare (Titmuss 1974: 31). It also produced a system of immense complexity. Linking health insurance to the market introduced a wide disparity of treatment, dependent upon the worker's salary and type of employment. Employees working in areas of public service deemed important to the regime enjoyed more benefits than other workers. The industrial working class enjoyed more benefits than agricultural workers. Those categories of workers left unprotected by the system were dependent on a poor law system or charity. In 1937 only 46 per cent of industrial workers and 24 per cent of those employed in agriculture were covered by health insurance (Cherubini 1977).

The regime tried to bring some order to the insurance chaos through the creation, in 1943, of the Istituto Nazionale per L'Asicurazione contro Malattie (National Insurance Sickness Institute) (INAM) which brought under one umbrella organisation many of the insurance funds which had previously been the product of collective agreements. As well as providing sickness insurance INAM would also provide medical treatment directly to the insured worker and his dependants. However, simply bringing together diverse schemes within one organisation did not achieve any kind of parity of treatment. The market-related differences continued within the administration of INAM.

Before INAM became fully operational, the Fascist regime had collapsed leaving the way open for a complete overhaul of the system along democratic and egalitarian lines. However, it would be another thirty-five years before such a plan became a reality.

Alongside the measures described above, the Fascist regime's concern for the size of the population and the quality of the racial stock led to the creation of a number of organisations which had, as part of their function, concern for health-related issues. One such organisation was the Opera Nazionale Maternita ed Infanzie (National Agency for Maternity and Childhood) (OMNI). Established in 1925, OMNI was concerned with the health care of mothers, children and families. Its major objective was that of increasing the rate of growth of the population and ensuring its health through co-ordinating a range of activities focusing on the family. This was part of a series of measures intended to provide Mussolini with six million 'bayonets' and a population of 60 million by 1950 (Terranova 1975).

The return to democratic government in 1945 should have provided Italy with the opportunity of creating a fully democratic welfare state. The British Beveridge Report had been widely discussed amongst the various resistance movements in Italy which, once the hostilities had ended, were determined to set the Italian state on a similar road. In 1947, the D'Aragona Commission was set up to make recommendations for a reform of the system of social insurance. The D'Aragona Commission's report did not constitute a Beveridge plan; however, its approach was clearly innovative and inspired by the principles of equity and efficiency (Ferrera 1984). Health reform was a central element of the report, the key theme of which was the need to unify the administration and delivery of health care. The ideals which inspired the D'Aragona Commission were also reflected in the work of those charged with drawing up the post-war Constitution. Article 32 of the Constitution states that 'The Republic provides health safeguards as a basic right of the individual and in the interests of the community' (see Hernandez 1965; Delogu 1967).

Despite the D'Aragona Commission, the exhortations of the Constitution and numerous official and unofficial reports, the system of health care, along with the rest of the welfare system, remained unchanged for over two decades. Health care was largely left to the private sector by way of contracts between large numbers of health insurance funds and independent doctors, hospitals and pharmacists. Rather than seeking to reform it, the government was content to extend the system to previously excluded categories of workers. About two-thirds of the population were covered by the insurance funds in 1955; a decade later the figure had reached over 90 per cent (Franco 1993). The failure to reform the health service was a disaster both for the health of the nation and for public finances. The major weaknesses of the health system organised on the basis of insurance funds were as follows:

- The right to health care was based upon one's position in the labour market and not on citizenship;
- the system was highly fragmented with literally hundreds of funds having direct or indirect responsibility for health services;
- treatment within and between the various funds was extremely variable in terms of services covered and the length of care provided;
- there were significant regional disparities, with the towns and cities of the north being better endowed with physicians, hospitals and other medical services than were the towns and cities of the south;
- the funds were constantly in a state of financial crisis, with the state having to relieve the deficits as a result of the lack of co-ordination between the financiers and the providers of health care; and
- concerned as they were with providing insurance against risks of sickness, there was no place in the health system for preventive medicine.

The organisation of health care on this basis continued for so long because it served a useful purpose in the clientelistic politics which characterised the system of power created by the Christian Democrats and their allies (Terranova 1975; Cazzola 1976). This combination of particularism and clientelism has been identified by numerous authors as the defining characteristic of the Italian welfare system (Ascoli 1984; Paci 1989).

Pressure to reform the system became overwhelming during the latter years of the 1960s and the early 1970s. Both the insurance funds and the hospitals were in a constant state of financial crisis with quality of health care well below the standard achieved in other countries with comparable levels of expenditure. The government sought to tackle the problem with partial measures when what was needed was complete root and branch reform.

One such partial reform was introduced into the hospital service in 1968. This removed the anomaly of having the hospitals within the remit of the Ministry of the Interior rather than the Ministry of Health. It also attempted to broaden the role of hospitals beyond that of therapeutic and diagnostic care which they had traditionally performed. Perhaps more importantly, the legislation sought to introduce a form of planning into the hospital service by giving the regions (then not formally created) the responsibility for planning and co-ordinating both public and private hospitals in order to achieve specific objectives.

The reform of the hospital service was rather like placing the cart before the horse. The real problem facing the service stemmed from the lack of an adequate system of primary health care to regulate demand for hospital care more than any inherent problem in the hospital sector itself. Not surprisingly, therefore, the problems of the health care system were not substantially affected by the reform.

Not deterred by the failure of this partial approach, the government tried, on yet one more occasion, to resolve the health care problem short of complete reform. This occurred in 1974 when a measure was taken to transfer to the regional governments the increasing debts which the sickness funds had incurred with the hospitals. This measure, however, made future reform an inevitability in so far as it removed the pretence that the financing of health care was anything other than the direct responsibility of the state. In removing the major item of expenditure from the sickness funds, the next step – removing the sickness funds themselves – became much easier (Cosmacini 1994).

The reform, when it came, was the product of a highly unusual set of circumstances. At a superficial level there appeared to be a growing consensus between left and right that reform was necessary and both looked to the British National Health Service as their role model, but for slightly different motives. The right, alarmed by the growing cost of health care, looked to the British system as a way of rationing care and reducing costs. In the changed political climate at the time it was probably the 'least worst' of the possible alternatives. The left admired the British system because of the equality it manifested in terms of both finance and access.

The second unusual circumstance was the nature of the coalition which governed Italy during the period in which the reform was enacted. A government of national solidarity was put in place to confront an intense economic crisis and the growing threat of terrorism from both the extreme left and right of the political spectrum. The government of national solidarity consisted of a left of centre governing coalition dependent upon the abstention of the Communist Party in parliamentary votes. The price the Communists extracted for such support was a series of social reforms, of which health care was the most important. Whether the reform would have been forthcoming without the pressure from the Communist Party is a matter of conjecture. The way in which support quickly evaporated within the centre and right parties once the immediate crisis was over suggests that far more concessions would have been made to vested interests had not the Communists played such a central role in maintaining government stability during the vital period leading up to the reform.

THE PRINCIPAL FEATURES OF SERVICE DELIVERY AND ADMINISTRATION

Primary health care

The first point of contact for the ordinary citizen with the health services is normally through the general practitioner (GP). There are 63,000 GPs who are liberal professionals contracted to the local health authorities (LHA) (about 7 per cent; just over 4,600 of this number are paediatricians) and who are paid on a per capita basis. Each GP is allowed a patient list of no more than 1,500 but in practice such a list size is rare and the average is in the region of 857 patients. The result is that there are over 4 million visits to GPs each year with the average patient making about seven visits per year; 387 million prescriptions are dispensed and 410 million requests for specialist care or analysis are made. It is the GP who provides access to pharmaceutical products, visits to specialists, diagnostic tests and hospital care (Ministry of Health 1990).

Other areas of primary health care are controlled by the communal authorities and include care provided by a network of over 3,000 family advice centres available to mothers, and mothers to be; and occupational medicine.

One of the major developments which has taken place since the inception of the National Health Service is the growth in the role of the voluntary sector in health care. The 1978 Act which created the health service contains provisions to encourage the health authorities to enter into agreements with and foster the development of voluntary organisations. As a result of this, and subsequent legislation, the voluntary sector has been extremely active in the spheres of care for the elderly, mental health, drug dependency, AIDS, and disability. Nevertheless, as observed above, the extent of voluntary activity, though growing, still lags behind that of other West European countries.

Secondary care

Hospital care absorbs the lion's share of health service expenditure accounting for over 60 per cent of the total. The hospital sector is similar to that of many of the health care systems discussed in this book in that it manifests clearly the public/private mix. From a legal perspective, hospitals can be divided into three groups: those directly managed by the LHA and therefore firmly located within the public sector; hospitals within the public sector but outside LHA control; and those which are contracted to provide services. The latter group includes teaching hospitals controlled by the universities and private hospitals contracted to the LHAs.

The total number of hospitals is 1,774, 65 per cent of which are public and the remainder private, with a total of 437,739 beds. Looked at from the point of view of the distribution of beds between the different types of hospital, a slightly different picture emerges. Whilst the private sector accounts for 35 per cent of hospitals, it provides only 15 per cent of beds. This is due to the smaller size of the hospitals in the private sector.

Italy, in common with many other countries in the developed world, has experienced a steady rise in the rate of hospitalisation over recent decades. In 1961 the rate was 997 per hundred thousand of the population. In 1971 it had risen to 1,617. It rose further to 1,778 in 1981. Since 1981 there has been a steady decline, to reach the figure of 1,711 by the end of the 1980s. The causes of the rise in the rate of hospitalisation are many and varied and a detailed analysis of them is beyond the scope of this chapter. A broad explanation can be found in a complex of demographic, epidemiological, technical-scientific, organisational and political factors. The encouraging aspect is that there appears to be a decline in the rate of hospitalisation in the 1990s. This decline can be explained by the steady improvement in recent years in the quality of both primary health care and care provided by social services. However, once again these improvements have been patchy. In some areas the quality of care in both sectors has improved markedly as genuine attempts at integrating services and improving social work training have come to fruition. In others, however, particularly in the south, little noticeable improvement has occurred. The now famous psychiatric reforms of the late 1970s have also complicated the picture somewhat. The closure of many psychiatric hospitals significantly reduced the availability of beds. The release into the community of large numbers of psychiatric patients without the necessary community care facilities has increased demand for beds in other sectors of the service.

Administrative arrangements

The major feature of the National Health Service as created by the 1978

Health Service Act was administrative decentralisation in so far as service delivery is almost totally undertaken at the local level.

Local level

By far the most important organs of the health service are the Unità Sanitaria Locale (USL), or local health authorities. These provide almost all health services and spend well over 90 per cent of the health service budget. They vary in size on a national basis, from a minimum of 50,000 to a maximum of about 200,000 inhabitants. Because of the fragmented nature of communal government in Italy, the 673 local health authorities had to be superimposed on a structure consisting of 8,032 communes. The complexity of local government can be illustrated by reference to the diversity in size of local government units. About 6,000 of the communes, nearly 74 per cent, have populations of under 5,000. Only about 163, 2 per cent, have populations between 50,000 and 250,000. Eleven of the largest cities between them cover 20 per cent of the entire population (Rotelli 1991; Spence 1993). As a consequence of these enormous disparities in size, the regional governments were obliged to create LHAs in three different ways: by amalgamating a number of smaller communes into a single LHA; by dividing the large urban communes into several LHAs; or coinciding a LHA with an existing communal structure.

Not only were the LHAs to be the main service providers, but they were also to be the main instrument through which democratic participation was to occur. To facilitate such participation, the LHAs were created with elected assemblies. However, plans to have the assemblies directly elected by the local population were rejected early in the legislative programme in favour of indirect election from members of the assembly of the interested communes. The assembly in turn elects the management committee of the LHA, which is composed of between four and six members, depending on population size.

Of all the aspects of the health service, the organisational structure of the LHAs has received most criticism. Those wishing to create a system of democratic medicine were disillusioned from the beginning by the failure to achieve direct elections to the assemblies. Over the fourteen-year life of the health service the LHAs degenerated, in the vast majority of cases, into instruments of party patronage and nepotism. Very rarely were people nominated to the management committees because of any knowledge, expertise or even interest in health care. The primary consideration was nearly always one of maintaining the balance of power between the political parties at the local level and giving reward to party hacks. The ideal of democracy in the health service had, in other words, been abandoned in favour of 'partitocracy' (Ferrera 1986; Freddi 1984). In such a climate, the massive funds controlled by the LHAs were ripe for utilisation in the patronage and corruption which the Italians refer to as *sottogoverno*, literally undergovernment, and which have been brought to light as part of the judicial enquiries into the *tangentopoli* (della Porta 1992).

In 1989 the 637 LHAs in Italy employed around 621,000 people of which 373,264 were medical staff (59.9 per cent); 1,281 (0.2 per cent) non-medical professionals; 178,806 (28.7 per cent) technical staff; and 68,514 (11 per cent) administrative staff. The ratio of health service staff to the overall population amounts to 10.8 for every thousand. If one adds to the overall number those groups employed in the private sector, the total employed in the health sector increases to almost 800,000.

Regional level

The twenty regional governments have responsibility for planning and co-ordinating health care at a regional level through the determination of regional health plans. They have to ensure the equal distribution of health services within their territory and ensure that services are provided on a cost-efficient basis. Health issues for which the regions have specific competence are prevention and environmental health; veterinary health and hygiene; and the education and training of medical staff other than doctors. The regions also have a good deal of legislative autonomy, particularly with regard to the structure, size and financial control of the LHAs (see Figure 3.3).

National level

Under the 1978 Health Service Act, a number of important tasks were, because of their nature, left to the central government. Chief amongst these were the setting of national objectives and standards in health care and ensuring equality of access to care across the national territory. These issues are covered in the National Health Plan. The central government is also responsible for controlling the supply and quality of pharmaceutical products; entering into international agreements on health issues and the control of personnel functions such as education and training, and the setting and regulation of salaries and conditions of employment.

Statutory bodies have been created in order to supply the government

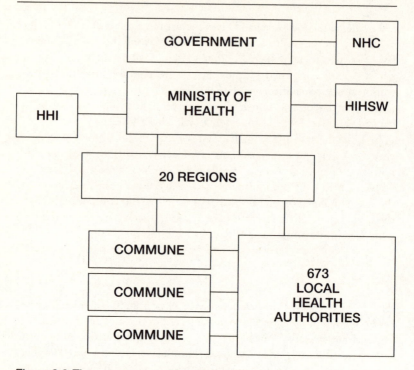

Figure 3.3 The organisation of health care

with expert information on a number of issues. The most important is the National Health Council (NHC) which makes a significant contribution to the formulation of health policy in general and the National Health Plan in particular. Its responsibility lies both in the formulation of the plan and in monitoring its implementation to ensure national standards. The NHC is composed of forty-five members representing the regions, interested departments of central government such as the Health Ministry, the two finance ministries, the Ministry of Labour and Social Security, the Ministries of the Interior, Defence, Industry, Agriculture and Scientific Research. Also included are representatives from two other statutory bodies attached to the Ministry of Health. First, the Istituto Superiore di Sanità (ISS: Higher Health Institute) provides the major source of scientific and technical information and support and is charged with responsibility for research into AIDS, for example. Second, the Higher Institute for Health and Safety at Work (HIHSW) advises the Ministry on the safety and health implications of new technology and industrial techniques.

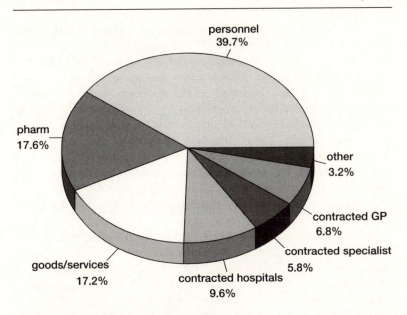

Figure 3.4 Health expenditure by category
Source: Ministry of Health (1990)

FINANCING ARRANGEMENTS

Health expenditure has remained constant for a number of years. On this basis one could say that one of the principal objectives of the 1978 reform has been achieved. However, the point that was raised at the beginning of the chapter is worth repeating. The problem with the NHS in Italy is not that it spends too much; rather, what it spends, it spends badly. The proportion of the GDP spent on all health care in Italy is about 7.6 per cent, a figure which compares favourably with those of all its European partners but one which appears beyond the wildest dreams of American health care planners (see Chapter 7).

The largest share of the health service budget, just under 40 per cent of the total, goes on personnel. The next largest item of expenditure is that dedicated to pharmaceutical services, followed by, in descending order, goods/services, contracted hospitals, contracted GPs, contracted specialist doctors, others (hotel services, etc.) (see Figure 3.4).

The financing of health care is determined on an annual basis by the Finance Act, which decides the level and sectoral distribution of all public expenditure. The proportion of the budget allocated to health care is distributed through the Fondo Sanitario Nazionale (FSN: National Health Fund), to the regional governments and through regions to the LHAs. The money distributed by the FSN is raised through general taxation and charges. The principal objectives of the reformers in establishing the FSN was to control health expenditure by determining in advance its allocation to specific services and administrative centres and closely monitoring their budgets; and to distribute resources in such as way as to remove historical inequalities between both geographical regions and particular services. The previous system, based upon the insurance funds, was incapable of such an exercise. Unfortunately, the FSN has not had a great deal of success in ensuring that either of these objectives have been met.

A number of factors go together to explain this lack of success. The first is that the central government, due to the clash of vested interests, proved itself incapable of issuing a National Health Plan. The service had been in existence for ten years before the first plan emerged. In the absence of such plans, eradicating the historical inequalities proved almost impossible. Second, a product of the above, was that the amount of money allocated to the FSN was always well below that which the regions, and through them the LHAs, needed to perform their services. The consequence was that the LHAs overspent their budgets by a quite substantial margin. The administrative inefficiency of the LHAs, alluded to earlier, was also a major contributory factor to such monetary shortfalls. In the short term the deficiencies in income were covered by borrowing from banks or delaying payments for services. In the longer term the deficits were paid off by the government by way of special finance bills, which negated much of the point of financial planning (Brunetta and Tronti 1991).

Attempts to control health expenditure have, in recent years, led to the introduction of charges to patients for particular services. The Italians refer to such charges as tickets and they are placed mainly upon prescriptions, X-rays, pathology tests and other forms of diagnostic and specialist treatment. The government has given particular attention to the burgeoning cost of the pharmaceutical bill in its attempts to control health expenditure. Italy is one of the largest spenders per capita on pharmaceutical products in the EU; only France and Germany have a higher rate of consumption. The amount of income generated by such co-payments is very small when measured against the overall health bill. In typical fashion the government introduces such charges and then makes concessions when faced with criticism, to the point where so many groups are exempt that the exercise is rendered almost pointless. Since 1981, the government has introduced well over thirty measures regulating co-payment for prescriptions, reflecting the government's difficulties in this area.

Recently, the government has sought to tackle the problem by taking supply side measures by forcing doctors and pharmacists to supply generic drugs instead of highly priced named products. Even this has not been without its problems as pharmaceutical companies are threatening to rethink their investments in Italy because of the reduced profit they claim will result from these measures.

Other attempts to control the health budget are made more difficult because of deficiencies elsewhere in the welfare system. Alternatives to hospital care are restricted by the lack of sufficient nursing homes for the elderly. Overall responsibility for such nursing homes is located in the Ministry of the Interior through its control of the local authorities, which either utilise their own nursing homes or contract them from the private sector; the majority of the latter are run by non-profit religious organisations. Charges for such nursing are based on a means test.

CONTEMPORARY ISSUES IN HEALTH POLICY

The Italian health care system is once again in a state of flux. It has become obvious to supporters and detractors alike that the ideals of the 1978 health reforms are far from being realised. Overbearing bureaucracy, inefficient and corrupt political control, combined with the alienation of many doctors, have brought the service to the point where public support has reached an all-time low. It should be added, however, that it is support for the practice that is low and not the ideals or principles, which still have strong public support.

In 1992 the government introduced major reforms of the system which, if no radical changes are made, will mirror the changes introduced into the health service in the UK in the mid-1980s. These include fundholding GPs; the development of self-managed hospitals; the remodelling of LHAs to remove political control and introduce private management techniques; and measures to increase competition between public and private sector providers. The LHAs and hospitals will in future be designated as *aziende pubbliche*.

The system will give added responsibility and power to the regional governments, forming them into a kind of 'holding' responsible for many of the functions which previously were delegated to the LHAs. One of the major changes with regard to the regions has been in the area of finance. Any budget deficits incurred at the local level now have to be covered by the regional and not the national government. This is intended to impose greater financial discipline on the regions and, through them, the LHAs. The regions, in the new organisation, will have far greater powers and responsibilities for planning, investment, controls over the LHAs and ensuring the quality of service than at present.

The LHAs have been stripped of many of their functions, most notably with regard to the management of the hospital service. Gone also is the role of the local politicians. The LHAs will in future be controlled by managers employed on private sector contracts. The new managers, or to give them their correct name, Director-Generals, will have the responsibility for all the affairs of the LHAs.

A similar change has taken place with regard to the public hospitals. Their management will in future be independent of the LHAs and they will have their own Director-Generals. They will contract their services to the LHAs in the same way that private hospitals do in the present system. The government's intention is to produce a fifty–fifty balance between public and private hospitals in any one region. Hospital finance is also undergoing a radical transformation. In the past the hospitals were financed according to a patient's length of stay. This led to different charges being made by hospitals of different sizes and legal status. The intention is clearly to create 'managed competition' within the hospital service in the hope of driving down costs. The system of finance will be closer to the American diagnostic-related groups than to the British system based on resource groups.

The new arrangements for GPs are, as in the UK, intended to render them more conscious of the financial costs of their decisions, particularly with regard to hospital referrals and prescriptions. There is also the intention of attracting doctors to work in groups with other professionals in health centres, an aspect of primary health care in which Italy lags behind most of its European neighbours.

All the above proposals have yet to be put into practice. Some movement has taken place with regard to the changing management structures of the LHAs and hospitals but so far it has been quite small. The creation of fundholding GPs is still in the distant future.

Privatisation

Reference has already been made to the complicated nature of the public/private mix of health care in Italy. The largely private provision of public-funded health care developed under the health insurance funds as they became increasingly dependent on public money. Much to the annoyance of those on the left of the political spectrum, the situation was not

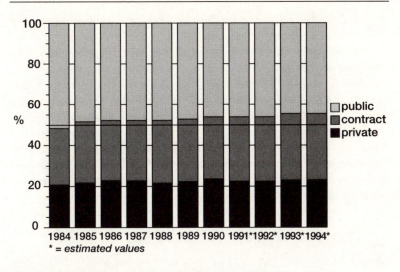

Figure 3.5 Public/private mix in health care, 1984–94
Source: Capri and Ricciarda (1993)

changed by the 1978 reform and there continued to be a public/private mix in which publicly financed services were delivered by private contracted providers. Well over 70 per cent of patients in private hospitals and clinics are financed by public money. Figure 3.4 (p. 69) shows that contracted hospitals, specialists and GPs account for over 22 per cent of public expenditure on health care.

Though most popular discussion in Italy has concentrated upon the effects of maladministration by the LHAs on the quality of health care, there can be no doubt that private providers have had something of a vested interest in ensuring that the public sector did not function as efficiently as it might. Patients dissatisfied with the quality of services provided by the public sector would turn to the private sector and receive the care from the people who should have provided it in the first place. This was particularly true of GPs and hospital doctors contracted to the public sector on a part-time basis. Under the current rules, people waiting in excess of three days for treatment in the public sector can turn to the private sector and have their costs repaid by the health authority.

Figure 3.5 maps the actual and probable direction in which the health care system is travelling. There are three possible mixes: private/private, public/private and public/public and, if the projected trends are accurate, the public/public mix will fall below 50 per cent of the total in the near future.

From the point of view of the health care mix, therefore, Italy has a starting point which is much closer to a quasi-market for health care than was the case in Britain in the mid-1980s. What was lacking in the Italian case was the kind of financial and quality controls that such a complicated public/private mix required. The reform measures alluded to above are designed to install these controls; to remove the influence of politicians; and to secure a more active role for patients and other service users. If and when the proposals become active, it remains to be seen whether the next step is the further reduction of the role of the public sector by replacing public finance with private insurance.

REFERENCES AND FURTHER READING

Almond, G. and Verba, S. (1963) *The Civic Culture*, Princeton: Princeton University Press.
Ascoli, U. (1984) *Il Welfare State, All 'Italiana*, Milan: Franco Angelli.
Banfield, E. (1958) *The Moral Basis of Backward Society*, New York: Glencoe Free Press.
Brunetta, R. and Tronti, L. (1991) *Welfare State and Redistribuzione*, Milan: Franco Angelli.
Capri, S. and Ricciarda, G. (1993) 'Public/private mix and international competition', in C.E.M. Normand and J.P. Vaughan (eds) *Europe without Frontiers: The Implications for Health*, Chichester: John Wiley.
Cazzola, F. (1976) 'I palastri del regime', *Rassegna Italiana di Sociologia* 17 (3): 426–52.
Cherubini, A. (1977) *A la Storia della Previdenza Sociale*, Rome: Editori Riuniti.
Cosmacini, G. (1994) *Storia della Medicina e della Sanità nell' Italia Contemporanea*, Rome: Editori Laterza.
Costa, G. and Pronta, A. (1993) 'La mortalità per classe sociale: differenze o disuguaglianze', *Polis*, 4: 425–45.
della Porta, D. (1992) *Lo Scambio Occulto*, Bologna: Il Mulino.
Delogu, S. (1967) *Sanità Pubblica, Sicurezza Sociale e Programmazione Economica*, Turin: Einaudi Editore.
Ferrera, M. (1984) *Il Welfare State in Italia*, Bologna: Il Mulino.
Ferrera, M. (1986) *La Salute Che Noi Pensiamo*, Bologna: Il Mulino.
Fox, J.(ed.)(1989) *Health Inequalities in European Countries*, Aldershot: Gower.
Franco, D. (1993) *L'Espansione della Spesa Pubblica in Italia*, Bologna: Il Mulino.
Freddi, G. (ed.)(1984) *Salute e Organizzazione nel Servizio Sanitaria Nazionale*, Bologna: Il Mulino.
Hernandez, S. (1965) *Per Una Sistema di Sicurezza Sociale*, Bologna: Il Mulino.
Hine, D. (1993) *Governing Italy*, Oxford: Oxford University Press.
IREF (1986 and 1988) *Rapporto sull' Associazionismo Sociale*, Milan: Franco Angelli.
ISTAT (Istituto Centrale di Statistica) (1990) *Annuario Statistico*, Rome: ISTAT.

King, R. (1985) *The Industrial Geography of Italy*, London: Croom Helm.

Ministry of Health (1990) *Relazione sullo Stato Sanitario del Paese*, Rome.

Paci, M. (1989) *Pubblico e Privato nei Moderni Sistemi di Welfare*, Naples: Liguori Editore.

Paci, M. (ed.)(1993) *Le Dimensioni della Disuguaglianza*, Bologna: Il Mulino.

Piperno, A. (1986) *La Politica Sanitaria in Italia: Tra Continuita e Cambiamento*, Milan: Franco Angelli.

Rotelli, E. (1991) *Le Martello e L'incudine*, Bologna: Il Mulino.

Spence, R. (1993) 'Local government in Italy', in J.Chandler (ed.) *Local Government in Liberal Democracies*, London: Routledge.

Terranova, F. (1975) *Il Potere Assistenziale*, Rome: Editore Riuniti.

Titmuss, R. (1968) *Commitment to Welfare*, London: Allen and Unwin.

Titmuss, R. (1974) *Social Policy: An Introduction*, London: Allen and Unwin.

Vertone, S. (1994) *La Cultura degli Italiani*, Bologna: Il Mulino.

Vineis, V. and Capri, S. (1994) *La Salute non è una Mercè*, Turin: Dollati Boringhieri.

Chapter 4

The Netherlands

Roger Ottewill

The current Dutch health care system can be likened to a patchwork quilt. It consists of a wide variety of structures, both public and private, funding arrangements, and delivery mechanisms, all of which are held together by a number of underlying principles. These include an emphasis on obligations and responsibilities and on solidarity, accommodation and co-operation between the many different interests which have a stake in the system. In addition, although rarely expressed in these terms, implicit in the system are notions of universality and comprehensiveness and health as a social right. However, in seeking to realise these values, the state has traditionally worked with and through legally independent corporate bodies rather than establish organisational structures of its own. In the words of Kirkman-Liff and Maarse: the Dutch health care system is 'built on private sector institutions, but regulated to achieve public goals' (1992: 24). Such an approach facilitates the current moves towards a more market-orientated approach in which the role of the state is likely to be diminished.

Despite the complexity and fragmentation of the Dutch health care system, the services to which every member of the population has access are of a high quality and are technologically advanced. As Tiddens et al. point out: 'Both the training of all personnel who are employed in the system and the material facilities, in the form of buildings and apparatus, meet the highest standards' (1984: 373). This is not surprising given that the Netherlands is a highly developed and relatively wealthy society. Nonetheless, those responsible for the development and delivery of health care face major challenges arising, in part, from the changing context within which they have to operate.

THE CONTEXT OF DUTCH HEALTH CARE

The demographic structure

With a population of 15,341,553 (as at 1 January 1994) and a land area of 33,936 square kilometers, the Netherlands is one of the most densely populated countries in Europe. The population density is 452 persons per square kilometre. Consequently, from a geographical point of view, access to health care facilities, such as hospitals and clinics, is relatively easy. For example, the majority of the population can reach a hospital from their home within forty-five minutes.

Like the population of most developed countries, that of the Netherlands is rapidly ageing. In 1960 only 8.7 per cent of the Dutch population was aged 65 years and over, by 1993 this had increased to 13.1 per cent and by the year 2000 it is estimated that approximately 14 per cent will be classified as elderly. By the year 2010 the figure will·be 15 per cent, and by the year 2030, 23 per cent. Clearly this has far-reaching implications for the nature and scale of the demands placed upon the health care system. Already there is an acute shortage of beds for psychogeriatric patients.

The situation is exacerbated by an increasingly unfavourable dependency ratio. In 1980 the total dependency ratio was 50.6 and the aged dependency ratio was 17.3. The latter is expected to increase to 22.1 per cent by the year 2010 and 37.8 per cent by the year 2030.

Epidemiological trends

Turning to the health status of the Dutch population, during the twentieth century there have been significant improvements in the infant mortality and life expectancy rates. Details are provided in Table 4.1.

During the past three decades the average amount of alcohol consumed in the Netherlands has tripled from 2.6 litres per head of population in 1960 to 8.2 litres in 1990. Thus, not surprisingly, there has been a significant increase in the number of those suffering from alcohol-related problems.

There is also concern over the mental health status of the Dutch population. Currently, between one in three or four people experiences some form of psychological problem, and one in six seeks treatment. It is expected that by the year 2000 this will have risen to one in four. Social and economic factors such as child abuse, sexual abuse and long term unemployment are seen as the causes of this trend.

On a more positive note, the percentage of the population over 15 years

Table 4.1 Selected measures of health status, 1900–90

Year	Infant mortality % of live births	Life expectancy at birth (male) years	Life expectancy at birth (female) years
1900	14.05[e]	51.0	53.7
1930	6.53[e]	61.9	63.5
1950	2.67	70.5	72.8
1960	1.79	71.6	75.5
1970	1.27	70.9	76.6
1980	0.86	72.5	79.2
1990	0.69	73.8	80.1

Source: Central Bureau of Statistics, *Statistical Yearbooks*
[e] = estimate

who are regular smokers reached a high point of 70 per cent in 1970 and subsequently fell to 39 per cent of males and 31 per cent of females in 1990.

The major causes of death are heart disease (approximately 45 per cent), various forms of cancer (approximately 27 per cent), respiratory diseases (approximately 7 per cent) and traffic accidents. By comparison with most other European countries the Netherlands has a very high male mortality rate for deaths caused by malignant neoplasms.

Cultural traditions

Inherent in Dutch society are the values of private initiative and independence, coupled with those of self-help, caution, obligation/responsibility, solidarity and toleration, all of which are reflected in the way in which health care has evolved and is currently organised.

The importance attached to private initiative, independence and self-help can be seen in the creation and subsequent development of the Dutch health care system, with the state maintaining a watching brief and only intervening when circumstances demanded it. This means that there has been a heavy emphasis on the principle of self-regulation by the agencies concerned rather than control by the state.

Another important value has been caution. The Dutch believe in the efficacy of incremental (i.e. gradual) change in order to minimise risk as opposed to radical change. Consequently, the health care system has developed relatively slowly with every proposed change being debated and reflected upon for a long period before being implemented or discarded. Thus, the system has never been subject to the dramatic root and branch reforms experienced in some other countries. For example, the current reform programme was initiated in 1988 and is not expected to be fully implemented until the second half of the 1990s.

Within Dutch society, the stress on obligations means that responsibilities rather than rights tend to take centre stage in discussions on health care. In drawing attention to this value, Kirkman-Liff and Maarse demonstrate how the participants in the health care system 'are bound together by mutual, interlocking obligations' (1992: 24). At the most basic level providers are obliged to care for all patients, who are under an obligation to pay for the care they receive. Practical expression is given to the second of these obligations through the elaborate and complex insurance arrangements which underpin the funding of much of the Dutch health care system. According to Kirkman-Liff and Maarse: 'These obligations tie all participants together in a private sector structure which ensures that all members of society receive care, all providers receive compensation for their efforts, everyone with limited means can afford insurance, and the cost of the system will be kept as low as is reasonable' (ibid.).

Linked to the value of obligation is that of solidarity. As Kirkman-Liff and Maarse have shown, within the Dutch health care system there is a high degree of mutual dependence. This can be seen, for example, in the principle of 'income solidarity' whereby the insured are required to pay a premium related to their income rather than to their likely use of health care facilities. As a result, there is a considerable amount of cross-subsidisation whereby those on high incomes who make relatively little use of the system subsidise those on low incomes who do.

Last, there is the value of toleration. In recent decades the Netherlands has become renowned for its acceptance of different lifestyles and its permissiveness with respect to individual behaviour. As a result, it has experienced, on the one hand, very high levels of sexually transmitted diseases, drug abuse and related health care problems. On the other hand, due in part to the liberal attitude of the Dutch to sex and sexuality, it has the lowest teenage pregnancy rate in Western Europe. Liberal attitudes have also meant that the Netherlands has been at the leading edge of the debate surrounding controversial moral issues, such as abortion and euthanasia, and of policy initiatives in these spheres. It is therefore not surprising that in 1993 the Netherlands became the first nation to legalise euthanasia, albeit with very stringent safeguards.

Social factors

Traditionally, Dutch society has been highly compartmentalised, with the population being divided into a number of well defined groupings. This phenomenon is known as *verzuiling* ('pillarisation') and it has resulted in most kinds of organisation, including those devoted to health care, being founded on distinctive religious or socio-political bases. These are a Protestant, a Roman Catholic, and a secular or general (subdivided into a socialist and liberal) *zuil* or 'pillar'.

With the increasing urbanisation and secularisation of society during the last two to three decades, the salience of the social groupings on which the 'pillars' are based has weakened. Nonetheless, from a historical point of view, their influence on the manner in which the health care system has developed should not be underestimated.

Other trends associated with the urbanisation and secularisation of Dutch society are a reduction in the size of families, greater mobility and an increasing divorce rate. This means a growing number of single-person households. From the point of view of health care provision, greater reliance is having to be placed on formal health workers and less on informal carers.

At the same time, as van Es points out, service users are now 'better educated, better informed, more self-confident and more demanding than in the past' (1990: 292). In short, their expectations are greater. They expect a better quality of service and to be treated as equals by health care professionals. They are also more likely to complain if they are dissatisfied with the service they receive, or if they do not receive the service to which they feel they are entitled. Clearly, this places additional demands upon the health care system.

The governmental and political setting

In formal terms, the Netherlands is a constitutional monarchy with its system of government based on the principle of parliamentary democracy. Parliament (the States-General) consists of two chambers. The members of the upper or first chamber are indirectly elected. Members of the lower or second chamber are directly elected using a system of proportional representation. Due to the proportionality inherent in the electoral system and the relatively large number of cleavages in Dutch society, the party system is fragmented, with the result that governments are invariably coalitions. On taking office, the coalition government will agree a broad policy statement, which serves as a guideline for the various departments. The department responsible for health care is the Ministry of Welfare, Health and Culture (recently renamed the Ministry of Public Health, Welfare and Sport). However, in recent years, health has become such an important political issue that it is, in the words of van Es, 'no longer exclusively the concern of the Minister of Welfare, Health and Cultural Affairs, but . . . a theme which is the responsibility of the entire cabinet' (1990: 298).

The Dutch political system is described by Lijphart (1968) as 'consociational'. This is intended to capture the high degree of accommodation which exists in the relations between the political parties and the degree of collegiality inherent in the public policy-making process. Such a style of policy-making is congruent with the 'complex corporatist framework' (Flynn 1993: 69) through which policy is implemented. In the case of health care policy this can be seen in the existence of a relatively large number of advisory boards, which are considered in more detail later in the chapter. Consequently, despite the traditional divisions within Dutch society, the political system is both viable and stable and a high degree of support can generally be secured for proposed legislation on aspects of health care and other topics of public concern.

Turning to the sub-national tiers of government, the Netherlands is a decentralised unitary state with a well developed two-tier system of local government. For this purpose, the country is divided into twelve provinces and approximately 700 municipalities. Each province has its own representative body, the provincial states. These are entitled to issue ordinances concerning the welfare of the province and to raise taxes. They also seek to promote and protect the interests of the province, when these are threatened by internal and external developments.

Each municipality is governed by a municipal council, the members of which are directly elected. The council has the right to issue by-laws concerning the welfare of the municipality and may levy taxes.

All three tiers of government – national, provincial and municipal – play a part in the operation of the Dutch health care system. This extends from policy-making and planning to aspects of service delivery.

Economic performance

Although the Dutch enjoy a high standard of living, in recent decades the rate of economic growth has tended to fall. This has been due to the impact of international developments, such as the oil crisis of 1973, which resulted in higher rates of inflation and unemployment as the government took steps to deal with the situation. Moreover, in the Netherlands economic problems have been exacerbated by budget deficits.

Table 4.2 Share of national resources devoted to health care, 1960–90

Year	Total spending on health % of GDP	Public spending on health % of GDP
1960	3.9	1.3
1970	6.0	5.1
1980	8.3	6.5
1990	8.1	5.9

Source: Central Bureau of Statistics, *Statistical Yearbooks*

At the same time, as the data in Table 4.2 illustrate, since the 1960s health care has developed into one of the most important components of the economy. Significantly, about 10 per cent of the Dutch labour force is now employed in the health care sector. This reflects not only economic and demographic factors such as the tendency for spending on health care to increase at a faster rate than spending generally, due to the ageing of the population, but also underlying political and cultural developments. In particular, it is a manifestation of the fact that, with the growth of state involvement in health care, people's expectations regarding their health status are now higher than they have ever been.

THE DEVELOPMENT OF STATE INVOLVEMENT

The origins of state involvement can be traced back to the cholera epidemics between the 1830s and 1860s and the general distress among the population at large during the first half of the nineteenth century. This combination of factors resulted in considerable pressure being exerted on the government to take steps to alleviate the situation. In 1865, government, under the leadership of the far-sighted Thorbecke, responded by securing the enactment of no fewer than four pieces of legislation which laid the foundations of the state's role in health care and initiated what has been described as 'quality control by government' (Rutten and van der Werff 1982: 171).

Two of these dealt with medical and pharmaceutical practice respectively and stipulated that in future only appropriately qualified persons would be allowed to practise. Another dealt with the conditions that needed to be met before someone could practise as a physician, pharmacist or midwife. These included the acquisition of qualifications which could only be gained by passing an examination before a government commission following a period of approved training.

The final piece of legislation made provision for state supervision of health care generally and, in so doing, laid the foundations of a state health inspectorate. Responsibility for exercising the supervisory role was to be exercised by state health inspectors. The inspectors were public employees with a medical qualification, each of whom was appointed to serve in a particular province. They were required to ensure the observation of the law with respect to clinical practice and to advise the Minister on health conditions in their province and to propose measures for dealing with them. Although during the remaining decades of the nineteenth century the state health inspectors endeavoured to raise the profile of public health, as Querido points out, they 'were largely frustrated in their work [and] their organisation did not develop' (1968: 34). This was mainly due to opposition from national politicians and a relative lack of concern at local level. Nonetheless, their efforts did result in various legislative measures being enacted during this period, of which the Epidemic Diseases Act of 1872 was undoubtedly the most important.

By the beginning of the twentieth century, due to rapid social and technological developments and the emergence of radicalism, support for public health measures had grown. At this point two developments are worthy of note.

First, by making school attendance compulsory and prescribing that no child was to be admitted to school without written proof of vaccination against smallpox, the Education Act of 1900 effectively made childhood vaccination compulsory. Second, the machinery for the state supervision of health was overhauled. Under the provisions of the Health Act of 1901, supervision was to be exercised by:

- the Central Health Council, consisting of four chief health inspectors and three nominated members;
- four chief health inspectors, operating at national level;
- provincial health inspectors; and
- health committees, in municipalities with a population of more than 18,000, with responsibility for monitoring the health status of the inhabitants and the quality of the health care facilities.

Due to complaints about its effectiveness, the status of the Central Health Council (renamed the Health Council) was changed, in 1919, to that of an advisory body. Its membership was substantially increased to include health experts and representatives of employer and employee organisations in the health field and its role was to proffer advice and guidance on health care matters to the Minister, whether invited to do so or not. From a contemporary perspective, the change of status was significant since it marked the beginning of a process which subsequently led to a proliferation of advisory bodies within the Dutch health care system.

Other inter-war developments included the Medical Discipline Act of 1928, which established a system of courts for dealing with cases of alleged misbehaviour on the part of physicians; the introduction of child guidance clinics during the late 1920s; and the Sickness Insurance Act of 1930, which made provision for those whose earnings were below a certain level to receive financial support during periods of sickness. This period was also characterised by significant progress in the development of socio-medical services due primarily to scientific and technical advances in medicine and health care generally and to an increasing acceptance of the principle of social justice.

Somewhat ironically, however, it was not until the German Occupation (1940–45) that the next major step in state involvement in health care was taken. This was the Sickness Funds Decree of 1941. The Decree legitim-ised a variety of principles, on which one of the key components of the arrangements for funding health care continues to operate, namely the sickness fund system. The sickness funds originated in the Middle Ages and were essentially a form of self-help whereby workers contributed an amount whilst in work and were provided with financial assistance and the services of health care providers when they were sick. There was a rapid expansion of funds during the nineteenth century, with doctors often taking the lead in establishing them. By 1940 the number had grown to 650 and approximately 50 per cent of the population were insured for health care purposes by this means. However, since the system 'had grown like Topsy' there were considerable differences in the way that they oper-ated and the benefits available to contributors. The time was ripe for a reform of the system.

The principles inherent in the provisions of the Decree were:

- a standardised and codified approach to the operation of the funds;
- the sick funds to act as intermediaries between the users and providers of health care services;
- the guarantee of either services or benefits in kind, not financial remuneration;
- the requirement that those whose income falls below a certain nation-ally prescribed level and their dependants are compulsorily insured through the funds;
- premiums related to ability to pay; and

• supervision of the funds, initially by a commissioner appointed for this purpose.

After the war, the government decided, in keeping with the value of caution referred to earlier, to make no fundamental changes to the sickness fund system, even though, while it was in exile, it had prepared a blueprint for a health care system very similar to the British National Health Service. In other words, 'the government found a going concern which seemed preferable to a new experiment' (Querido 1968: 83). But although the system ensured that everyone had access to health care, it did not automatically ensure that there would be improvements in the quantity and quality of care.

During the 1950s the only development of any consequence was the Health Act of 1956, which established the Central Council for Public Health, to advise the Minister on administrative and organisational aspects of health care. This was to operate alongside the Health Council, which was now charged with providing the government with advice on the scientific aspects of health care.

Thus, up until the 1960s, state involvement in the health care system was relatively limited. However, from this period onwards there was a significant and, for the Dutch, dramatic increase in state intervention. This was prompted by a number of concerns, in particular the disproportionate increase in health care costs relative to other sectors of the economy; the uneven and inequitable geographical distribution of resources and health care facilities; the unbalanced growth of the health care system, with curative, institutionally based services expanding rapidly and ambulatory care and health prevention being left behind; the duplication of, and excess capacity within, hospitals; and the lack of cohesion and collaboration between the various components of the system. Much of the blame for this state of affairs was placed on financial arrangements. Since these were mainly based on the principle of fee-for-service, with hospitals being automatically reimbursed by sickness funds and private insurers for the costs incurred, they encouraged referrals to specialists and expensive and excessive forms of treatment.

During the 1960s and 1970s, three aspects of the health care system were subject to increased intervention by the government. These were insurance arrangements and funding; the cost of health care; and supply side issues, such as the quantity and quality of health care facilities (i.e. capacity).

With respect to insurance arrangements and funding, the operation of the sickness fund system was revamped by the Sickness Fund Act of 1964 and the Health Insurance Act 1966. However, this legislation made no significant changes to the principles established by the Sickness Fund Decree of 1941. Of greater importance was the Exceptional Medical Expenses (Compensation) Act (AWBZ) of 1968. The objective of this piece of legislation was to insure the entire population against the risk of incurring exceptional expenditure on health care services. Initially, these were institutionally based services (i.e. long-stay hospital care), but from 1980, the provisions of the Act were extended to cover home nursing services and from 1982, ambulatory mental health services.

Turning to costs, under the provisions of the Hospital Tariffs Act of 1965, a Central Agency for Hospital Tariffs was established. This was made up of representatives of bodies concerned with the fixing of hospital tariffs. It was charged with the issuing of guidelines for the fixing of tariffs for hospital services, nursing homes, home nursing schemes and ambulance services. Although the Agency was more concerned with monitoring the cost calculations of health care providers than with regulating tariffs, its establishment was a watershed in that it marked the first stage of a process which has led to substantial government control over the costs of health care provision.

Intervention in the supply side of health care was characterised in the early stages by a proliferation of policy documents. The first of these, the *Report on National Health Care*, was issued in 1966. During the remainder of the decade reports on primary and basic health care services followed.

In 1974 the government published what proved to be a far more significant document, the *Memorandum on the Structure of Health Services*. In this the government set out its broad policy aims and strategies for the future of health care. These were to correct the unbalanced growth in the system by strengthening primary health care; to improve the coherence of the system through the application of the concept of regionalisation; and to remedy the disproportionate increase in health care costs by exercising greater control over them. According to Rutten and van der Werff: 'This document has to be considered as a salient point in the development of the health services in the Netherlands and as a first step on the road to a government controlled system' (1982: 183).

The legislative measures which preceded and followed the *Memorandum on the Structure of Health Services*, substantially extended the role of the state in the supply side of health care. They included:

• the Hospital Facilities Act of 1971, which provided for the establishment of a Commission on Hospital Facilities and the preparation of a national hospital plan;

- the Revised Hospital Facilities Act of 1979, which provided for the closing down of hospital facilities;
- the Health Care Facilities Act of 1982, which enabled the state to be more involved in the planning of health care facilities; and
- the Health Care Tariffs Act of 1982, which provided for the regulation of all health care charges.

Also of importance, with respect to supply side issues, was the introduction of the annual *Financial Review* of health care, in which the government formulates policy proposals for future years and indicates the level of expenditure for the year ahead. In addition, in 1982 the Ministry of Health and Environmental Protection was combined with the Ministry of Cultural Affairs, Recreation and Social Work to improve the co-ordination of health and social care.

Since the early 1980s, right-of-centre coalition governments have sought, within this legislative and administrative framework, to stabilise the real cost and to increase the cost-efficiency of health care. Specific measures taken during the 1980s included:

- the introduction of stringent controls over capital developments (i.e. investment in new hospital buildings and equipment);
- budget ceilings (i.e. cash limits) for revenue expenditure;
- a reduction in the number of hospital beds;
- control over the fees paid to specialists;
- limitation of the number of doctors and physiotherapists working for sick funds; and
- attempts to hold down the price of drugs.

Although none of these measures was entirely successful and a number were abandoned as impractical soon after their introduction, as the data in Table 4.3 indicate, the government was partially successful in securing a degree of stabilisation.

Nevertheless, in the Netherlands, a basic problem for governments in seeking to control total spending on health care has been the fact that the bodies responsible for planning, financing and providing services enjoy a considerable degree of autonomy, operate at a variety of levels and have their own agendas.

As a result of continuing concern with the situation, during the second half of the 1980s two commissions were set up by the government to investigate aspects of the health care system. The first was established in 1986 and was chaired by Professor Dr W. Dekker (former chief executive officer of Philips). Its brief was to consider the structure and regulation of

Table 4.3 Health care developments,1983–88: selected statistics

Category	1983	1984	1985	1986	1987	1988
Gross cost of health and social care	38.8	39.2	39.2	39.4	39.8	40.1
Spending on hospitals	11.1	11.2	11.3	11.5	11.5	11.7
Spending on drugs, aids and appliances	2.8	3.0	3.3	3.6	4.0	4.2
Spending on ambulant care	6.6	6.7	6.9	7.2	7.5	7.7

Source: Based on Abel-Smith (1991: 87, Table 31)
Note: Figures in constant 1983 prices – guilder billions.

the system. The second, established in 1990 and chaired by Professor A. J. Dunning (Professor of Cardiology, Academic Medical Centre, Amsterdam), was charged with considering the range of services which the system should provide for patients. Since the analyses and recommendations of these commissions form part of the current debate on the future direction and organisation of the Dutch health care system, they will be discussed in a later section.

THE PRINCIPAL FEATURES OF SERVICE DELIVERY AND ADMINISTRATION

At the grassroots level, the Dutch have, in the past, made a distinction between what they termed the four 'echelons' of health care: the basic echelon; the first echelon; the second echelon; and the third echelon. These still provide a useful framework within which to consider the different types of health care, and each is considered in turn.

The basic echelon embraces elements of both public health and primary health care. It comprises a mix of preventive and caring services designed to prevent ill health and promote the health of the population as a whole as well as to meet the health care needs of certain vulnerable groups. Responsibility for these essentially 'extramural' (i.e. non-institutionally based) activities is primarily exercised by the municipal authorities, either individually (i.e. municipal medical and health services) or collectively (i.e. district health services).

The activities include:

• general health measures, such as those designed to combat infectious diseases and their transmission; to control the quality of foodstuffs and

environmental pollution; and to secure the collection and analysis of epidemiological data;
- health education and promotion initiatives, including anti-smoking, drug and alcohol abuse programmes, which are being undertaken by special municipal and local bureaux for health promotion;
- youth health care, covering children being educated in both ordinary and special schools, and students;
- occupational health;
- mental health care; and
- ambulance services.

The first echelon consists of a relatively large segment of the primary care sector in the Netherlands and encompasses most of the non-specialised extramural and preventive facilities. The two principal groups of services making up this echelon are those provided by general practitioners (GPs) and those provided by employees of what are known as cross societies (i.e. home nursing associations).

With respect to GP services, all residents are required to register with a GP. The extent to which they are able to choose their GP is considered later.

Although there is an adequate number of GPs to meet the requirements of the population, their geographical distribution is still in need of improvement. Traditionally, GPs have worked on their own on a single-handed basis. Increasingly, however, they are recognising the value of collaboration. Consequently, many now work in group practices and over 20 per cent of GPs are based in health centres and work on a team basis with other professionals, such as dentists, pharmacists, physiotherapists and nurse midwives. Access to these health care workers is either direct (e.g. dentist, midwife) or indirect, that is via the GP (e.g. physiotherapist).

GPs are primarily responsible for the provision of personal curative care for minor acute disorders and continuing care for chronic disorders of all patients registered with them. They also act as a 'gatekeeper' to the second and third echelons. This role is buttressed by the 'rule that specialists can only be consulted after referral by a general practitioner' (van Es 1990: 289).

The cross societies are a peculiarly Dutch phenomenon, and they combine a caring with a preventive role. Originally they were linked to one of the 'pillars' referred to earlier (white-yellow cross – Roman Catholic; orange-green cross – Protestant; green cross – secular), thereby reflecting their origins. However, during the 1970s there were moves through amalgamation across the religious divides (a process of 'uncolouring'), towards a geographical/population-based system. The societies provide their members with district nursing, maternity and child health care services; home nursing aids and appliances; and information on sickness, convalescence, disability, old age and death.

Mention should also be made of the relatively high number of home births in the Netherlands. One of the principal reasons for this is the expertise of Dutch midwives, who 'form the core of the home birth system' (Torres and Reich 1989: 407). They receive specialist professional training in midwifery for three years, which is far longer than that provided in many other countries.

The second echelon incorporates most secondary and tertiary care services, that is all hospital-based specialised facilities for both in-patients and out-patients. It also includes ambulatory mental health care.

Almost all consultants and specialist services are hospital based. Access is via a GP referral, but patients are free to choose their consultant and hospital once they have been referred by their GP. Within hospitals consultants are generally organised into single-specialty firms that lease office space from the hospital authorities and employ their own clerical staff. Like GPs, consultants are independent practitioners.

The vast majority of hospitals are owned and managed by not-for-profit bodies, which are either Roman Catholic or Protestant (approximately 60 per cent of hospitals come into this category) or secular in their origins. This has meant that in many urban areas there have often been three main hospitals in close proximity, each providing a similar range of specialist diagnostic and treatment facilities. In recent years, however, the duplication of hospitals has been reduced by mergers. Between 1988 and 1993, for example, the number of hospitals fell from 181 to 157.

Whatever the origins of a hospital, responsibility for determining policy is vested in an independent governing board. The board members, who are either elected or co-opted, are 'respected members of the local community' (Grunwald and Mantel 1992: 108). They draw up the contracts with consultants and appoint a board of management and heads of service. In the larger hospitals the board of management generally includes a director of patient care and a director of management, with responsibility for administrative and financial matters.

The few remaining hospitals are owned by municipal and provincial authorities and, in the case of nine university teaching hospitals, by the national government.

Cutting across the distinction based on the ownership of hospitals is one based on function. In some hospitals, designated general (of which there were 111 in 1994), a wide range of specialties are available, including surgery, gynaecology and obstetrics, ophthalmology and neurology. In other hospitals, designated special (thirty-seven in 1994), services are restricted to those required by a particular category of patient (e.g. children) or to those required for a particular health care need (e.g. eyesight). As in other developed countries, the average length of stay in hospital is falling, and is currently about ten days.

With respect to ambulatory mental health care, the key role is increasingly being played by the regional institutes for ambulatory mental health care (RIsAGG). Each RIsAGG serves a population of about 250,000. The principal roles of the RIsAGG are advice, prevention, counselling and treatment. In performing these roles, RIsAGGs:

- channel patients, who have been referred to them by a GP or social worker, to the most appropriate form of help and, where necessary, treatment;
- provide a 24-hour on-call service for help in crisis situations;
- support other professionals working in this field; and
- disseminate information on various aspects of mental health.

Complementing the work of the RIsAGG are nearly twenty consultation bureaux for alcoholics and drug addicts. As indicated earlier, alcohol and drug abuse is a major problem for the Dutch.

The third echelon embraces facilities and services for long term or permanent care, both intramural and extramural. These include rehabilitation centres and homes for those with learning disabilities, and for elderly people who are severely mentally infirm.

Not surprisingly, as befits a highly developed and sophisticated health care system, the labour force is both large and complex. Table 4.4 provides details of the number of people active in various health care occupations. Traditionally, the professional service providers, in particular doctors, have possessed a considerable amount of autonomy and exercised a great deal of power. However, as Flynn points out, 'recently . . . medical dominance has been threatened and constrained at various points in the system' (1993: 73). Clinical activity, for example, has been constrained by the need for hospitals to operate within budget ceilings which, as mentioned earlier, were introduced during the 1980s. Moreover, professionals are being increasingly subject to control by health care managers.

At the intermediary level, there are two groups of agencies contributing in various ways to the operation of the health care system. First, there are provincial health councils (established in 1956) consisting of health care experts and representatives of private and professional organisations. These are responsible for stimulating and co-ordinating health care activities in

Table 4.4 The size of the health care labour force: selected professions

Professional group	Total	Year
Doctors:		
General practitioners	6,379	1990
Specialists	12,210	1990
Social physicians	2,176	1990
Other physicians	15,277	1990
Dentists	7,900	1991
Nursing staff:		
Hospital based	94,786	1993
Psychiatric nurses	29,655	1993
Other nurses	104,040	1993
Midwives	1,194	1991
Physiotherapists	10,659	1993
Speech therapists	2,717	1993
Pharmacists	2,087	1993

Source: Central Bureau of Statistics, *Statistical Yearbooks* and Ministry of Public Health, Welfare and Sport, *Care in Numbers 1995*

their province. Second, since the 1970s the provincial states have had a regional planning role. However, according to Flynn, they have been ineffective in exercising this role 'because of the plurality and independence of providers and financiers' (1993: 69).

At national level, overall responsibility for health care matters is currently held by the Ministry of Public Health, Welfare and Sport. The principal roles of the Ministry are in the spheres of:

• policy-making;
• inspection and regulation (e.g. investment in technologically advanced equipment by hospitals); and
• planning (e.g. the capacity and distribution of in-patient facilities).

In performing these roles the Ministry receives support and assistance from the Public Health Supervisory Service, various advisory bodies and a number of self-regulatory bodies.

The Public Health Supervisory Service, currently comprises the:

• Medical Inspectorate of Health;
• Medical Inspectorate of Mental Health;
• Commodities Inspectorate;
• Inspectorate of Drugs;
• Veterinary Inspectorate;

- Alcohol Legislation Inspectorate; and
- Environmental Protection Inspectorate.

Within their sphere of responsibility the roles of the various inspectorates include advising the Minister and Director-General of Health; ensuring compliance with statutory regulations; providing individuals and the public at large with advice; and dealing with complaints about institutions and health care practitioners.

As mentioned earlier, another feature of the Dutch health care system at national level is the plethora of advisory bodies, some of which have a self-regulatory function. Both advisory and self-regulatory bodies serve as mechanisms whereby all the various interests with a stake in the health care system can play a part in policy-making and implementation. The principal features of the five most important bodies of this kind are summarised below.

National Advisory Council for Public Health

This was established in 1956 and was originally named the Central Council for Public Health. It is responsible for advising the Minister on matters of a general or organisational nature and facilitating co-operation between the Minister and public and private bodies active in the health sphere. Half the members represent private and professional organisations and the other half are public employees with particular expertise in the areas within the Council's terms of reference. In recent years, it has provided advice on the organisation of psychiatric services and the emergence of private clinics.

Hospitals Council

This was established in 1971 and originally named the Council on Hospital Facilities. It gives advice on all aspects of the planning and building of hospitals.

Health Council

This was established in 1901 and originally named the Central Health Council. It advises the Minister on scientific aspects of medical matters and health care generally. It issues an annual advisory paper in which it identifies new developments with potential, and existing clinical technologies which have become partially or completely redundant.

Table 4.5 Interest groups within the Dutch health policy community

Title	Initials	Interest represented
Federation of Health Care Organisations in the Netherlands	NZF	health care generally
National Hospital Association of the Netherlands	NZR	hospitals
National Association for Home Care and Home Nursing	LTV	cross societies
Dutch Patients/ Consumers Federation	NP/CP	service users
Association of Dutch Social Health Insurers	VNZ	sickness funds
Association of Private Health Insurers	KLOZ	private insurance companies
Royal Dutch Medical Association	KNMG	doctors generally
National Association of General Practitioners	LHV	GPs
National Specialists Association	LSV	hospital consultants
National Dutch Association of Nursing Personnel	Bureau NU'91	nursing

Sickness (Health Insurance) Fund Council

This was established in 1948. It is composed of thirty-five members, one-fifth of whom are appointed by the Minister; one-fifth by representatives of employers' organisations; one-fifth by representatives of employees' organisations; one-fifth by sickness fund organisations, and one-fifth by 'collaborators' (i.e. individuals and institutions engaged in the provision of health care). Their principal responsibilities are:

- regulating and supervising the activities of the sickness funds;
- approving agreements (other than those relating to fees and charges) between the sickness funds and health care providers;
- administering the General Fund into which the compulsory sickness funds' insurance contributions are paid; and
- advising on the application of the provisions of the legislation governing different aspects of compulsory health insurance.

Central Agency for Health Care Tariffs (COTG)

This was established in 1965 as the Central Council for Hospital Tariffs. It is the forum within which the collective bargaining on the fees and charges payable to health care providers takes place and it determines the annual prospective budgets within which hospitals have been required to work since 1983.

Interacting with these statutory agencies and bodies are a number of organisations which represent the interests of institutions and personnel working within the health care system. The most important are listed in Table 4.5.

Collectively, all these bodies and organisations comprise what can be described as the Dutch health care policy community. An ongoing issue for the members of this community is the financing of health care.

FINANCING ARRANGEMENTS

The funding of the Dutch health care system embraces elements of the social insurance, private insurance and taxation models. In outline it is an insurance-based system, incorporating the principles of compulsion and of discretion, with substantial contributions from taxation.

This is illustrated by the information in Table 4.6. Here the principal components of the current funding arrangements are summarised. An elaboration of these arrangements is provided in the notes that follow that table.

Table 4.6 Funding arrangements

Key	Basis of funding	Type of care/service	Administrative agencies	% of pop'n covered
(a)	Compulsory insurance contributions + tax subsidy	short term/acute hospital care + GP services	sickness funds	60
(b)	voluntary insurance premiums	ditto	private insurers	34
(c)	compulsory insurance premiums	ditto	agencies	6

Table 4.6 (continued)

(d)	voluntary insurance premiums	care/services not covered by other insurance + out of pocket expenses	private insurers	n.k.
(e)	compulsory insurance contributions + tax subsidy	long term care + child health care + mental health care	sickness funds + private insurers	100
(f)	taxation	public health + social services	national, provincial, municipal government	

Notes

(a) Under the provisions of the Health Insurance Act 1966, approximately 60 per cent of the population, whose income does not exceed a nationally determined limit (at the time of writing this is 58,950 guilders per annum, approximately £24,000), are required to obtain their basic health insurance from one of the forty non-profit-making sickness funds. Most of the funds, which continue to enjoy considerable legal and administrative autonomy, operate in a particular geographical area, where they have a monopoly. Thus, there is little competition between them.

The sickness fund scheme is compulsory and is designed to ensure that no one is denied access to services on grounds of cost. For those in employment, the premium of 8.35 per cent of earnings is shared between the employee (1.10 per cent) and employer (7.25 per cent). These income-related premiums are collected by employers, who pay into the sickness funds. Members of the insured's family who are not working are insured free of charge. In other words, the premium is paid out of public funds. Those under 65 years of age who are in receipt of certain benefits or allowances pay a premium of 1.4 per cent.

Everyone covered by this insurance is entitled to a variety of health care services free of charge at the point of delivery. These include short term treatment (up to a maximum of one year) by medical and nursing staff and the provision of drugs and appliances in general and psychiatric hospitals; maternity services; consultations with, and treatment by, general practitioners; pharmaceutical services; and some dental treatment. Thus, those covered under this scheme receive benefits in kind as opposed to the reimbursement of health care charges.

(b) For the remainder of the population, basic health insurance is obtained, on a voluntary basis, from one of seventy competing private health insurance companies, which are either for profit or not for profit in the way that they operate. There are two main categories of person covered by this means.

First, those over the income level, who are under the age of 65 and not classified as 'high risks', purchase insurance direct from private insurers on either an individual or a group basis. With respect to the former, premiums are adjusted for risk, particularly age.

Second, anyone over the income level and the age of 65 or classified as 'high risk' (whatever their age) is placed in a risk pool. This means, in effect, that their premium is subsidised by the other purchasers of private health insurance. Such an arrangement was introduced by the government in 1989, since 'high risk' individuals, especially the elderly, were faced with steep rises in premiums, which could have had a deterrent effect. In so doing it imposed 'social insurance conditions on private insurers' (OECD 1992: 91).

Since private insurance is voluntary, individuals may decide to cover some of the risk themselves. However, very few cover the whole of the risk in this way. Whatever they decide, unlike those covered by the compulsory scheme they are responsible for meeting their bills for health care in the first instance. If insured, they can then recover the amount paid from their insurance company.

(c) Employees of the national government and of provincial and municipal authorities are insured for health care purposes as part of their contracts of employment. Dependants and those in retirement are also covered by this scheme. Contributions are income-related and are shared between employer and employee. The scheme is implemented by eleven agencies. It covers a similar range of services as the sickness fund scheme, but provides for the reimbursement of health care charges, like private insurance, rather than benefits in kind.

(d) Supplemental health insurance is available to cover the costs involved in paying for treatment and services which are not covered by the basic health insurance or provided directly from public funds.

(e) On the grounds that everyone might need, at some stage in their lives, very expensive services and that for even the wealthiest the costs involved could be prohibitive, their availability is ensured under the provisions of the Exceptional Medical Expenses (Compensation) Act or AWBZ of 1968. The services concerned are:

- long term (i.e. more than one year) hospital-based care;
- child health services;
- mental health care including that provided by RIsAGG;
- home health care, including that provided by cross societies;
- medical appliances and dressings;
- programmes for those suffering from a physical or mental disability; and
- since 1992, medicines (although in some cases patients are required to make a contribution towards the cost).

The cost is met from income-related premiums (currently 8.85 per cent of income up to a ceiling) and the scheme is administered by the sickness funds and private insurers.

(f) A variety of basic echelon health care and related programmes are directly funded out of tax revenues by governmental agencies operating at national, provincial and municipal levels, including the provision of social and related services for elderly people.

Turning to the bases on which health care providers are reimbursed for services rendered, again the picture is relatively complex.

GPs are paid on a capitation basis (i.e. an amount per person regardless of the amount of care and range of services provided) for patients covered by the sickness funds; and on a fee-for-service basis for patients with private insurance and for public employees. Levels of capitation fee, which are the same throughout the Netherlands, are negotiated between the VNZ (representing the sickness funds) and organisations representing the interests of GPs. There is a higher rate of fee for the first 1,600 patients and a lower rate for the remainder. Patients are required to register with a GP with whom their sickness fund has a contract. In return the patient receives care which is free at the point of delivery.

Privately insured patients and those insured under the scheme for public employees are free to consult any GP of their choice. They are then expected to pay the fee, which reflects the amount of care received, and claim it back from the insurance company or agency, unless they have decided to bear the risk themselves.

Cross societies receive their income from payments under the AWBZ and, to a small extent, from fees paid by clients.

With respect to hospital services consultants are paid, in the main, on a fee-for-service basis by both sickness funds and private insurers. Thus, as Maarssen and Janssen point out, they, like GPs, 'work as commercial entrepreneurs' (1994: 20). Hospital running costs, including the salaries and wages of non-medical employees, are met from the annual global budgets, negotiated with local sickness funds and insurance companies and approved by the COTG.

In the case of private hospitals, capital expenditure (i.e. investment) on new buildings and equipment is normally financed by borrowing from banks. Until now, loans from the banking system have been guaranteed by the government. Depreciation and interest payments are included in the charges levied by the hospital. Investment by public hospitals is financed by government grants.

The complexity of the financial regime under which the Dutch health care system operates reflects, in part, past attempts by the government to ensure that, although the system is essentially within the private sector, no one is denied access to health care on grounds of poverty and that there is a reasonable balance between the supply of and demand for services. Not surprisingly, however, as the complexity of the regime has increased there has been a growing number of calls for its simplification. Indeed, it can be argued that this desire for simplification is one of the most pressing of the contemporary policy issues in Dutch health care.

CONTEMPORARY ISSUES IN HEALTH POLICY

Many of the issues which currently occupy high positions on the Dutch health care agenda are by no means new or unique to the Netherlands. Of particular concern are the following:

- the complexity of the system, both in financial and administrative terms, which makes it expensive to operate;
- the unco-ordinated nature of the financial arrangements;
- the lack of financial incentives to promote efficiency;
- the rigidity of the system, which inhibits innovation and experimentation;
- the widening gap between public expectations and demands, and the availability of resources;
- the overemphasis on institutional care, with relatively high average lengths of hospital stay, and the consequent failure to give greater attention to the use of ambulatory and community care; and

- the lack of co-ordination of care for groups of clients, such as the elderly and chronically sick, who often require a wide variety of services.

As indicated earlier, during the late 1980s and early 1990s two commissions, chaired by Dekker and Dunning, were established to examine and report on different aspects of the health care system. It is their diagnoses and recommendations which have shaped the subsequent debate on the future of health care in the Netherlands.

In their report, *Willingness to Change* (March 1987), the members of the Dekker Commission criticised the existing arrangements on the grounds that they contained too few incentives for efficiency; too little scope for competition between service providers; and too little genuine choice for service users. They were also critical of the extent to which the government regulated insurance premiums and the income of providers.

At the heart of the Dekker proposals (later renamed 'Plan-Simons' after the Minister for Health), which were strongly influenced by the ideas of the American health economist Alain Enthoven, was a system of regulated competition between insurers who would purchase care selectively from competing providers. More specifically, they incorporated the following principles:

- Health care would remain a 'social right'.
- Service users and providers would be made more cost conscious.
- There would be a degree of consumer choice.
- There would be greater competition between 'care insurers'.
- Competition between health care providers (i.e. GPs, consultants, hospitals) would be introduced.
- Insurers would act as intermediaries between the insured and health care providers.
- There would be a reduction in government regulation and greater reliance on market forces.

Under the proposals:

- The whole population would be insured on a compulsory basis for what are termed 'basic health services', embracing both acute and long term care in hospitals and the community.
- The sickness funds and private health insurers would be merged.
- Each person would be able to choose his/her insurer, who would not be permitted to refuse him/her or adjust the premium to reflect risk.
- Approximately 70 per cent of the cost of the insurance would be met from contributions by adults at income-related standard rates.

- Children would be covered by their parents' contributions.
- Contributions would be collected centrally and distributed to the insurers according to numbers insured and their risk status.
- The remaining 30 per cent of the cost of the insurance would take the form of a flat rate payment by the person insured and this would vary between insurers, although each insurer would have to charge the same amount for every person insured (i.e. they could not vary the payment in accordance with risk).
- Insurers would be able to determine which health care providers those they insure could use.
- In addition to the basic insurance, individuals would be able to take out, but only with the same insurer, supplementary insurance for dental care, physiotherapy and related services.

The Dekker Commission's report generated a great deal of debate and it took a year for the cabinet to decide its response. This was eventually contained in a policy paper entitled *Change Assured* (March 1988). In accepting the main thrust of the Dekker Commission's proposals the cabinet indicated its intention to restructure the insurance system and inject a degree of regulated competition into the health care system. In so doing, it hoped to secure greater cost-effectiveness and efficiency in service provision, while retaining the principle of health care as a social right.

Following the general election of 1989 the new centre-left government coalition made some modifications to the detailed proposals of its predecessor, but 'decided to continue with the main thrust of the reform' (OECD 1992: 87). In keeping with the Dutch tradition of incremental change, the 'Plan-Simons' is unlikely to be fully implemented before the mid to late 1990s, with the pace of reform being slowed 'by discord within the governing coalition' (Maarssen and Janssen 1994: 21).

To complement the Dekker Commission, that chaired by Dunning was charged with examining how to put limits on new medical technologies and how to deal with problems caused by scarcity of care, rationing of care, and the necessity of selection of patients for care. Underlying this task was the recognition that it was extremely difficult to decide what should be included in the package of 'basic health services' that lay at the heart of the Dekker proposals.

In their report, entitled *Choices in Health Care* (1991) Dunning and his colleagues recommended that the cabinet should use four criteria in determining whether or not particular forms of care should be included in the basic package:

- Is it necessary care, from the community point of view?

- Has it been demonstrated to be effective?
- Is it efficient?
- Can it be left to individual responsibility?

Clearly, these criteria, presented in the form of questions, beg more questions than they answer. Nonetheless, they do represent a serious attempt to get to grips with what many commentators consider to be an intractable problem.

Inherent in their other recommendations – which relate to waiting lists and the rationing of care, new technology, the appropriate use of health care, and procedural issues – are the principles of openness and the need for more informed public debate and systematic evaluation of different kinds of clinical intervention.

Other issues associated with the reform process include the demand for more rigorous and detailed management information and costing systems; the equipping of health care managers with the skills they need to operate effectively in a more competitive environment; the types of mechanism needed for quality assurance purposes in the health care marketplace; and growing concern over whether the most vulnerable groups in society will receive the care they need in such an environment. As things stand at present, many commentators are either unable or unwilling to predict, with certainty, how and in what ways the reforms will affect the behaviour patterns of service users, insurers and service providers. It does seem likely, however, that in seeking to deal with one set of issues, another set will, 'Hydra-like', emerge in its place.

CONCLUSION

Although the Netherlands does not have a 'national health service' in the generally accepted meaning of that term, it does have a health care system which ensures that no one is denied access to health care on the grounds that they cannot pay for it or for any other reason. Consequently those responsible for health care in the Netherlands face many of the issues and dilemmas associated with systems funded primarily out of taxation. Not surprisingly, therefore, the response of the Dutch has been similar to that in other countries. However, whether the injection of more competition and choice into the system and the making of the rationing process more explicit will ease the situation remains to be seen.

REFERENCES AND FURTHER READING

Abel-Smith, B. (1991) *Cost Containment and New Priorities in Health Care*, Aldershot: Avebury.

Flynn, R. (1993) 'Restructuring health systems: a comparative analysis of England and the Netherlands', in M. Hill (ed.) *New Agendas in the Study of the Policy Process*, London: Harvester Wheatsheaf.

Grunwald, C. A. and Mantel, A. F. (1992) 'The Netherlands', in *European Health Services Handbook*, London: The Institute of Health Services Management.

Kirkman-Liff, B. L. and Maarse, H. (1992) 'Going Dutch', *Health Service Journal*, 102, 24 September: 24–7.

Lijphart, A. (1968) *The Politics of Accommodation, Pluralism and Democracy in the Netherlands*, Berkeley: University of California Press.

Maarssen, A-M. and Janssen, R. (1994) 'Reforming health care in the Netherlands', *Health Services Management*, 90, 1: 19–21.

OECD (1992) *The Reform of Health Care: A Comparative Analysis of Seven OECD Countries*, Paris: OECD.

Querido, A. (1968) *The Development of Socio-Medical Care in the Netherlands*, London: Routledge and Kegan Paul.

Rutten, F. and van der Werff, A. (1982) 'Health policy in the Netherlands. At the crossroads', in G. McLachlan and A. Maynard (eds) *The Public/Private Mix for Health. The Relevance and Effects of Change*, London: Nuffield Provincial Hospitals Trust.

Tiddens, H. A., Heesters, J. P. and van de Zande, J. M. (1984) 'Health services in the Netherlands', in M. W. Raffel (ed.) *Comparative Health Systems: Descriptive Analyses of Fourteen National Health Systems*, London: Pennsylvania State University Press.

Torres, A. and Reich, M. (1989) 'The shift from home to institutional childbirth: a comparative study of the United Kingdom and the Netherlands', *International Journal of Health Services*, 19 (3): 405–14.

van Es, J. C. (1990) 'Background and development of the health care system in the Netherlands', in A. F. Casparie, H. E. G. M. Hermans and J. H. P. Paelinck (eds) *Competitive Health Care in Europe: Future Prospects*, Aldershot: Dartmouth.

Chapter 5

Sweden

Bernard Jones

The provision of health care in Sweden must be seen in the context of the whole welfare state. Logically, health and, say, social security may be separate. In reality the dynamic which produced the Swedish health service was the same dynamic which produced the rest of the social welfare matrix.

The Swedish welfare state, giving protection 'from the womb to the tomb', and in particular the Swedish health services have flourished for decades, having been built up since the 1930s. They have been held up as examples of what a welfare state could and should look like. They have been used to demonstrate what social democracy can achieve in a liberal democratic state. They have been effective.

In the early 1990s, however, two things occurred which changed the picture. First, the centre-left government which had run Sweden for most of the previous sixty years was replaced by a centre-right coalition. Second, Sweden and its people were hit by the global recession and began, for the first time in living memory, to worry about money: resources for the welfare state, previously provided on a generous scale, began to be rationed. The centre-right coalition was replaced in 1994 by a new centre-left coalition and thus some of its policies were not, at the time of writing, being implemented. The Social Democrats had still, however, to face up to the problems of tight finances and the imperatives of demography.

This chapter tells two stories: the story of the growth and operation of the paradigm health service; and the story of the changes taking place as the Swedes come to terms with what may be a fairly grim close to the twentieth century. Because Sweden has been the paradigm in so many ways these stories are of interest both as comparisons and contrasts. Comparisons may be made with, say, the UK which went about the task of creating universal health care in the same sort of way. Contrasts may be made with, say, the USA, which adopted a very different model.

THE CONTEXT OF SWEDISH HEALTH CARE

The demographic structure

The population of Sweden, only 7 million in 1945, had reached a peak of
8.35 million in 1985 and is estimated to decline to 7.71 million by 2025
(OECD 1992). At one point there was considerable concern that the
fertility rate had declined to a figure below that needed for population
replacement, the 1983 figure of 1.6 children per woman being insufficient
for this purpose, but by 1990 the fertility rate had risen to 2.1 children per
woman, the point at which population stabilises (*Economist*, August 1991).
There is a low infant mortality rate of 5.8 deaths per thousand live births.
This can be compared with the European average and the UK figure, both
of which are about nine deaths per thousand.

Life expectancy is high. For men the 1990–91 figure was 74.8 years,
behind only Japan and Ireland, while for women the figure of 80.4 years
was behind only Iceland (80.5 years). The combination of increasing lon-
gevity and relatively low fertility implies a significant change in the overall
population structure. In 1985 16.9 per cent of the population was aged
over 65 years. The OECD estimates that this figure will rise to 22.2 per
cent by the year 2025 and will accompany a significant rise in the proportion of the population aged over 80 years.

Epidemiological trends

Whilst Sweden is among the healthiest nations of the world, there are
health problems. Increased rates of sick leave and early retirement probably
indicate a rising morbidity rate, although there may well be other, possibly
contingent, social factors. The main disorders are those associated with
advanced industrialised countries, due not so much to infections and malnutrition as to environment and lifestyle. Tobacco smoking, alcohol consumption and overeating, all often associated with stressful living patterns,
are responsible for a high proportion of the cardiovascular conditions and
cancers which are the predominant diseases.

Cultural traditions

Among the younger element the 'freedom', popularly associated with
Sweden, leads to a culture which includes drug abuse and sexual promiscu-
ity, both of which have health care implications. AIDS is a growing problem and much work on the frontiers of social work and health care is

needed, particularly in the larger cities such as Stockholm, the capital city, and Malmö.

Social factors

Sweden's standard of living is among the highest in Europe. It is the materialist counterpart to the USA with the added feature of a much more even distribution of both income and wealth. Although Sweden has achieved a relatively high level of social equality, there are nevertheless differential incidences of disease and injury between social groupings. Some employment categories, lower income groups, unemployed persons, single people and the rising proportion of immigrants encounter and fall prey to greater health hazards than others.

The governmental and political setting

The Scandinavian states, in general, have been termed the 'consensual democracies'. Sweden is a rich, stable, parliamentary democracy. Although it is clearly a part of the capitalist world, it is unaligned politically and militarily, and its neutrality during the second world war, coupled with the long period of almost continuous centre-left Social Democratic government from the early 1930s to the early 1990s, have given the Swedes the chance to develop a welfare state organised on rational and corporatist principles which has frequently been held up to the world as a model of how a society can be enriched by a beneficent state.

The liberal democratic Constitution of Sweden has developed steadily from the early nineteenth century. In the seventeenth century Sweden was a world power but since 1814 has maintained neutrality. In the eighteenth century there was a period of parliamentary government followed by a short spell of royal absolutism, but the Constitution of 1809 placed restraints upon the King and since 1975, although titular head of state, his political powers have been nil. The government has been responsible to the *Riksdag* (parliament) since 1917 and in the case of deadlock it is the Speaker of the *Riksdag* who assumes the initiative for policy and control.

Sweden is a unitary state. The *Riksdag*'s laws apply throughout the whole state territory and can cover all aspects of the affairs of the Swedish people. In practice there is a degree of local autonomy which shows itself partly as freedom of local authorities to interpret a skeleton or framework law in ways appropriate to the locality, and partly as the freedom of local authorities to make their own regulations in such matters as parking.

It would be a mistake, however, to suppose that local government in

Sweden is nothing more than this might indicate. Local government also has the freedom to take initiatives in any way not specifically reserved to another authority, and to proceed with those initiatives until challenged successfully by a local resident through a quasi-legal process. This major freedom arises from the Constitution. Local government is a serious matter to the Swedes, outspending central government in the ratio of two to one, with the major services of health and education being in the control of local authorities.

Local government plays an important role in providing health care. There are two basic levels: first, the municipality or commune of which there are 286 each with a minimum population of around 8,000; second the county or region, of which there are twenty-six including Gotland, Göteborg and Malmö which serve as unitary authorities. The counties and municipalities all have councils and there are elaborate arrangements for co-ordinating their activities both at local level and *vis-à-vis* the local activities of the state.

The national parliament, the *Riksdag*, has 349 members, 309 of whom are elected from constituencies. The remaining forty seats are allocated so that party proportionality is achieved. Any party which gains at least 4 per cent of the overall vote or 12 per cent in any one electoral district will be represented in the *Riksdag*. In practice this has meant that a five-party system has evolved at both local and national levels, with seats being gained in such a way as to keep the Social Democrats (a centre-left party) in national control from the early 1930s until September 1991 except for the period from 1976 to 1982. From 1991 to September 1993 a minority centre-right coalition led by Carl Bildt was in power. This was replaced in September 1994 by a Social Democratic government led by Ingvar Carlsson who rules with the support of the Communists.

Locally there have been variations on this theme, the urban areas inclining more to the centre-left and the rural areas more to the centre-right.

There is no upper house. The government finds its support in the *Riksdag*, and the constancy of the Social Democratic support over such a long period, set against the background of neutrality in international affairs, meant that Sweden was often held up as the model of a welfare state created by popular will expressed through the parliamentary process. With electoral turnout figures usually over 90 per cent, the legitimacy of the government could not be questioned (at least from liberal democratic premises).

The fact that recent government has ruled in a minority situation implies, perhaps, some weakening of legitimacy. Whether centre-right (1991–94) or centre-left (post-1994), the coalition nature of government has reduced the ideological underpinning, and the liberal-left consensus, throughout Scandinavia, has been undermined in the face of financial difficulties.

Nevertheless the main shape of the welfare state and in particular the health services remains unchanged. This forms a major problem for the Swedes and is among the reasons contributing to the recent relative instability.

Participatory aspects

The Swedes show great respect for their government (local and central) and for its institutions. The high legitimacy has already been noted and it is worth adding that there are provisions for referendums (again both local and national) but that these provisions are rarely used. The satisfaction felt by the Swedes is due, in part, to the system of ombudsmen which enables grievances to be investigated and redressed, but more importantly keeps government officials on their toes. It is also due to the efforts which are made both centrally and locally to involve interested parties in discussions and to make few moves without a feeling that consensus has broadly been achieved.

It has already been noted that over 90 per cent of electors tend to exercise their right to vote. Moreover, it has been estimated that 10 per cent of Swedish adults play some active part in the democratic process, which is high by comparison with other similar states. This activity is an integral part of the corporate state. Much of it is associated with local government and is, therefore, strongly related to the provision of health care services.

Economic performance

Sweden's economic performance has been generally good, and compares favourably with that of the other countries considered here. However, the growth of the welfare state in general, and the health care system in particular, has been at a faster rate than industrial growth in recent years and this has led to increasingly severe budgetary deficits and, in turn, to financial constraints upon welfare spending.

For any government such changes imply two problems. The first is economic: there must be a restructuring of the productive economy and the fiscal system in order to maintain GDP and government revenue from a smaller working population. The second is a service problem: within the health care system there must be a redirecting of resources from younger to older persons. In practical terms these problems are being solved by governments throughout the world by general resource squeezes on health care services and by specific consideration of the effectiveness of provision for the elderly.

Sweden is among the highest-spending states on health care. In 1987 the expenditure on health care of £1,002 per person had fallen in real terms by 5 per cent since 1977, but still left the Swedes behind only the United States of America, Switzerland and West Germany. The figure was more than double the figure for the United Kingdom, although this comparison must be treated with caution as there are differences in statistical methodology and definitions.

Another important indicator of health care spending is the number of beds per thousand of the population. Here again Sweden has a relatively high level, with about twelve beds per thousand people. One-third of these are for short term somatic (physical) conditions. One half are reserved for long term somatic conditions. The remainder, roughly 15 per cent, are for psychiatric care. In addition there are about seven places per thousand people in long-stay municipally run homes for the elderly. This state provision of nineteen beds per thousand (roughly 2 per cent) for the sick, the mentally ill and the elderly is among the highest in the world.

The cited 1987 health care expenditure figure of over £1,000 per person corresponds to a high proportion of GDP. In 1991 this proportion was 8.8 per cent, and in this Sweden was third only to USA and West Germany. The high figure is possible only because the Swedes accept high taxes: the overall rate of 57 per cent of GDP can be compared with the European Community average of 41 per cent. Whether the Swedes can maintain this high level of taxation, and therefore welfare provision, is a matter of conjecture: the exchange-rate crisis of September 1992 resulted in an effective devaluation which will have implications, as yet unclear.

THE DEVELOPMENT OF STATE INVOLVEMENT

In common with all developed countries, the crucial changes in the nature and structure of the welfare services date from the period of industrialisation. In Sweden this occurred in the late nineteenth and early twentieth centuries: 50 per cent of the population were primarily dependent on agriculture as late as the first world war. Sweden was one of the last of the West European states to industrialise, but when it did so its changes were comparatively rapid and it was able to avoid some of the problems encountered elsewhere and to learn from the experience of others with respect to addressing those problems which remained.

Until the nineteenth century, therefore, it was possible for the embryonic welfare services to exist with a minimum of state direction, control or finance. The institutions of Church and family provided the majority of help for the poor and aged until the eighteenth century, when each parish (then the local unit of organisation) was expected to assume responsibility for its poor. Interestingly the Lutheran reformation of the sixteenth century had taken responsibility for the sick away from the Church, but without properly organising a replacement. A decree of the early seventeenth century stated that sick people should receive care in hospitals, but it was not until 1752 that a national hospital fund, made up partly of donations and partly of the proceeds of indirect taxes, was able to endow Sweden's first recognisable hospital, the Serafimerlasarettet in Stockholm, an eight-bed hospital intended for the whole population!

The later secularisation of society that went with the liberal enlightenment and the beginning of the break-up of traditional values meant that the work of the Church, the state and the parishes was supplemented by voluntary effort not necessarily inspired by religious beliefs. In 1765 the local authorities were empowered to raise funds and create general hospitals, and in the next century about fifty of these, each with about twelve beds, were provided.

Such trade, industry and commerce as there was employed only 20 per cent of the workforce up to about 1840, and a guild system dating back to medieval times saw in part to the needs of members and their families who had fallen on hard times. This system could not cope with the stresses that went along with the changes that began in the early nineteenth century with land reform and were exacerbated by rapid population growth. To some extent the USA cushioned the effects: over a million people emigrated during the second half of the century, roughly a quarter of the population at that time. Real problems remained, however, as people left the land without a corresponding increase in the opportunities afforded by industry.

The Local Government Reform of 1862 institutionalised the secularisation, making the local authorities responsible for poor relief but failing to provide the economic wherewithal to cope in times of stress. Relief was generous in times of plenty but restricted when depression ruled. At the same time the already existing rudimentary nucleus of a public health service was being extended. The newly created counties were to be responsible for all medical care with the exception of care for the mentally ill, who became the responsibility of the state.

These reforms were perhaps the last of the old era. Mats Forsberg suggests that the modern development of the welfare state in Sweden can be categorised into three epochs, beginning in the 1880s when the combination of liberalism and the growing labour movement meant that the causes of distress were seen to be rooted not in the shortcomings of individuals but in the inequities of the social system. This was an important conceptual change as it implied that the goal was not the immediate relief of distress (although that, of course, remained important) but the ultimate restructuring of society, and its benefits and burdens, on the principle of equity. Although Forsberg was discussing social services, his analysis is relevant to the development of health care. Without the recognition of societal responsibility for the problems of individuals, and the commitment to collectivism which this implies, the health care system could never have been developed on such generous lines.

However, such changes do not come overnight and about a century elapsed before the conceptual shift of the 1880s became the enacted provisions of the 1980s. Moreover, in contrast to those in many other polities, the legislative changes did produce real benefits for Swedish people.

The second epoch began in 1932 with the initiation of social welfare programmes by the Social Democratic Party which took office in that year. In addition to social insurance, housing, family and social services and education, these programmes included the 'rolling reforms' in health care. The programmes were gradually implemented through legislation over the next forty years. Thus, the period from the 1930s to 1970s was characterised by important but incremental growth.

The third epoch, according to Forsberg, began relatively recently with the Social Services Act which came into effect in 1982. The importance of this act was threefold. Its immediate effect was to strengthen the services of the state; it modernised the theory underlying means tested benefits; and, through its mechanisms for providing feedback, it ensured that society will be changed in accordance with information about how people live. Inevitably, these changes had an impact on health care. As well as reaffirming the commitment to collectivist responsibility for the promotion and maintenance of health, they influenced the way in which certain disorders were viewed. Conditions such as heart disease, lung cancer and AIDS, which could be construed as carrying a measure of 'victim responsibility', are products of a society in which the preconditions of stress, social acceptability and sexual freedom obtain.

THE PRINCIPAL FEATURES OF SERVICE DELIVERY AND ADMINISTRATION

Primary health care

Primary health care is organised at local level and provides a range of services through the primary care districts. These are of variable size, with populations ranging from 5,000 to 50,000. Each district has at least one local health care centre and at least one nursing home for long term care. All clients are out-patients.

The professional staff include doctors (district physicians) who are mainly GPs but, particularly in the larger health centres associated with larger districts, may also be specialists. These doctors provide medical treatment, advisory services and preventive care. Appropriate treatment is also provided by associated nurses and midwives, who between them run clinics for such things as child and maternity care.

The district health centres are also responsible for a range of mass health screening activities such as routine health checks on 4-year-old children, vaccination services, and cervical and breast cancer tests.

Separate from the health centres, but clearly a part of the primary health care system, are the school health services provided by the municipalities. Regular health checks are a feature of the system.

For employees in large organisations, both public and private sector, the occupational safety system provides appropriate check-ups and first-line care. The industrial health services cover 70 per cent of all Swedish employees and are thus of major significance.

Although there are frequent client referrals from the primary sector to hospital-based specialists, the policy is that as many patients as possible should be cared for in their own homes. To this end the nursing staff in the primary health care services co-operate with social workers employed by the municipalities to provide home care services for the sick and disabled.

Secondary health care

Several districts comprise a county, and the hospital services are mainly organised on a county basis. Usually counties have one large central county hospital with a wide range (fifteen–twenty) of specialties and several smaller district county hospitals which have at least four specialties, always including medicine, surgery, radiology and anaesthesiology. There is not necessarily one district hospital for each primary health care district, but the district county hospitals are geographically located to minimise travel for patients and their visitors.

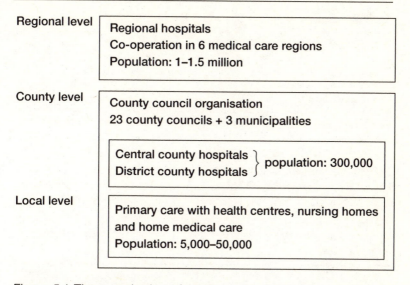

Figure 5.1 The organisation of health and medical care services in Sweden: regional, county and local levels

Sweden is divided into six medical care regions each with a population in excess of a million. These generally comprise several counties, and have at least one regional hospital which functions as a research and teaching centre in addition to having a range of highly developed and probably highly technical specialties. The control of these regional hospitals is in the hands of the counties which have agreements between themselves over funding and regulation of activities.

Psychiatric hospitals are special-purpose. There are, however, two relevant policies which are currently having an impact. The first is a policy to merge psychiatric with somatic care hospitals as much as is practicable. The second is to reduce the number of beds for psychiatric care. These policies will clearly have an impact on the volume of home care to be provided by both the municipal social services and by the district care centres. Figure 5.1 summarises the basis of regional, county and district health care provision.

In 1989 there were just over 100,000 beds available in medical institutions. Table 5.1 illustrates their distribution.

The average hospital stay is illustrated in Table 5.2, which demonstrates clearly the relative length of psychiatric in-patient care.

Table 5.1 Beds in medical institutions, 1989

Type of care	No. of beds
Somatic short term care	35,000
Somatic long term care	56,000
Psychiatric care	15,500

Source: Fact Sheet on Sweden, 76. Stockholm, Swedish Institute, October 1991

Table 5.2 Average hospital stay, 1990

Type of hospital	No. of days
Medical wards	8
Surgical wards	6
Psychiatric wards	46

Source: Fact Sheet on Sweden, 76. Stockholm, Swedish Institute, October 1991

Table 5.3 Categories of clinical personnel, 1990

Physicians	28,000
Dentists	12,700
Nurses	108,000
Assistant nurses	70,000
Physiotherapists	10,700
Psychologists	5,500

Source: Fact Sheet on Sweden, 76. Stockholm, Swedish Institute, October 1991

Staffing the health care system

Approximately 450,000 persons, 10 per cent of all Swedish employees (albeit many part time), are involved in health care! In common with most health care systems, these employees absorb a large proportion of the total health care spending. So one way of categorising expenditure, the question of how the service level is achieved, is predominantly driven by staffing. Table 5.3 shows the utilisation of clinical personnel in 1990.

Table 5.3 demonstrates the preponderance of nurses and assistant nurses who between them constitute nearly 76 per cent of the total of 235,000 clinical staff. Doctors and dentists amount to 17 per cent, with the remaining supporting staff coming to around 7 per cent. The table is not exhaust-

Table 5.4 Education and training period for doctors

Programme	Period (years)
Basic study programme	5.5 (medical school)
Internship	1.75 (hospital-based)
Postgraduate training	4.5 (average)
Total	11.25–12.25

Source: based on *Fact Sheet on Sweden*, 76. Stockholm, Swedish Institute, October 1991

ive as it omits, for example, radiologists and some other categories of paramedical staff, but the significance is clear. The largest group of staff is nursing.

Beyond the 235,000 clinical staff are more than 200,000 non-clinical staff who make up about 48 per cent of the whole.

The implications of these figures for possible future policy changes are twofold. First, any substantial changes in the pattern of service will have direct repercussions on the employment of nurses. Second, any changes in the way that support services are offered, for example cleaning, building maintenance or grounds maintenance, will have quite serious overall effects on the general pattern of Swedish employment.

The education of doctors is lengthy, the full training period, as undertaken by most physicians, occupying between eleven and twelve years (see Table 5.4). The postgraduate training, taken after the initial licence to practise, qualifies physicians as specialists or general practitioners.

The National Board of Health and Welfare exerts control over the supply of doctors in two ways. The first is by regulating the overall number entering one of the six medical schools. The current figure is an annual intake of about 865 students. The second is by controlling, through a 'block system', admissions to the postgraduate courses.

The six teaching institutions which provide the medical training are linked to regional hospitals. They also serve, along with the universities, as a focus for medical research. This, in total, is currently funded at almost £1 billion, half of which comes from the central government.

The role of the county councils

The county councils were established in the mid-nineteenth century specifically to run hospitals for physical diseases. Since this beginning, the county level of local government provision has been closely associated with health care and has had its range of responsibilities increased. In the mid-1960s the counties took over responsibility for all services provided for out-patients (including the provision of general practice) and psychiatric care, which until then had been a central government responsibility.

The important Health and Medical Services Act of 1983 consolidated changing practices and extended the health care responsibilities of the county councils to such an extent that between 75 per cent and 80 per cent of their total expenditure is currently under this heading. The counties are required to undertake the following duties:

- the promotion of health for residents in their areas;
- the provision of access to good medical care including, where necessary, the provision of appropriate transport;
- the planning and development of the health and medical care services with regard to the aggregate needs of the county population; and
- the inclusion in planning of consideration of the health care services provided by industry, by private practice and by the municipal school medical services.

The legislation also gives the patient certain rights to information about his or her state of health and the availability of investigative procedures and treatments. A good deal of sensitive information is held on county and central computers and the patient has identity protection. The registers maintained include the Central Cancer Registry, the In-patient Registry and the Registry of Congenital Malformations.

There is special legislation covering the needs of the mentally ill, but all other patients have the right to discontinue medical treatment if they so wish. Patients are afforded protection through the supervisory role of the National Board of Health and Welfare which is responsible for health and medical personnel. The National Medical Disciplinary Board investigates charges of misconduct by such staff.

The role of central government

Although the counties have such an important role in the planning and delivery of health services, the central government is responsible for overall policy goals in the social welfare field. It is also responsible for the macro-economy and thus for the overall levels of funding available to the health and social care systems.

The political government comes from and is responsible to the *Riksdag* (as mentioned on p. 106). The administrative arm of government works through the Ministry of Health and Social Affairs and a set of relatively

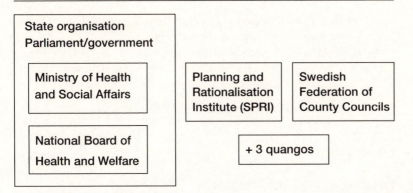

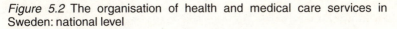

Figure 5.2 The organisation of health and medical care services in Sweden: national level

independent administrative agencies, the chief of which is the National Board of Health and Welfare. Figure 5.2 illustrates this and also includes several bodies to be discussed later.

The Ministry of Health and Social Affairs is responsible for drawing up guidelines for health care and health insurance as well as other services of a social welfare nature. It also prepares government business where necessary.

The National Board of Health and Welfare is the central administrative agency responsible for such cognate matters as:

- monitoring and evaluating developments and experiments in health and medical care;
- co-ordinating knowledge and experience in the field of social policy; and
- acting as the government's expert adviser in this field.

The Swedish Planning and Rationalisation Institute of the Health and Social Services (SPRI) works on planning and efficiency measures. It also supports appropriate research and development in health care administration and undertakes any special investigations. It is funded jointly by central government and the Federation of County Councils. The latter federation also has a co-ordinating role to play.

Other government agencies include:

- the state-owned National Corporation of Swedish Pharmacies, Apoteksbolaget, responsible for the purchasing and distribution of drugs;

- the Medical Products Agency, Lakemedelsverket, which is responsible for the registration and control of drugs; and
- the Swedish Council of Technology Assessment in Health Care (SBU) which reviews and evaluates the ethical, medical and economic impacts of existing and developing health care technology.

This apparatus of interrelating, co-ordinating and co-operating organisations which spans the range from the political to the technical is entirely typical of the Swedish approach to government and administration.

FINANCING ARRANGEMENTS

Funding the service

The primary funding of health and medical care costs is from income taxes raised by the county councils. These taxes run at around 13.5 per cent of personal income and cover just over 60 per cent of the total cost of health and medical care.

The national government contributes a further 15 per cent, which is awarded differentially to the counties to compensate for inequities in income levels. Thus, just over three-quarters of the funding of direct health care is from local and central taxation.

As shown in Figure 5.3, the state takes responsibility for education, psychiatry and research, contributing a further 12 per cent. The remaining 12 per cent comes from health care insurance (8 per cent) and patients' fees (4 per cent). Health care insurance is an hypothecated tax, that is, specially designated or 'earmarked'. Inasmuch as county-level local government is primarily responsible for health care, then the bulk of its taxes may likewise be seen as hypothecated. This is a *de facto* classification rather than *de jure*. Governments, in general, prefer non-hypothecated taxes as this increases their freedom of manoeuvre.

The health insurance system confers three rights on Swedish citizens in return for payments made:

- medical and health care;
- sickness benefit; and
- parental benefits.

Of these, the two latter are on a generous scale. Sickness benefit works out at 90 per cent of normal income and is paid by the state after the employer has covered the first fourteen days of sickness. For persons not in employment there is a guaranteed minimum benefit. Parental benefit provides for

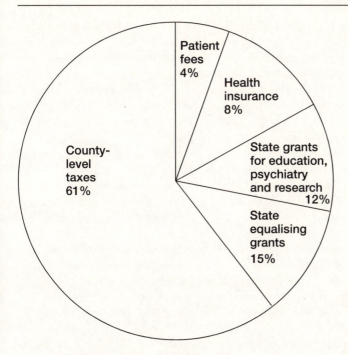

Figure 5.3 Sources of health care funding

up to ninety days per year leave of absence per child if either the child or the person who normally looks after the child is ill. This benefit is paid at the same rate as the sickness benefit.

The medical and health care benefits must be described more fully as they interrelate with the charging system. Where a person enters hospital as an in-patient, a charge of about SEK70 (about £6.50 or $10) per day is made and this is paid by the social health insurance service to the county council.

An interview with a general practitioner, whether in the private or public sector, costs the patient around SEK100. This fee covers the consultation together with any necessary documentation; any immediately necessary tests such as X-rays; any immediately necessary treatment such as radium therapy; referral to a specialist; and the cost of the first specialist consultation. Clearly the charge is nowhere near sufficient for this package. The balance is paid by the total health revenues, including the health insurance element.

A smaller charge, around SEK50 per visit, is made for treatment such as physiotherapy, provided that it has been prescribed by a doctor and is given by a public employee. A charge of SEK90 is levied on each prescription for drugs, although life-saving drugs are free. Some other services, such as birth control counselling, are also free. Travel to hospital is subsidised for adults undertaking long journeys and for children with their accompanying adult. Moreover, there is an important safety net in that there is a limit of SEK1,500 per year on the amount that any person must pay in various forms of charges.

With respect to dentistry, the position is rather different. Charges are levied according to an established scale whereby the patient pays 60 per cent of treatment costs up to SEK3,000, 50 per cent of treatment costs from SEK3,000 to SEK7,000 and 25 per cent of treatment costs beyond that limit (although all dental treatment for children and young people up to the age of 19 years is free).

This discrepancy between the charging patterns for medical care and dental care has resulted in a very different pattern of public and private provision. For medical provision, approximately 95 per cent is public (although 17 per cent of initial visits to doctors are in the private sector). For dental provision, the division between the public and private sector is fifty–fifty.

There is no tradition of income generation either from the sale of services or from local charitable activities such as bazaars or raffles. There are currently no plans for any form of national lottery. Nor is there a tradition of charitable bequests, contributions or donations. The Swedes are highly taxed and see no need for such activities.

Expenditure on health care

Spending on health care can be considered in two main ways. One way, that concerned with staffing, has already been discussed. The second is with reference to the pattern of care provision: on what services is the money spent?

From the data in Table 5.5 and its associated pie chart (Figure 5.4) a number of points emerge which are worthy of expansion. First, the 'general' and two 'somatic' categories absorb nearly three-quarters of health care costs. Second, long term somatic care costs only just over half as much as short term somatic care despite the fact that long term care has 56,000 beds compared with 35,000 for short term care. The relative cost ratio is therefore just about 35 per cent. The relative cheapness of long term care is due to the higher staffing ratios associated with short term care, including

Table 5.5 Distribution of health and medical care costs, 1989

Type of care	% OF SEK 98,000 million
Somatic short term care	25.4
Somatic long term care	14.0
Out-patient primary care	12.2
Psychiatric care	6.3
General and medical services	35.5
Dental care	4.7
Other	2.0

Source: Fact Sheet on Sweden, 76. Stockholm, Swedish Institute, October 1991

the very high staffing ratios used for theatre time, and also to the generally higher utilisation of technology with short term patients.

Lower staffing ratios and low-tech therapies also explain the comparatively low cost of psychiatric care, where the level of costs is similar to that of the long term somatic care.

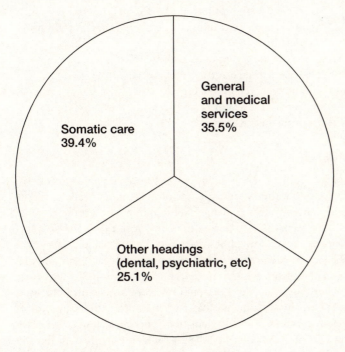

Figure 5.4 Health care expenditure, 1989

CONTEMPORARY ISSUES IN HEALTH POLICY

Current problems

There are two related problems associated with the current system. First, from central government's point of view, there are serious difficulties associated with financing. These difficulties are due to both the current recession and, more long term, to the changing ratio of 'dependants' to 'producers' caused by demographic trends.

Second, the esteem in which the health care system traditionally has been held, a positive factor when it comes to bidding for resources, is now being challenged by growing public discontent.

The Swedish Institute in 1991 listed the main weaknesses of the health service as follows:

- lack of integration between health services, social services and health insurance (especially sickness benefits, early retirement pensions and occupational injury insurance) and, within the health sector, between primary care and hospital care;
- in the primary health care system, the failure of GPs to act as 'gate-keepers', resulting in a high proportion of direct referrals to hospitals;
- great emphasis placed on institutional care, which may not always be effective and efficient;
- long waiting lists for some types of treatment, such as cataract removal, hip-joint replacement and coronary bypass surgery;
- sometimes, a limited choice for patients;
- insufficient incentives for health personnel to improve the productivity and efficiency of the health sector.

The winds of change

An important document, *The Swedish Health Services in the 1990s* (HS90), published in 1984 by the National Board of Health and Welfare, set the scene for the changes which demography and public pressure would impose on the system. In considering the content of this report it is important to note that it was published under the Socialist government which had been returned to power in 1982 after a six-year break; and that the economic problems which characterised the late 1980s and early 1990s were but clouds on the horizon. Optimism could still hold sway. The changes that the document advocated were thus the result, not of economic despair but of rational calculation. The calculation was, in fact, the product of a project set up in 1978 and which published an interim report, *Health in Sweden* in 1982.

The report recommended that health care developments should be guided by three general principles:

• Health care must be characterised by active health policies.
• Allocation of health care resources should be determined by the needs of the population.
• Demands for health care resources must be weighed against other demands, particularly those relating to socio-economic and employment goals.

The survey went on to deal with three main areas: health policies, including a drive towards preventive efforts; the structure of the health care system; and the planning of staffing and associated education.

The introductory chapter concluded with the message that people must be given greater knowledge, greater freedom of choice and responsibility for their own health and the possibility of influencing it.

The messages of the report were entirely consistent with the structure of the health care system as so far described and the trends which have been noted. The health care system at the end of the 1980s was recognisably that defined by the 1983 Health and Medical Services Act as modified by the report's enactment in the Health Policies Act of June 1985.

The early years of the 1990s have, however, seen a flurry of important documents which are relevant to the field of health care, and which reflect both the new priorities of the post-1991 government and the new constraints of less economic optimism. The *Public Health Report 1991*, published by the National Board of Health and Welfare, was the second in a series begun in 1987. The Foreword summarises it thus: 'the health status of the population as a whole is improving but . . . certain groups are lagging behind. There are still dramatic social differences in health related living habits.'

Within the context of the World Health Organisation strategy 'Health for All in Europe by the Year 2000' the report states that the regional and social health imbalances, if corrected by a movement to a uniform status associated with the healthiest category (senior salaried employees), would result in a 60 per cent decline in morbidity, from 33 per cent to 13 per cent. The economic impact of such a change is obvious.

The findings of the report have been summarised in earlier sections of this chapter. Cancers and cardiovascular conditions associated with smoking, alcohol and overeating are the chief diseases and there are worries about the increase in suicides and alcoholism, both of which are indicative of poor mental health.

The concluding section listed the problem of waiting lists in some specialties and cited difficulties with discharge from psychiatric and emergency somatic care because of lack of care and support facilities outside the hospital. All these problems, the report suggested, have been addressed to some extent but needed to be tackled further.

In March 1992, *Health and Medical Care in Sweden* was published by the Ministry of Health and Social Affairs over the signature of Under-Secretary of State Mr Goran Rådö. The following problems with respect to the health care system were identified:

- Patients have little freedom of choice between different hospitals and health centres.
- Hospitals have long waiting lists for certain kinds of surgery (e.g. hip replacements, cataract removal).
- Productivity is low.
- Elderly patients remain in emergency hospitals after their treatment has been completed owing to a shortage of nursing home capacity and home help personnel.
- In spite of the high cost of health and medical care, there are several fields in which improvements are needed, e.g. psychiatric care and care of the aged, where not all patients can as yet have individual rooms in nursing homes.
- Despite the expansion of primary health care which has taken place in recent years, Swedish medical care still has quite a strong hospital bias.

The document went on to list the changes in progress. First, 1992 saw the introduction of a 'caring guarantee' for about ten diagnoses which promises treatment in either a county or a private hospital within three months at the county's expense. If a municipality cannot make appropriate after-care provision for discharged patients, it will have to pay the hospital for keeping the patient.

Second, with respect to GP services, there is a move towards equality of provision on the basis of one GP to 2,000 residents. Patients will have a choice of GP and remuneration will be, primarily, on the basis of patient choice. There will also be weightings for the proportion of elderly patients on a GP's list and some 'achievement-related' remuneration. Patients who bypass their GPs and go directly to hospital, without referral, will pay a much higher fee.

Last, a purchaser–provider type of internal market will be widely introduced after successful, albeit limited, experiments in three county council areas. Hospitals, as providers, will have a manager and a senior consultant but no politically appointed governing body. Counties, as purchasers, will pay for the treatment on a patient by patient basis and will also, as owners of the hospitals, make the major investment decisions. This will almost certainly mean the closure of some emergency hospitals, a procedure likely to evoke opposition. Day surgery will be encouraged, thus reducing the overall level of hospital beds. Furthermore, because patients have more choice, the hospitals themselves are becoming more sensitive to patient preference, carrying out regular surveys and taking other quality assurance measures.

Two other major experiments are planned. In some municipalities the health care and social insurance allowances are to be merged, thus permitting authorities to use the sickness allowance to purchase treatment and rehabilitation. The intention is that this should result in an overall cost saving.

In addition, there would be a Government Commission, which was due to report in 1994, to examine the funding of medical care over the remainder of the century and to investigate three models of medical organisation. These models may be characterised briefly as follows:

- greater autonomy for hospitals within the overall control of the counties;
- fundholding group general practices; and
- compulsory medical insurance, thus removing the need for counties to have their taxation powers.

With respect to the first two models, the influence of the British experience is evident and, with respect to the third model, the American influence is apparent. The change in government during 1994, however, resulted in suspension of the publication of the report: the principles on which it was based were clearly contrary to the rhetoric of the centre-left. Nevertheless it will be surprising if some such moves are not carried through because of the very urgent need to address the economic side of the fiscal–demographic problem.

Care of the elderly

The demographic aspect of the problem is also being addressed. Nils Fernow draws attention to the massive reduction in long-stay beds for the elderly from nearly 130,000 in 1982 to only 98,000 in 1990, a 25 per cent reduction over the period. Beds in retirement homes showed an even more dramatic decrease if the figures for the over-eighties are considered. The reduction was from twenty-two per hundred to ten per hundred.

The responsibility for caring is being transferred from the county medical services to the municipal social care services. It is also being recognised that there is an important role to be played by the family. The 1992 reforms allow for payments to be made to relatives and friends who abstain from paid employment in order to care for an elderly person. Old people will, of course, become ill and will need treatment by the medical services, but one outcome of these reforms is that expensive medical care will not be misapplied by maintaining unnecessary long-stay beds.

CONCLUSION

The pattern of Swedish provision and expenditure is not dissimilar to that of other developed states. The trends which must be allowed for in looking at policies for future provision include the declining proportion of younger people, and therefore a potential reduction in the proportion of expensive short term care, and the increasing proportion of older persons, and thus the likely considerable increase in the need for longer term care. There is also concern about the number of psychiatric patients. Disquiet over the costs of health care and debate about the optimum methods of treatment are evident in Sweden as they are in all other developed health care systems.

REFERENCES AND FURTHER READING

Cochrane, A. and Clarke, J. (1993) *Comparing Welfare States: Britain in International Context*, London: Sage Publications.

Fernow, N. (1992) 'Swedish elder care in transition', *Current Sweden* 392, Stockholm: The Swedish Institute.

Forsberg, M. (1984) *The Evolution of Social Welfare Policy in Sweden*, Stockholm: Swedish Institute.

Heidenheimer, A. J., Heclo, H. and Teich Adams, C. (1990) *Comparative Public Policy: The Politics of Social Choice in America, Europe, and Japan*, New York: St Martin's Press.

OECD (Organisation for Economic Co-operation and Development) (1990) *Health Care Systems in Transition*, Paris: OECD.

Rådö, G. (1992) *Health and Medical Care in Sweden*, Stockholm: Ministry of Health and Social Affairs.

Swedish National Board of Health and Welfare (1991) *Public Health Report 1991*, Stockholm.

The National Board of Health and Welfare (1985) *Swedish Health Services in the 1990s*, Stockholm.

Vagero, D. (1992) 'Women work and health in Sweden', *Current Sweden* 387, Stockholm, Swedish Institute.

Chapter 6

The United Kingdom

John Kingdom

Most British health care is provided by the state-run National Health Service (NHS) which is tax funded and free at the point of delivery. Although it has always existed alongside a fee-charging private sector alternative, the great majority of ordinary citizens can expect to come into contact with the NHS at some time in life, if only upon entering and leaving it.

The NHS is an intensely political institution. Perhaps more than any other part of Britain's welfare state it has enshrined the values of collectivism over those of individualism, a fact which has placed it in the front line of the left–right confrontation. It invariably features prominently in popular debate, usually as a central factor in general election campaigns. It is also a nexus of interest group activity, bringing together professional associations, voluntary associations, trade unions, large business interests including multinationals, and a variety of promotional groups concerned with particular patient categories, public health, the environment and so on. Political salience is heightened by the fact (confirmed repeatedly in opinion surveys) that it remains the most highly regarded part of the welfare state. Consequently it is impossible to understand the NHS merely as an organisational structure reflecting rational processes and values; virtually no part of its architecture has been untouched by the interplay of political forces.

THE CONTEXT OF BRITISH HEALTH CARE

The demographic structure

Overall, Britain has experienced a major demographic transition over the last hundred years, moving from being a country with high birth and death rates to being low on both counts. Broadly the reasons for this are

Table 6.1 Population size, 1951–2031

Year	UK population (millions)
1951	50,290
1961	52,807
1971	55,928
1981	56,352
1991	57,801
2031	62,096 (projected)

Source: Social Trends 18, London, HMSO, 1988, p. 28, Table 1.9; *Social Trends* 24, London, HMSO, 1994, p. 22, Table 1.2

Table 6.2 Elderly population, 1901–2021

Year	% of population over 75
1901	1.4
1931	2.1
1951	3.5
1971	4.7
1981	5.8
1991	7.0
2001	7.5
2011	7.5
2021	8.1

Source: Annual Abstract of Statistics, London, HMSO, Central Statistical Office, 1992

advances in medical technology and general improvements in socio-environmental factors. Table 6.1 depicts a steady population increase in the post-war era.

Perhaps the most important aspect of this development for the NHS is the increasing number of elderly people. The trend and projected trend for males and females over 75 years is shown in Table 6.2. This greying trend is accentuated by a decline in the birth rate, as shown in Table 6.3. However, this is not projected to fall below the annual death rate until 2028 (*Social Trends* 1994: 21). There are major financial implications to what has been termed a 'demographic time bomb'. In the first place, on average a person over 75 years consumes around nine times the amount of health care resources used by the average person of working age (DHSS, 1983). Moreover, many of the conditions suffered by this group are of a chronic

Table 6.3 Birth rate, 1901–90

Year	Annual number of live births per 1,000 population
1901	28.6
1931	16.3
1951	16.0
1971	16.1
1981	13.0
1990	13.9

Source: *Annual Abstract of Statistics*, London, HMSO, Central Statistical Office, 1992

Table 6.4 Dependency ratio, 1951–2013

Year	Children under 16 years and people of pensionable age per 100 of the working population
1951	57
1991	63
2013	79 (projected)

Source: *Social Trends* 24, London, HMSO, 1994: 23

nature not amenable to hospital cure, so that treatment costs cannot be expected to fall.

These costs are borne by the working population through taxes. The number of people of working age increased from 32.6 million in 1975 to 35.5 million in 1991. However, after peaking in the near future, it is projected to fall to 34.6 million by 2031. The proportion of those dependent on the working population is rising. In 1951 there were twenty-one people of pensionable age to every 100 of working age. By 1991 this had reached thirty, and is projected to reach forty-six by 2031. By combining the number of children under 16 years with people of pensionable age it is possible to determine the dependency ratio (Table 6.4). (This ratio is even higher if one includes a figure for unemployment, which hovers around 3 million.)

Epidemiological trends

During the twentieth century Britain has seen an epidemiological shift comprising various elements. First there has been a dramatic fall in the incidence of infectious diseases linked with mortality and morbidity rates, particularly during childhood. Many of these are associated with poverty and include tuberculosis, the enteric fevers, cholera, smallpox, scarlet fever, measles, whooping cough and diphtheria. Economic, social and medical developments have contributed to the decline.

Yet the scourge of infectious diseases has not been eliminated. From the 1970s there have been significant rises in food poisoning and acute meningitis notifications. There have also been signs of increase in the incidence of tuberculosis, particularly amongst the poorer sections of society including ethnic minority communities.

A further area of increase is in conditions associated with the general ageing of the population: chronic and degenerative in nature, they include coronary heart disease, strokes and arthritis. Other areas of increase reflect modern conditions and include allergy-related diseases such as asthma, mental disorders, alcohol-related conditions, solvent abuse and accidents. Finally there are diseases new to Britain such as Lassa fever, hepatitis B and legionnaire's disease. Overshadowing all is the spread of HIV infection and AIDS, though its actual incidence remains small in relative terms.

Cultural traditions

Modern British social culture is a product of a tradition of monarchic and aristocratic rule which was challenged in the eighteenth and nineteenth centuries through the industrial revolution, which saw the rise to dominance of a capitalist bourgeoisie. However, rather than overthrow the old order the bourgeoisie was largely assimilated into its ranks. The rise of expensive fee-charging public schools, offering to give the aristocratic virtues to the sons of the rough-talking northern businessmen, helped ensure that Britain remained a highly elitist and class-conscious culture. At the same time the expansion of trade gave Britain an unrivalled world hegemony through the most extensive empire the world has ever seen. The British ruling class was a world ruling class. This was white male dominance at its most naked. The persistence of a titled aristocracy, a non-elected chamber in parliament (the House of Lords) and an elaborate monarchy symbolises the adherence to an elitist tradition.

In fact, what is termed *British* culture is, to a large extent, *English* culture. The UK comprises four nations (effectively provinces today), England, Wales, Scotland and Northern Ireland, but from early times the unity of the UK was seen by the English as vital for security. The Welsh and Scottish nations were subjugated over history by conquest. The UK was formally established in 1800 with the parliamentary union of Great Brit-

ain and Northern Ireland under Westminster. However, the Irish continued to chafe under the English yoke. In 1921 partition saw the birth of
the Irish Free State, which drifted free leaving only Northern Ireland as
part of the union. The troubles over Northern Ireland, where a Protestant
majority clashed with the Catholics, have continued to blight UK politics.

The twentieth century has seen the dismantling of the empire and a
decline in Britain's world position both economically and politically.
However, delusions of grandeur have tended to persist. This has in large
measure contributed to the UK's difficulty in coming to terms with its
place in the modern world and has caused problems with membership of
the European Union. There is a deep unease within the political class
about the loss of national sovereignty of a nation that could once lay a valid
claim to rule the world.

The inter-war depression years were faced with a non-revolutionary
stoicism which has been repeated during the 1980s and 1990s when unemployment stands at unprecedented heights. Throughout recent decades,
not only has the population avoided any serious social unrest, but it has
repeatedly rejected the Labour Party, with its social democratic agenda, in
favour of the Conservatives who, under Margaret Thatcher and then John
Major, have offered the most right-wing programme of the post-war era
and perhaps of the century.

The significance of this culture for the welfare state in general, and for
the NHS in particular, has been considerable. The provincial constitutional set-up means that, although health services are broadly the same
in England, Wales, Scotland and Northern Ireland, there are certain organisational differences. At the ideological level, it can be argued that the post-
war social democracy was grafted on to the elitist nineteenth-century
liberal state so that its institutions were never well embedded in popular
culture. When the New Right, led by Margaret Thatcher, took control of
government in 1979 it was not difficult to denigrate the welfare state and
dub its recipients 'scroungers'. Although the popularity of the NHS was
the most difficult bastion to storm, it was not to escape the reform agenda.

Social factors

Britain is a class-based society, the deference of the lower classes strengthening this. Moreover, during the past decade there has been considerable
talk in academic and journalistic circles of the emergence of an underclass:
a category of people living outside mainstream society, unable to enjoy its
benefits and unwilling to accept its social responsibilities and duties
(Morris 1994). Unlike the US, where this is seen largely as a racial issue

(with blacks forming the underclass), the British case is a function of un-employment (though race and gender factors play a part). At the same time, the 1980s and early 1990s have seen a disproportionate rise in the salaries of top managers and a broadening of the gap between the richest and the poorest.

Unemployment has become a chronic social problem. Although the manner of calculation was manipulated during the 1980s by a government wishing to present a more favourable picture, the figure hovered around 3 million for much of the period. Where jobs have been created they are often of a low-paid, part-time, menial nature. There has been a regional dimension to this development, with the greatest prosperity confined to the south-east.

Britain has for long been a sexist society. The great majority of positions of power in the state and in civil society have been occupied by men. Similarly, the role of women within the home has been one of depend-ence on a male breadwinner. A rise in single-parent families, where the parent is usually female, links the gender issue with that of the underclass.

Britain is also a racist society. To some extent this is a legacy of the era of empire when world leadership helped foster a culture of racial superiority. The problem was intensified when, with the break-up of the empire and the creation of the British Commonwealth, citizens from the ex-colonies were encouraged to come to Britain to take menial jobs in the employ-ment market.

For much of the post-war era religion has been a waning force in an increasingly secular society. However, as Britain has become a more multi-ethnic society there has been some growth in non-Christian religions. There has also been a marked propensity since the 1980s for the Church of England to become more outspoken on political and social issues, with much criticism of the government's social and economic policies.

The governmental and political setting

Although there are calls for change, the British political class generally takes pride in the fact, highly unusual amongst developed democracies, that the polity lacks a formal written constitution. This is not to say there is no constitution, but it can only be discovered through a combination of powers granted under the ancient Royal Prerogative, statutes passed by parliament, common law decisions in the courts, the authoritative opin-ions of learned experts and, finally, conventions. Although the last of these exists in all polities they assume a particular importance in the UK. This means that such constitution as the UK does possess is a product of hundreds of years of history; the past remains wedded to the present in a manner not found in polities which have seen popular revolutionary renunciations of an undemocratic past. This may be lauded as preserving the wisdom of the ages. It may also be seen as a means of preserving an elitist state. British citizens have no bill of rights to protect their freedoms. There are no entrenched rights of political participation to protect local democracy or trade union membership. Rather than a freedom of information Act there is only official secrets legislation. Indeed, in the UK we find the most secret and closed form of government in the western world.

General elections to the House of Commons (effectively the senior house) take place within a five-year period of any government succeeding to office and at a date of its own choosing. The electoral system is nonproportional. Each constituency returns a single member who does not require an absolute majority; merely more votes than any other candidate ('first past the post'). This is said to conduce two-party politics and means that the party with most seats will generally form the government. Coalitions may occur for reasons of national emergency, such as war, but tend not to occur in normal circumstances. Although there are calls for them, Wales and Scotland have never had separate assemblies. Northern Ireland did have such provision at Stormont but direct Westminster rule was imposed in 1972.

The two major parties are the Conservatives on the right and Labour on the left. There is a third party, the Social and Liberal Democrats, which, although receiving much electoral support across the country, falls victim to the electoral system and gains relatively few parliamentary seats. There are also nationalist parties in Wales and Scotland which, with their geographically concentrated support, do relatively well from the system.

Evidence of deference within the political culture comes in the fact that the Conservative Party (essentially the party of capital) has enjoyed the lion's share of office throughout the century. In this sense, modern British political history displays a pattern of single party government. The other chamber in parliament is the House of Lords, where membership is based on noble birth or political patronage through the appointment of life peers.

Beyond the formal structure of state power lie well-established pressure group networks. Britain is sometimes termed a pluralist democracy though the elitist culture means that not all can enjoy equal access to the seat of power. The inequality has fostered the idea that a dilute form of corporatism, or a corporate bias (Middlemass 1979), had evolved with unions and capital playing a formal role in the policy-making process. This had relevance for welfare, with professionals exerting a dominant influence over policy and was particularly evident in the NHS where the medical profession enjoyed privileged access to power (Eckstein 1960).

However, the range of groups interested in health policy extends well beyond the medical professionals. Within the NHS are many other employee interests, usually organised as trade unions. In addition there is a vast health industry comprising developers who build hospitals, manufacturers who equip them and of course the multi-million-pound pharmaceutical industry. Even beyond this stratum of interest there are those whose activities can be *harmful* to health, the tobacco and alcohol industries, the convenience food manufacturers, the farmers at times, and so on. There is also an increasingly vocal lobby favouring more private provision of health care; this comprises not only those who would provide services but the powerful financial interests who would stand to gain through the development of private insurance systems.

In short, whether policy is about the provision of services or the regulation of activities with health implications, there are numerous interests active in the health arena.

Post-war political developments have been very important for the NHS. For much of the period Britain experienced consensus politics, where the two main parties shared a broad measure of agreement on the role of the state, the management of the economy and social policy. This was the Keynesian social democratic settlement where political battles were largely about means rather than ends. Consensus on the NHS lay at the very heart of this and entailed agreement on the basic goals of universality, free accessibility and comprehensiveness. However, the consensus was not to prove as enduring as had been thought. The Thatcher era, beginning in 1979, was to see a fundamental questioning of the very principle of the social democratic state. The economic context helps explain this development.

Economic performance

Economic buoyancy has been central to the UK welfare state. Anthony Crosland, prominent Labour politician and intellectual, argued in an influential book, *The Future of Socialism* (1956), that growth was an essential prerequisite of socialism. Only with improvements in their own material standards would the wealthy accede to the necessary redistribution of wealth.

The possession of a vast trading empire and early leadership in the process of modern industrialisation made the British economy in the eighteenth and nineteenth centuries mighty indeed. From the mid-nineteenth century, rivals, in the form of the US and Germany, began to erode this hegemony but the UK entered the twentieth century in a relatively powerful position. Being committed to parliamentary socialism and the protection of workers within a capitalist system rather than its overthrow, the left, in the form of the Labour Party created in 1900, did not threaten this economic order. However, the prosperity was not to last for ever.

The burden of two great wars left the UK economy considerably weakened and dependent upon the US, but in the early decades of the post-war era it was possible to enjoy the benefits of a long boom of world capitalism. This boom was based upon free trade, the monetary stability of the Bretton Woods agreement and a belief in Keynesianism. Yet, although British-based multinationals were second only to those of the US, the domestic economy did not match those of competitors; the era proved one of relative decline. When, in the mid-1970s, economic collapse shook the western capitalist world, the British frailty was exposed.

The diagnosis of the New Right in the mid-1970s was that the problem was not world capitalism but the welfare state: it imposed a burden on profitability and sapped the vitality of ordinary people. In 1979, after a so-called winter of discontent, marked by widespread public service strikes, the country returned a Conservative government with its mission to roll back the state, end welfare state feather-bedding, repudiate Keynesianism and return to a nineteenth-century style economic monetarism. The broad thrust of the strategy was a reduction of the public sector borrowing requirement, which would entail cuts in welfare spending. Reform of the high-spending NHS was central to the programme and the period was marked by even more intense politicisation of the subject of the nation's health.

Health care beyond the NHS

We cannot fully understand the British NHS without recognising the variegated landscape of health care in which it subsists. Its creation did not entail the abolition of private or voluntary provision. In addition, there remains a little-recognised, but important, informal sector. Hence a person requiring medical treatment has, at various points, a number of possible alternatives to the NHS.

The informal sector

This comprises networks of families, colleagues and friends. In pre-industrial days families took on a wide range of responsibilities for caring for their sick, elderly and disabled. Today they continue to do so though this informal level of health care is little recognised and rarely funded by the state. Beyond the family, people at work advise each other, school-teachers care for children, support groups offer psychological help and so on. One politically significant aspect of this is that the informal caring role tends to fall disproportionately upon women.

The voluntary sector

Although sometimes ignored in studies, the NHS has made extensive use of voluntary endeavour both by individuals and by organisations. NHS hospitals even appoint organisers of such services. The associations, often engaging thousands of unpaid workers, add important cogs to the health care machinery and, through the receipt of government funds and the concept of partnership, are virtually part of the NHS itself.

The role of voluntary societies was important in the early development of state welfare, though today they have grown well beyond the nineteenth-century paternalistic image. Many are high-profile, well organ-ised and politically active organisations such as, say, Age Concern, the Royal National Institute for the Blind, the Terrence Higgins Foundation and so on. Many are run by well-known figures regarded as authorities in their areas, consulted by governments and appearing in the media as pundits.

Broadly the societies fulfil two functions: service provision and fund raising. However, as side effects they fulfil many others such as educating public opinion, identifying unmet needs, offering informed criticism of state policy and acting as pressure groups. As service providers they can enhance diversity, pioneer new services and even enter areas the state cannot reach (for example drug-dependants living at the fringes of the law or members of sexual minorities seeking anonymity in a prurient society).

However, although relying heavily upon state subsidies (Webb and Wistow 1982), the societies tend to see their role as complementary rather than as an alternative to state provision.

The private sector

This is a diverse sector going beyond private hospitals, private practices and health insurance companies. It also includes provision for part-time contracts for NHS consultants, allowing them to devote time to private patients and the existence of 'pay beds' in NHS hospitals. Practitioners such as dentists and chiropodists may see patients privately and pharmacists ply their trade as shopkeepers as well as dispensing for the NHS. In addition there are the giant commercial drugs companies and equipment manufacturers who supply the NHS as well as manufacturing a bewildering range of products for direct sale to the public.

The balance between the parts of the health care system tends to be in a state of continual flux, with particular turbulence since the early 1980s.

THE DEVELOPMENT OF STATE INVOLVEMENT

The earliest, and perhaps most important, developments in state involvement in the health of the nation came in the area of public health. State health care, as such, evolved at three levels: the hospital, general practitioner services and community care.

Public health

The emerging bourgeoisie of the nineteenth century soon realised that the germs causing diseases such as cholera and tuberculosis took a more egalitarian view of social life than they themselves did. Although breeding in the bodies of slum dwellers, germs could invade the nostrils of the wealthy and even, as the death of Prince Albert grimly demonstrated, enter the blue blood of royalty. Hence the century saw a great movement for sanitary reform spearheaded by Edwin Chadwick, an acolyte of the leading utilitarian thinker, Jeremy Bentham, which resulted in a number of major Public Health Acts. Across the country local sanitary boards were created with responsibility to ensure adequate sewerage and clean water. In 1894 these responsibilities were taken over by the newly formed all-purpose elected local authorities. They also municipalised many of the private water companies and assumed various environmental responsibilities such as the burial of the dead, the administration of slaughterhouses, town improvement, the regulation of trades dealing with noxious substances, street cleaning, waste disposal, slum clearance and town planning.

Hospitals

Many early hospitals were provided by voluntary bodies on the basis of charity, often with endowments from wealthy philanthropists. The best of these developed a high degree of specialisation and offered medical teaching. From here came the prestigious teaching hospitals, such as Saint

Bartholomew's in London. Other hospitals were pioneered by the Poor Law authorities within the workhouses, to be taken over by elected local government in 1929. These were funded by local taxes (rates) and tended to offer more rudimentary provision.

It was the second world war which saw the major incursion by the central state with the establishment of an Emergency Medical Service in which the government effectively took over all hospitals. Being generally hard pressed for funds (there were political limits on the amount available from the rates, and charity was drying up) they were in no position to resist. This was to prove the precursor of the NHS.

General practitioner services

Literally as well as metaphorically the poor man's physician, the role of the general practitioner evolved from that of apothecary, working as a corner-shop business treating patients for fees. Some workers obtained health insurance through friendly societies, trade unions and commercial under-takings, though women and children were largely excluded. A major state incursion came with the 1911 National Insurance Act which established a national health insurance system modelled on that operating in Bismarck's Germany. The system was co-ordinated at the centre by a National Insur-ance Commission and administered locally by the existing insurance agencies which, anxious to maintain their role, gained new status as ap-proved societies. Premiums were deducted from wages along with contri-butions from the state and the employer, the insured acquiring rights to full treatment from a doctor though not (with the exception of TB sana-toriums) hospital treatment.

GPs were placed on a local panel and paid on a capitation basis rather than on the basis of treatment given. The Act also made provision for sickness benefits to cover loss of earnings for a limited period. However, it was restricted to manual workers earning below a specified wage. Others without the means to pay (including dependants of the insured) continued to go without.

Unlike that of Germany, the system was to be fully funded; contribu-tions were supposed to finance treatment as in commercial insurance. There were political reasons for this. Within British society there re-mained a strong vein of Victorian self-help ideology which feared state involvement on the social front. Coupled with this was profound disap-proval from business interests of any increases in state expenditure.

Even so, political opposition remained. Many employers, particularly those of servants, were angered and even got their servants to complain.

The British Medical Association (BMA), the professional association representing the upper reaches of the profession, was also sceptical, though the more humble GPs stood to gain and were enthusiastic. In the view of the left, including the fledgling Labour Party, the scheme was too parsimonious and insufficiently redistributive, the employee contribution being higher that those from employer or government.

One important consequence of the new scheme was the revelation of unsuspected levels of disease within the population, particularly amongst women. This strengthened the case for a more comprehensive system and the inclusion of hospital treatment.

Community health care

In Britain this constitutes a residual category of services which are not hospital or GP based. They include home nursing, health visiting, family planning clinics, the school health services, vaccination, health education and many others. The common characteristic is that they are, for the most part, received by individuals within a community context. Development came largely in response to industrialisation. Many services were pioneered through voluntary endeavour by individuals and societies, though most were later taken over by local authorities. For example, the first district nursing service was started in Liverpool in the late 1850s by a local philanthropist.

Central government also played a part. Free vaccination was introduced by parliament in 1840, though the local Poor Law authorities, offering a ready-made national framework, were used to administer the service. Up to the beginning of the twentieth century, midwifery could be practised by any woman who saw it as a way of making a living. However, an Act of 1902 established professional and training requirements. The school medical service evolved unevenly through the actions of various school boards set up under the great Education Act of 1870. The Boer War of 1899–1902 exposed the poor health of the nation's children and led to responsibility being given more formally to newly created local education authorities in the Midwives Act 1902.

Gradually local authorities took over many of the services, with their medical officers of health, whose roles were originally associated with public health, assuming the major responsibility. This illustrated the complementarity of community care and public health.

The period from the end of the first world war was one of consolidation but the second world war saw further developments. Infant, child and maternity services were expanded but the evacuation of children from urban to rural areas placed extreme pressures on rural authorities and voluntary societies. In a few years a wide range of nurseries and hostels had emerged. There were also developments of maternity homes and residential nurseries, usually staffed by volunteers. Local authorities found themselves responsible for administering programmes of free school meals and milk, a school medical service and vaccination programmes. When the NHS was created it inherited a well-established system of community health care under the control of local government (Ottewill and Wall 1990: 25–64).

Creating the NHS

The second world war, like the first, revealed considerable inadequacies in the quality of health care available to ordinary people, with women by far the worst off. Evacuation of women and children from the poorest areas of the cities in the summer of 1939 exposed to middle-class gaze the reality of poverty, malnutrition and limited access to running water and sanitation present in Britain. Consequently, much wartime domestic debate focused on health care, and a broad consensus emerged on the need for a fully-fledged, comprehensive service once post-war reconstruction began. Such a debate was, of course, good for the morale of working-class families who were being asked to fight and die for a society that had offered them very little.

An important impetus came in the Beveridge Report of 1942. Ostensibly on the subject of *Social Insurance and Allied Services*, it was widely regarded as a blueprint for a new welfare state. Amongst its basic assumptions was a comprehensive and free national health service available to all. Perhaps even more impelling motivation came from surveys amongst a beleaguered population, revealing massive public support for such a service.

Yet subsequent events can be seen as a classic example of pressure politics. If a camel is a horse designed by a committee, the NHS, shaped by several committees and subject to advice from numerous interests, including doctors' associations, trade unions, local authorities, voluntary hospitals, academics and politicians, was scarcely less curious an animal. Structure and authority were the major issues faced in the debate. A health service must be accessible; within easy reach of all. Again, because health is so vital to quality of life there was a self-evident case for democratic control. Such considerations pointed to administration by Britain's elected local government system, a case strengthened by its important pioneering role in hospital and community health care. Indeed, a wartime

White Paper from the coalition government, with the support of doctors, proposed such a model.

However, the post-war debate saw factors other than rationality at play. The doctors, with a monopoly of esoteric knowledge, formed a powerful interest. They were unwilling to submit to democratic (or bureaucratic) control and were able to gain significant concessions. One of these was selective breeding of a new species of constitutional animal, the hospital authority, a non-elected local authority with members appointed by ministerial patronage, and guaranteeing strong representation of the doctors themselves. The influential teaching hospitals preserved considerable independence, keeping their endowments and their governing boards. In addition doctors were allowed to continue to treat fee-paying private patients in NHS hospitals.

Similarly, and contrary to early ambitions, general practitioner services also evaded local authority control. Initially, plans envisaged local authority health centres employing GPs as salaried state employees (like teachers) but, in the final settlement, they were to preserve their independent contractor status, still paid on a capitation basis. The system was to be run by local bodies called executive councils composed of one-half lay representatives (appointed rather than elected) and one-half from the profession.

Failing to gain responsibility for hospitals or GP services, the elected local authorities were left with a residual category of community health services of less interest to the medical profession.

The provisions in the legislation applied to Wales and England. In Scotland a separate Act also followed the tripartite principle, overall NHS responsibility lying with the Secretary of State for Scotland.

The Labour minister charged with the responsibility for the final tortuous negotiations was Aneurin Bevan. In retrospect, his reputation as a left-wing radical seems tarnished with many concessions to the medical establishment. However, he was confronted with the alarming possibility of complete breakdown in health care. Holding a power of veto, the profession appeared fully prepared to boycott the service. His central aim was to establish a universal free system of medical care, and this he achieved. By international standards the structure was to be judged a success. In the consensus era of post-war politics few would dispute the status of the NHS as the proud flagship of Britain's social democracy.

Key features before the 1980s

Key features of the new NHS included a high degree of centralisation, a geographically dispersed administrative structure, a tripartite organisation, a corporatist style of policy-making, lack of a clear managerial structure and a weak system of democratic accountability.

Centralisation

The most clear demonstration of the centralism of the system lay in the financing arrangements. This was the major concession made by the medical profession; the price of preserving their clinical autonomy. On the principle of he who pays the piper calls the tune, centralisation offered considerable directive power to the government. In this way the NHS was made free from 'the contingencies of local history and parochial vision' (Strong and Robinson 1990: 11). The centralisation also meant that there would, at least in theory, be a responsible minister accountable to parliament.

Geographical dispersal

This came through an areal pattern based on fourteen regions subdivided into districts (some 200 by 1982). The fact that each was headed by a local board was intended to provide a degree of responsiveness to local community feeling. The regional pattern was also to form a basis for equalising the distribution of resources over the country. The 1960s saw the creation of large district general hospitals and each region came to have its own medical school.

Tripartism

There were three distinct organisational elements responsible respectively for hospitals, GP services and community care. The fragmentation was generally viewed as a fundamental flaw rather than a virtue, undermining the idea of a single unified service, and various attempts were made to improve co-operation, though these were largely judged as unsuccessful.

The Porritt Report of 1962 and a Green Paper produced by the Labour government in 1968 both considered transferring the whole system to local government but opposition from the medical profession ruled this out. In 1974 a major NHS reform sought a degree of unification in a different way by combining responsibility for community care with hospital administration under newly created unelected regional and area health authorities and district management teams. At this time the grand teaching hospitals were finally brought within the system and their boards of governors disappeared. Yet in one respect the unification was a fiction;

although the administrative boundaries were made conterminous, the merging of primary and secondary health care remained a dream. The executive councils were given the more patient friendly title of family practitioner committees (FPCs); the GP services stayed largely autonomous.

In Wales the tripartite system remained as in England. The Welsh Office, Whitehall's outpost for a range of functions, assumed both central department and regional responsibilities, with a Health and Social Services Department under the Secretary of State for Wales. In Scotland, however, reform was more radical. Here tripartism was eliminated, with fifteen health boards created to administer all three branches of the service. Ten of these were further divided into districts. However, there was no provision for collaboration with local government. Local health councils were created to represent consumer views and a Health Services Commissioner for Scotland began work on 1 October 1973. Reform in Northern Ireland came in 1973 and resulted in an even more integrated structure. The province was placed under four area health and social services boards responsible, as their name implies, for both health and social services. Beneath these were seventeen districts, broadly conterminous with local government. As in Scotland, there was no separate set of authorities dealing with GP services, which were under a Central Services Agency.

Corporatism

Corporatism arose as an outcome of the initial negotiations between government and the medical profession. The NHS seemed to reflect a conviction that doctor knew best not only in the consulting room but also in the corridors of Whitehall. The medical profession gained an entrenched position in medical policy-making, with representatives seated on numerous advisory bodies and consultative councils. Generally they retained a set of professional rights including control over training, initiation, disciplinary matters, conditions of work and level of remuneration. The pattern was replicated at local level with medical representation on various advisory bodies and even on the health authorities themselves. The arrangement was sometimes described as syndicalist.

Managerial weakness

This was a corollary of the power of the medical interests to resist non-medical direction at all levels. Reforms in 1974 made some attempt to address the problem by promoting more of a management ethos, an emphasis on planning, and talk of the need for equipping administrators and clinicians with new management skills. The new style was to be consensus management through multidisciplinary teams at each tier. Doctors and (for the first time) nurses had representation on both the regional and area authorities. District management teams were collectives, only able to move forward on the basis of conciliation and compromise. The NHS was to be run by groups of nominal equals; although doctors could not be commanded by a managerial class like factory workers they had at least been made members of teams.

Yet the reality of professional power remained indelible. At each tier the system remained ornamented with a web of advisory bodies to ensure that expert opinion would inform all policy deliberations. The reforms could even be said to have enhanced the power of the doctors by setting their voice 'into the concrete of the institutional structure even more firmly than Bevan's design had done' (Klein 1989: 95).

Weak democratic accountability

The failure to place health authorities under the control of elected representatives left the system in democratic deficit from the outset. The removal of community health care from local government in 1974 reduced the democratic element even further. Some attempt was made to mitigate the position through the creation of community health councils at district level to act as consumer watchdogs. Yet these had no executive authority, and were able only to advise and transmit information to members of their local communities; to bark but never bite.

However, from 1979 several features of the NHS were to be reshaped under the critical hand of the New Right.

THE PRINCIPAL FEATURES OF SERVICE DELIVERY AND ADMINISTRATION

The New Right impact

In 1979 Margaret Thatcher assumed the British premiership promising to rewrite the political script and bring down the curtain on the Keynesian era. The welfare state was a particular target: here, it was felt, bureaucrats and professionals were liable to self-seeking and profligacy with public money. With the Royal Colleges and the BMA amongst the most powerful pressure groups in the country, the NHS presented a particularly acute example of unrestrained professional power (Wilding 1982).

The first moves of the government were not dramatic. In 1982 following a 1979 White Paper, *Patients First*, the structure was simplified with new district health authorities (DHAs) replacing the old area and district tiers. This change seemed to place the value of small size before the values of efficiency and rationality vaunted in 1974 (Klein 1989: 136). It also jettisoned the goal of unification of health care and social services since the area tiers had shared territorial boundaries with local government and the general practice areas. Although the collaboration had never been entirely successful, this movement away from elected local government further reduced NHS democracy.

Patients First applied only to England and Wales, but it was still suggested that the Scottish system should seek a more simplified structure. The uneven population dispersal led to a protracted process of deliberation which was suddenly pre-empted in 1983 by the Scottish Secretary, who ordered the scrapping of the districts, leaving a direct relationship between the boards and the units.

However, the basic model of local non-elected authorities arranged hierarchically in a line management relationship under a central authority at Whitehall remained intact. The structure comprised the Department of Health and Social Security headed by a Secretary of State and some junior ministers; all responsible to parliament. Below were fifteen regional health authorities (RHAs) overseeing the work of a lower tier of some 200 DHAs. Within the districts a range of hospitals and community care units were subject to the general control of the DHA. Also in 1982 a system of efficiency scrutinies (designed by Derek Raynor of the retail chain, Marks and Spencer) which had been operating in Whitehall was extended to the NHS. In addition accountability reviews, between Minister and RHA, and RHA and DHA, were introduced.

Yet the prevailing ethos of consensus management explicitly contradicted the principle of lines of command and remained prey to the syndicalist designs of the clinicians. Hence, the reforms were to go further and did so through two of the most seismic items of the new agenda: managerialism and the internal market.

Managerialism

The government instigated an enquiry into NHS management by Sir Roy Griffiths, managing director of the supermarket grocery leviathan Sainsbury's. The Griffiths Report (1983) advocated replacing consensus management with general management in which one single figure gave the orders. It was stressed that the new general managers, who would head each health authority and health care unit (hospital, clinic, etc.), should not necessarily come from within the NHS; private sector appointments were to be encouraged. The new positions would carry a deliberate insecurity with performance-related salaries, short-term contracts, performance review and a knowledge that those not up to muster would be liable to removal. The prime task was to control the spending propensities of the professional and seek value for money.

Under the banner of resource allocation there was even an attempt to enter the sacred temple of clinical judgement through the use of 'clinical audit' and 'clinical budgeting techniques'. The challenge was symbolised in new language; hospitals became 'management units', nursing officers became 'directors', and employees discovered themselves to be 'resource factors' (Cousins 1987: 168). In the great health supermarket, patients were to become customers and, in due course, a patient's charter emerged informing them of their rights.

The shake-up went to the top to break the stranglehold of the Whitehall mandarins, unversed in the cost-conscious methods of business. Alongside the existing departmental hierarchy a management board rather like a board of directors was established to operate under a Health Services Supervisory Board chaired by the Secretary of State. Griffiths argued that the head of the management board, a kind of super general manager, should come from outside the public sector. However, the first appointment, Victor Paige, proved unable to function within the political environment and resigned in 1986. In 1988 a new NHS Management Executive (NHSME) (later renamed the NHS Executive) replaced the Management Board. This comprised senior managers and was chaired by an NHS chief executive. It was to be responsible for day-to-day management, working under the strategic direction of a policy board chaired by the Secretary of State and containing ministers, civil servants and a variety of prominent industrialists working on a part-time basis. The intention to make a separation between policy-making and management was symbolised by the relocation of the NHSME from London to the northern city of Leeds.

The reforms did not stop with general management. In 1983 a Whitehall circular on competitive tendering obliged health authorities to look to the private sector for certain support services such as laundry and catering. In the same year, and again in 1985, packages of performance indicators were introduced to measure efficiency. However, these generally focused on finance rather than health outcomes or patient satisfaction. New staffing targets were also set. In 1987 resource management pilot schemes, designed to make clinicians more cost conscious, were launched in six hospitals and six community health units.

Yet, within the health care arena and in society at large, the talk was of the NHS being in a state of crisis and in January 1988 the Prime Minister announced the establishment of a major review. The result was a much publicised White Paper, *Working for Patients* (DoH et al. 1989b), which sought to introduce market disciplines into the NHS by breaking the line management relationship between the NHS tiers and units. Less radical than some of the schemes promoted (Small 1989: 172), the essential thrust was towards the idea of an 'internal market' developed by US economist, Alain Enthoven (1988). However, its implications were far-reaching and radically changed the organisation which had been created in 1948.

The internal market

The internal market meant that, instead of central direction and formal planning (rational or otherwise), resource allocation outcomes within the NHS were to be the result of competition between a myriad of self-interested actors. If a market is to work then there must be buyers and sellers, a very simple distinction in the world of the retail trade. However, in the traditional structure of the NHS such a distinction had been deliberately obliterated; service was rendered on the basis of need, not purchasing power. Moreover, in a world of highly specialised knowledge, high-tech apparatus and obfuscating jargon, the ordinary people who were to be seen as the NHS customers could not be expected to exercise informed choice.

Hence, in the health care market, the sellers and buyers were to come from within the service itself: the health authorities, hospitals, GPs and other health care units would barter with each other for services on behalf of the patients. Sometimes they would be cast as *providers* and sometimes *purchasers*. Indeed, the internal market could also become an external one; purchasers could also turn to the private sector. The roles of health authorities and care units was to change dramatically.

Health authorities

Although the RHAs remained in being, their role as providers of common services to DHAs diminished. They did, however, acquire some responsibility for the GP services. DHAs became *purchasers*, assessing local needs and receiving budgets calculated on a weighted capitation basis; but their ability to control the provider units was restricted to the strategic use of the commercial carrot. Their main function was procuring health care for those within their districts from a range of providers (hospital and community care units) competing with each other for either block, cost and volume, or cost-per-case contracts (excepting teaching, which is funded separately). Not necessarily confined to the services within their own district, they can examine those available across the boundaries.

To make them more willing, or able, to operate in the new environment, the composition of the health authorities was changed by removing the principle of reserved places for the health service professions, local government nominees or trade union representatives. The tendency was for them to be replaced with local businesspeople. In addition, the role of the ordinary member was diminished as the division between members and officials was blurred by allowing chief officers to become executive members, sitting alongside an equal number of non-executive part-time members. Moreover, the paid chairpersons assumed an increasingly dominant position, making decisions on sensitive issues like merit bonuses (Small 1989: 69).

Hospitals and community units

These were to move from their line management relationship with the health authority to one of contract. Instead of being integrated parts of a local system they would be in competition with each other and of course with those in other districts and in the private sector. However, in perhaps the most controversial of the proposals in *Working for Patients*, the government was further to challenge the principle of strategic control by allowing hospitals and community units (and other units such as ambulance services) to opt out of health authority jurisdiction altogether to become self-governing NHS trusts, shaping their internal policy entirely on the basis of commercial self-interest.

The new trusts would have boards of directors rather like those of private companies with a composition similar to the new-style DHAs. Established in law as bodies corporate, with a separate legal existence from the health authority, they would have managerial powers not available to those remaining as directly managed units, including freedom from nationally determined terms and conditions of service for employees. They would derive their funds by selling services to health authorities, GPs and private patients, and could advertise. They could also acquire and dispose of assets and were permitted to accumulate financial surpluses for re-investment. They were to be free to determine their own management patterns and pay structures.

Amidst considerable political controversy a first fleet of fifty-seven self-governing trusts cast adrift from their health authority moorings on 1

April 1991. By 1994 some 96 per cent of hospitals and community units had trust status, with turnovers ranging from £15 million to £230 million per annum.

GP services

The 1989 White Paper sought tighter controls over GPs, making them more accountable to the FPCs (renamed Family Health Service Author-ities – FHSAs), which in turn became, for the first time, accountable to the RHAs. The role of the FHSAs was made more managerial and their composition changed to reduce the representation of the GPs themselves. Expenditure by GPs was to be controlled and any excess would require justification to the FHSAs, which could impose financial penalties upon malefactors. Other changes aimed to create competition for patients, who would be given easier means to change their GPs. The payment system was modified so that 60 rather than 46 per cent would be capitation based.

There was also a version of opting out; large practices were given the right to become fundholders. They would receive a budget from the RHA, calculated on the characteristics of their patient populations, and could shop around for the best deal for a range of services including diagnostic tests, out-patient treatment but excluding chronic or life-threatening acute care. Unspent funds could be retained for largely discre-tional professional use.

Community health care

Although the post-war story was one of decline for elected local govern-ment in health matters, the marketising policy envisaged their greater in-volvement in community health care. Again it was Roy Griffiths (1988) who provided the master plan in a report entitled *Care in the Community*. Government policy was announced in the White Paper, *Caring for People* (DoH et al. 1989a), to be followed by legislation in 1990 which applied throughout the UK. Local authorities were to take over from the hospitals much responsibility for a range of patient categories including the chron-ically sick, the aged and infirm, and the physically and mentally handicapped.

However, the essential role was not providing but enabling. Like health authorities they were to become purchasers of care packages from various sources including the NHS, the voluntary sector and the private sector (which could include the encouragement of home-based family support).

The informal and voluntary sectors

The 'Care in the Community' policy gave an enhanced role to informal and voluntary carers. In 1980 Health Minister Patrick Jenkin asserted:

> We cannot operate as if the statutory services are central providers with a few volunteers here and there to back them up . . . we should recognise that the informal sector lies at the centre with statutory services and the voluntary sector providing expertise and support.
>
> (quoted in Allsop 1984: 118)

Yet, while generally praising its efforts, the government was placing a greater burden on the voluntary sector. The care in the community initiative was the most obvious example of this. The concepts of partnership between the public and voluntary sectors gave way to contractual relationships. This also meant that the voluntary societies were in competition with the private sector. The voluntary societies complained loudly that they could not meet the extra demand placed on their fund-raising ability.

The private sector

The Thatcher government sought to stimulate the private sector in several ways. A modified contract, permitting consultants to earn up to 10 per cent of their NHS income privately, enabled many to take on such work for the first time. Simultaneously BUPA, the market leader in private health insurance, introduced generous fee increases. US medical insurance companies also enlarged their UK operations. Other measures included tax concessions for certain categories of medical insurance, charges for sight and hearing tests and contracting out of various services. Although there was no waiting list in her area, Margaret Thatcher ostentatiously chose to have an eye operation privately (*Guardian*, 27 February 1984); not a vote of confidence in the service of which she was the ultimate head.

The internal market and care in the community reforms offered further scope for the private sector, and there was sometimes official encouragement to state institutions to purchase private sector services.

The private hospital movement was stimulated. In 1976 they had provided 3,500 beds; ten years later the figure had reached 10,000 (Small 1989: 109). Research by the Office of Health Economics published in August 1992 revealed spending on private health care to be rising at three times the rate in the NHS (*Guardian*, 25 August 1992). However, the rise was generally in 'cold' surgery where costs were relatively low and profits high.

Back to the patchwork quilt?

The post-1979 NHS changes have placed emphasis on variety of forms of provision. While maintaining some recognisable features, the system established in 1948 has been subject to a relentless process of small changes which together add up to a considerable redrawing. It has been described as 'radicalism by stealth'.

Despite the centrally prescribed framework, there have been various innovations under local initiative adding to the diversity. Sometimes FHSAs have combined with community units, in other cases a split has been made between acute, family and community services which may even cover different geographical areas. In some districts the health care agencies are working closely with local authority social services departments in the areas of primary and community care. Again commissioning agencies may cover single districts or, an increasing tendency, combinations of districts. In some cases fundholding practices have been able to influence the pattern of acute care, some offering services only previously available in hospitals. Others have even made themselves into limited companies and employed the services of consultants.

The result of the reforms has been to create a patchwork quilt of agencies, many with more specific and narrow functions. Yet, ironically the idea of a 'patchwork quilt' was what the NHS was originally designed to erase through the contrary idea of a uniform 'seamless web'. To critics, variety and choice can mean inequality and even a two-tier system of health care.

FINANCING ARRANGEMENTS

The British NHS receives the lion's share of its funding from general taxation (around 80 per cent). The rest comes from national insurance contributions (around 16 per cent) and other fees and charges to patients (prescriptions, sight and hearing tests). In addition, further health expenditure (equal to around 12 per cent) comes from the purchase of over-the-counter medicines and private health insurance. Today total NHS spending is around £35 billion per annum. As Table 6.5 shows, the trend has been one of increase, both in absolute terms and as a proportion of total government expenditure.

The size of the global amount devoted to the NHS is the outcome of an annual public expenditure survey which has existed in various forms since the early 1960s. The process is overseen by a Public Expenditure Survey Committee (PESC) composed of Treasury officials and representatives from the various government departments including of course the

Table 6.5 NHS spending, 1981–92

Year	%	Total government expenditure (£billion)
1981	11.4	117.1
1986	11.8	162.3
1991	13.7	228.3
1992	13.8	254.1

Source: Social Trends 24, London, HMSO, 1994, p. 91, Table 6.21

Department of Health. The process is highly political with much inter-departmental competition and energetic lobbying from pressure groups including voluntary societies, professional associations, health authorities, health care units and business interests. In autumn 1993 the outcome of the PESC process and the consideration of tax proposals were combined in the UK parliament's first unified budget, making it possible (in theory) to consider expenditure plans in the light of overall fiscal and economic policy.

From 1974, following the international economic crises, a system of cash limits (on both revenue and capital expenditure), whereby planned funding levels would be held constant in cash terms regardless of inflation, was imposed throughout the public sector. This has applied to hospital and community health services but has left family practitioner services exempt, so that they are eligible for supplementary allowances during the year according to demand. In addition there may be earmarked grants for specific purposes such as reduction of waiting lists, treatment of AIDS or community care. The global sum is apportioned between the four countries of the UK: England, Wales, Scotland and Northern Ireland.

In England allocations were made to the regional health authorities through a formula devised by a Resources Allocation Working Party (RAWP) in 1976. This followed a weighted capitation principle, based upon population size, age and sex structure of a region, weighted to reflect regional differences according to two criteria:

1 perceived need for health care, using the standard mortality ratios (SMRs, number of observed deaths as a percentage of the expected deaths in an area) as a proxy, and
2 geographical factors such as costs of provision, cross-boundary patient flows, medical and dental education costs and the pattern of buildings and equipment.

The regions would then distribute funds to districts, having regard to the pattern of local need and costs. The application of the formula promoted a substantial transfer of resources from rich to poor areas. The essence of the system was rational planning under a central authority. However, the Thatcher reforms were to make important modifications to this principle. RAWP was phased out and replaced by a revised weighted capitation system (son of RAWP). The weighting given to SMRs was reduced from 1 to 0.5, with the effect of shifting resources away from areas of higher health care need (as measured by premature mortality) which were predominantly in the north, to those with lower need, which were mainly in the south where the Conservative Party enjoyed its greatest support (Sheldon et al. 1993: 835).

DHAs were to receive funds for their resident populations, paying each other directly for cross-boundary patient flows. Hospitals and community care units opting for self-governing trust status ceased to be directly financed and managed by the health authorities; their income came from contracts with health authorities and fundholding GPs, and by sales to the private sector.

Doctors in hospitals and community care units are salaried state employees. Their remuneration level is subject to review by an independent body, though the government is not bound to accept its recommendations.

General practitioners, as independent contractors, are paid an income plus practice expenses. They receive capitation payments, reflecting the number (and ages) of patients for which they are contracted, and fees for services such as night visiting and immunisation. Remuneration level is recommended by an independent doctors' and dentists' review body though, again, government is free to diverge from this. Following the *Working for Patients* White Paper, fundholding practices receive a practice budget with which to purchase certain hospital services. Non-fundholders are constrained within 'indicative prescribing budgets'.

Pharmacists are paid a dispensing fee for prescriptions and each year a representative body negotiates the size of the global sum for this with the Department of Health. The Department also aims to control the prices charged to the NHS by drug companies through a pharmaceutical price regulation scheme.

The 1988 review which led to *Working for Patients* was originally intended to focus on finance. However, a report from the Central Policy Review Staff (the government's think tank) on an insurance-financed health service scenario, leaked rather than published, so alarmed public opinion that Margaret Thatcher was forced into a famous declaration at her party's 1982 conference that the NHS is 'safe in our hands'. Fundamental changes were ruled out and reform largely confined to the way funds were allocated within the NHS, producing structural rather than financial reform (Klein 1989: 238). Hence, tax-funding, with services free at the point of delivery, remains the basis of NHS financing.

CONTEMPORARY ISSUES IN HEALTH POLICY

It is clear from the above that UK health care is fraught with political controversy. Much of this ostensibly concerns structure and finance, though behind these considerations lie deeper issues of accountability, ethics and even the pattern of power within society. Some tensions arise from the reforming moves of the New Right government but others have been present since the inception of the NHS. Several issues belong in both categories; an existing sore is aggravated by the new agenda. Space constraints prevent a full catalogue or analysis of these issues; this section offers only a brief identification of some which are seen as central.

Democracy and accountability

This is a prime example of the perennial issues. It has been held from the outset that a service so fundamental to the quality of life of all should be under democratic control, yet this has posed considerable problems. We have noted how medical opposition prevented local government gaining responsibility for the NHS. It was argued by Aneurin Bevan that elected authorities were unnecessary because democracy would be secured via Westminster; the Minister of Health would be the 'whipping boy' of the health service in parliament. Yet this was not to prove so. In spite of some attention by select committees, parliament has had very little impact on health matters (Ingle and Tether 1981: 148). When questioned in the Commons, ministers have regularly disclaimed responsibility, urging MPs to pursue matters with the relevant health authority.

The post-1979 reforms have added to the problem. The removal of the automatic right of representation of local councils on health authorities made the latter even less democratic than before. Allowing chief officers to become executive members diminished the role of the ordinary member.

The opting-out process itself was by no means democratic, the decision to seek trust status being made within the health care unit, leaving the local community and the health authority with no say in the matter.

In the community care reforms, the greater involvement of elected authorities could not necessarily be seen as increased democratisation of the services since the awarding of contracts on the basis of tenders is something which has traditionally lain with the local authority accountants and lawyers rather than with councillors.

In the absence of democratic avenues of complaint or redress there was nowhere to turn save to an arcane grievance procedure weighted in favour of the doctors and rusty with disuse. The creation in 1973 of an NHS ombudsman system did little to remedy the position. There have been some attempts in the 1990s to combat the democratic deficit by the production of various versions of a patient's charter. However, in the eyes of critics, these attempt to replace the essentially collective rights of citizenship with the individual rights of customers and can only be cosmetic.

Patronage

The nature of the health authorities meant that they were always open to the exercise of political patronage. The changes in composition following *Working for Patients* made them even more amenable to this. Indeed, in March 1986 Conservative Central Office (the headquarters of the Conservative Party) carried out a vetting process designed to root out chairpersons who had fought funding cuts, and sixty-two of them were effectively removed (by non-reappointment) (*Guardian*, 19 March 1986). By the end of the 1980s virtually all health authorities were chaired by those sympathetic to New Right ideology.

Management

The early managerial weakness of the NHS was a manifestation of the considerable political power of the medical profession which effectively demanded the right to professional self-government. For the New Right, managerialism was the solution. The use of general management to control professionals can always be expected to arouse controversy and this case proved no exception. For some it was nothing less than the most profound disruption to the NHS since its inception, going to the heart of the power structure. Not only did it challenge the traditional autonomy of doctors, it necessarily diminished the role of the health authority members.

The reforms fired intense political opposition, not only from the left but from the BMA, the august Royal Colleges (surgeons, physicians, nurses), and the Association of Nurse Administrators. They argued on the grounds that the NHS, which depended upon caring professions working together, could not benefit from the application of techniques from the hard world of competition and profit maximisation. However, they were also defending their own self-interest.

Criticism has continued to rage. The salaries the new managers have given themselves have been seen as excessive. There have even been exposures of serious corruption in areas such as contracting-out. In addition, the large increase in the number of managers has appeared to contradict government efficiency claims. Significantly, one of the most severe critics of developments has been Roy Griffiths himself who, in the third Audit Commission lecture in 1991, lamented the creation of 'yet another profession' in the NHS (Griffiths 1992).

The internal market

This far-reaching reform has aroused fierce criticism on many aspects from many sources. The Association of Community Health Councils articulated the view of many that the allocation of resources by market forces destroyed any idea of rational planning (ACHC 1988). As in all forms of competition there were losers as well as winners and there have been controversial closures of accident and emergency units, wards and even hospitals. In the case of GP services, controversy arises when the egalitarian principles of the NHS are undermined as fundholding GPs secure more speedy services for their patients than non-fundholders.

Financial problems also remain; research commissioned by the National Association of Health Authorities and Trusts revealed one in ten to be in financial crisis and facing the prospect of merger in order to avoid going to the wall (NAHA&T 1994).

Centralisation

Although the market rhetoric spoke of freedom from central control, in reality the trusts were being asked to turn away from a devil they knew (the health authority) towards the unknown one at the centre (the Department of Health). The managerialism also exerted a centralising force through the system of performance appraisal by the tier above, right up to the NHSME (Harrison 1988: 118–19).

How much to spend?

For the political right, the NHS is a drain on the economy; for the left, too little is spent. The objective fact is that the UK generally spends a lower proportion of national income on health care than other developed countries. The official historian of the NHS argued that, from the first, the problem has been 'not profligacy but resource starvation' (Webster 1988). As explained in Chapter 1, health service funding is about political values and choices rather than the technicalities of accounting. Nowhere can this be more true than in the UK, where NHS funding has sought to enshrine a commitment to equal access to health care for all based on need rather than ability to pay.

The original vision of the NHS had suggested a nation becoming healthier so that, over time, costs would actually fall. However, the opposite was to prove the case; as medical puzzles yielded their secrets before the onward march of the researchers ever more conditions became treatable, more and more expensive technology was developed and people lived longer, to present further medical conditions. Moreover, the nation became more health conscious and had higher expectations. Further spending pressure comes from the giant corporations, growing fat on NHS contracts by making equipment, building hospitals and feeding an insatiable appetite for drugs (the NHS spent £3.138 billion on medicines in 1991, *Guardian*, 25 August 1992).

In the New Right era this issue sharpened. Although the mission was to reduce state expenditure, and although the government's opponents (parties, groups and the health care professions) constantly lamented a lack of resources, health spending continued to rise throughout the decade and the basic principle of tax funding remained intact.

Even so, the gravamen of the opponents' case was that this remained insufficient in the light of rising demand. Parliament's Social Services Committee argued in 1988 that, merely to keep up with demographic and technological trends, NHS spending should increase in real terms by at least 2 per cent *per annum*. The figure was rejected by the government, which argued that greater efficiency could produce the required increases. However the committee argued that, even after allowing for efficiency gains, hospital and community health services remained underfunded by some £1.5 billion between 1980/81 and 1987/8. In contrast the demand-driven (non-cash-limited) family practitioner services experienced growth of almost 3 per cent throughout the 1980s (Social Services Committee 1988: para.12, viii).

Critics feared a drift towards a two-tier system, with the state providing a second-rate service for an underclass. Indeed Britain would need to spend another £10 billion per annum to come into line with the rest of the developed world (*Guardian*, 25 August 1992).

Who pays?

Given the general disposition of the government since 1979, it is perhaps surprising that funding from general taxation has been retained. Indeed, in opposition the Thatcher-led Conservatives had talked the language of privatisation. However, once in power a major report from a Royal Commission, established by the previous Labour government, made this politically difficult. The Merrison Report (1979) strongly endorsed the funding system, which was held to give extremely good value for money. A private insurance system would cost more, not least because of the huge expense of administration as well as the profits expected by the companies.

But although the popularity of the NHS means that governments repeatedly declare their commitment, alternative forms of financing such as private insurance or a fully-blown system of national insurance can never be said to be entirely off the political agenda. The leaked think-tank proposals in 1982 had revealed a government not unprepared to contemplate the replacement of tax funding with some form of health insurance.

Privatisation

Not surprisingly, the existence of a private sector alongside the NHS (and sometimes making use of NHS facilities) has been and remains intensely controversial. The left has seen it as a distortion of the NHS, denying it resources and making good health a commodity to be enjoyed by the rich rather than a right of all. In 1976, Labour Minister Barbara Castle waged a bitter battle with the doctors over the issue. She created a Health Services Board to oversee the phasing out of 'pay beds' in NHS hospitals and to control the development of private hospitals. She also sought to change consultants' contracts to encourage a full-time NHS commitment.

For the right, the private sector is a necessary feature of a liberal society. One of the first moves of the Thatcher government was the reversal of Castle's anti-pay-bed policy. It has been shown above that the reforms of the 1980s did much to revive private medicine and raised the intensity of debate.

Priorities within the NHS

The tripartite nature of the NHS (in England and Wales) has led to internal rivalry and uneven development. Considerable growth in the high-spending acute care hospital services has been at the expense of the 'Cinderella' services such as primary health care, preventive measures and health education. This pattern has reflected the power within the medical profession of the hospital physicians and the dominance of the medical model of health.

Since the 1980s, when professional power was challenged, there have been moves to reverse this trend. In July 1992 a White Paper, *The Health of the Nation*, outlined a major health promotion initiative. Five key areas (chosen from a possible sixteen) were identified – heart disease, cancers, mental illness, sexual health and accidents – and specific targets were set for achievement in a certain time (for example a cut of 15 per cent in the suicide rate by the year 2000). Improvements were to be secured through more healthy surroundings and lifestyles with action taken in homes, schools, workplaces, cities and the general environment. However, the policy could be construed as a means of diverting responsibility from the NHS and blaming people for their own ill health. Significantly, the White Paper ignored the health effects of poverty, an area where government economic policies could be implicated.

Health education tends to live uneasily in Britain's capitalist economy. In 1986 the government dissolved the Health Education Council, a quango prone to incur the displeasure of various industrial interests, particularly those associated with dairy produce, tobacco and alcohol. It was replaced by a Health Education Authority which was placed more closely under Whitehall control. At the beginning of 1995, the Authority's budget was reduced from £36 million to £6 million.

Inequalities in health

Despite its egalitarian principles, the NHS has perpetuated a degree of social injustice. Research has revealed working-class people to suffer more illness than the middle class yet, in an 'inverse care law', to be less successful in making use of the service (see for example Gibson 1981: ch. 5). In 1980, a government report revealed the depth of this inequality (Black 1980) and subsequent follow-up research, commissioned by the Health Education Council, confirmed that the position had actually grown worse (Whitehead 1987).

Inequality, both in health status and in level of provision, also relates to gender and race, with women and black people disadvantaged. The Conservative government emphasis on the informal sector and care in the community, often expressed in the rhetoric of family values, has been seen to contain strong sexist implications. 'Family' could be seen as a code word for women, particularly working-class women without access to private sector assistance in caring for their sick, aged and handicapped members (Phillips 1992: 71).

In addition, there have been significant geographical inequalities, with the broadly better-off regions of the south enjoying the more generous allocations. The RAWP formula was introduced to address this, though the revised system made this problem more acute and the debate does not go away.

Health, power and society

The question of political power underlies most UK health policy issues. The polity has often been portrayed as a pluralist democracy, though the dominance of the medical profession in the early post-war decades led some political scientists to speak in terms of welfare corporatism, with certain groups more favoured than others (Klein 1989). However, the medical dominance could also be interpreted in neo-elitist terms as a demonstration of professional power in modern society (Illich 1975: 165).

The New Right era was to see the power of the medical profession considerably reduced in an attempt to cut public spending. These developments accord more with the neo-Marxist analysis of James O'Connor (1973) who anticipated a 'fiscal crisis of the state' arising from an inherent contradiction between the modern capitalist economy and a welfare state. In this analysis the earlier high point of medical power can be seen as a feature of a limited period when the interests of doctors coincided with those of private capital (Navarro 1976). In the 1980s these separated as the welfare state became seen as a drain on profitability. Other health policies, such as a refusal to ban cigarette advertising, the restriction of democracy within the NHS and the persistence of private medicine, add further weight to the idea that capitalist interests lie at the real heart of power.

The placing of health care so clearly within the remit of the state thrusts it to a central place in the political life of a nation. While it is clear that the period of New Right government broke with the post-war social democratic consensus and raised debate to white heat level, the key issues are not essentially new. So long as the NHS retains its basic form, debate over fundamental questions of accountability and finance can be expected to continue. When such questions cease to be regarded as political issues the NHS will in all probability be no more.

REFERENCES AND FURTHER READING

ACHC (1988) *Financing the NHS: The Consumer View*, London: Association of Community Health Councils.

Allsop, J. (1984) *Health Policy and the NHS,* London: Longman.

Black, D. (1980) *Report on the Working Party on Inequalities in Health*, London: DHSS.

Cawson, A. (1982) *Corporatism and Welfare: Social Policy and State Intervention in Britain*, London: Heinemann.

Cousins, C. (1987) *Controlling Social Welfare*, Brighton, Sussex: Wheatsheaf.

Crosland, A. (1956) *The Future of Socialism*, London: Jonathan Cape.

Department of Health (1992) *The Health of the Nation* (Cm 1986), London: HMSO.

Department of Health and Social Security (1983) *Health Care and its Costs: the Development of the NHS in England*, London: HMSO.

Department of Health, Department of Social Security, Welsh Office and Scottish Office (1989a) *Caring for People* (Cm 849), London: HMSO.

Department of Health, Department of Social Security, Welsh Office and Scottish Office (1989b) *Working for Patients* (Cm 555), London: HMSO.

Eckstein, H. (1960) *Pressure Group Politics: the Case of the British Medical Association*, London: Allen and Unwin.

Enthoven, A. C. (1988) *Reflections on the Management of the NHS*, London: Nuffield Provincial Hospitals Trust.

Gibson, I. (1981) *Class Health and Profit*, Norwich: University of East Anglia Press.

Griffiths, R. (1983) *NHS Management Inquiry*, London: HMSO.

Griffiths, R. (1988) *Care in the Community: Agenda for Action*, London: HMSO.

Griffiths, R. (1992) 'Seven years of progress – general management in the NHS', *Health Economics*, 1 (1): 61–70.

Harrison, S. (1988) *Managing the NHS: Shifting the Frontier*, London: Chapman and Hall.

Harrison, S., Hunter, D. J. and Pollitt, C. J. (1990) *The Dynamics of British Health Policy*, London: Unwin Hyman.

Illich, I. (1975) *Medical Nemesis*, London: Calder and Boyars.

Ingle, S. and Tether, P. (1981) *Parliament and Health Policy: the Role of MPs, 1970–5*, Aldershot: Gower.

Klein, R. (1989) *The Politics of the NHS*, 2nd edn, London: Longman.

Merrison, Sir A. (1979) *Royal Commission on the NHS* (Cmnd 7615), London: HMSO.

Middlemass, K. (1979) *Politics in Industrial Society*, London: André Deutsch.

Morris, L. (1994) *Dangerous Classes*, London: Routledge.

NAHA&T (1994) *The Fourth Newchurch Guide to NHS Trusts*, Birmingham: National Association of Health Authorities and Trusts.

Navarro, V. (1976) *Medicine under Capitalism*, New York: Prodist.

O'Connor, J. (1973) *The Fiscal Crisis of the State*, New York: St Martin's Press.

Ottewill, R. and Wall, A. (1990) *The Growth and Development of the Community Health Services*, Sunderland: Business Education Publishers.

Phillips, A. (1992) 'Must feminists give up on liberal democracy?' *Political Studies*, 40 (special edn): 66–80.

Sheldon T. A., Davey Smith, G. and Bevan, G. (1993) 'Weighting in the dark: resource allocation in the new NHS', *British Medical Journal* 306 (27): 835–9.

Small, N. (1989) *Politics and Planning in the National Health Service*, Milton Keynes: Open University Press.

Social Services Committee (1988) *Sixth Report, Session 1987–8: Public Expenditure on the Social Services*, London: HMSO.

Strong, P. and Robinson, J. (1990) *The NHS under New Management*, Milton Keynes: Open University Press.

Webb, A. and Wistow, G. (1982) 'The personal social services: incrementalism, expediency or systematic social planning', in A. Walker (ed.) *Public Expenditure and Social Policy*, London: Heinemann.

Webster, C. (1988) 'Confronting historical myth', *The Health Service Journal*, 19 May.

Whitehead, M. (1987) *The Health Divide*, London: Health Education Council.

Wilding, P. (1982) *Professional Power and Social Welfare*, London: Routledge and Kegan Paul.

Chapter 7

The United States of America

Jim Chandler

The United States appears to have less government regulation of health care than almost any other developed state and many of its citizens have been horrified at the thought of what they see in Europe as 'socialised medicine'. However, the nation spends a higher percentage of its GDP on health care than any other liberal democracy even though many of its poorest inhabitants below the age of 60 years have virtually no capacity to buy health care and can expect to receive little or nothing through the public sector. The public health schemes that have been established are in serious financial difficulty. President Clinton thus embarked upon a major health reform in the United States with the intention of bringing the health care system of the country into a form that, to some degree, would resemble the previously reviled systems of the socialised medicine of Western Europe.

THE CONTEXT OF AMERICAN HEALTH CARE

The demographic structure

The United States is one of the largest nations, with a population of 258 million inhabitants in 1993. Europeans may often receive the impression that this population is predominantly centred in the large cities but despite the pre-eminence of centres such as New York, Chicago and Los Angeles, the country is as much a land of small towns.

A more accurate image is that of America as the 'melting pot of the world'. The indigenous Indian population was quickly outstripped by immigration from Europe and, in the nineteenth century, the population of the United States increased at a huge rate due especially to the arrival of Irish, Italian and East European people facing economic privation in their own countries.

In addition to the dominant European populations there also existed further groups, predominant among which were the Africans who had been brought over to the southern plantations as slaves. In the twentieth century immigration, often through illegal means, of Mexicans and South Americans has created a large but underprivileged Spanish-speaking sub-culture within the nation.

Epidemiological trends

United States citizens enjoy a higher life expectancy than most of the world's population, as can be expected from a highly developed industrial country. Life expectancy at birth in 1990 was estimated to be almost exactly the average for developed OECD states, at 72 years for males and 79.5 years for females. The infant mortality rate is, however, slightly higher than the European average (OECD 1987).

The principal causes of death in the United States are not dissimilar from European patterns. The most important causes of death are, in descending order of importance, heart disease, cancers, cardiovascular problems and chronic obstructive pulmonary diseases. The fifth most frequent cause of fatalities is accidents and violence. For individuals from birth to the age of 35 years, this latter is the most common cause of death (United States Bureau of the Census 1994).

Life chances in the United States are not, however, very evenly distributed. Although among white races, females have a life expectancy of 79 years and white males of 73 years, black males can expect on average to live only until the age of 65 years which is not that far from the world average life expectancy of 61 years, whilst black females have a life expectancy of 74 years. Such discrepancies in life expectancy between favoured and unfavoured social groups are replicated in other nations but are, nevertheless, a stark reminder of the effect of more advantageous lifestyles for favoured groups within the United States (United States Bureau of the Census 1994; OECD 1987).

The life expectancy of all groups in the population has been increasing slowly since the 1950s but prior to that date there had been a dramatic increase. In 1920 the average for the United States was 54 years but by 1950 this has grown to 68 years (United States Bureau of the Census 1986). It is argued by McKinlay et al. (1983) that much of this increase was due, not to the development of the medical system, but to public health measures and, in particular, improvement in the nation's diet as a consequence of greater prosperity. They point out that, whilst improvement in the nation's health seems to have slowed since 1950, during this period the cost of health care has increased dramatically.

Cultural traditions

Just as the structure of the population reflects the pattern of immigration, so too do the cultural traditions of the United States. Most groups, among the first waves of immigrants who arrived in the seventeenth and eighteenth centuries, were refugees from religious or economic oppression by aristocratic governments of Western Europe. Their values and the conditions they encountered in a largely undeveloped nation inclined them towards philosophies of individualist liberalism and egalitarianism. It was this culture which, in time, displaced and dispossessed that of the Indian inhabitants.

Successive waves of immigrants encountered a country in which the social and political values of individualism and dispersed government were well established and had, in general, to be accepted or modified to accommodate the interests of their own communities.

Not surprisingly, the United States was sympathetic to the ideals of the French revolution and gave sanctuary to the English radical, Tom Paine. All men — equality was yet to extend to women — were born with equal rights and were expected to make their way, for good or ill, in the world through their own individual exertions.

In practice, however, these values served to justify and underpin not socialism but a free enterprise capitalist culture of which the United States has long been considered the epitome. In fact, the United States is not as *laissez-faire* as this image might suggest, but there is an engrained enthusiasm for capitalism and aversion to socialist values.

Social factors

America is one of the most wealthy nations with a GDP per capita of $24,681. Wealth is not, however, evenly spread throughout the country. The poorest 20 per cent of the population command but 3.8 per cent of the aggregate income received within the nation, whilst the richest 20 per cent obtain 46.8 per cent of aggregate income (United States Bureau of the Census 1994). There are, therefore, sectors of American society which enjoy a standard of living better than any person has probably experienced since human life began. Many in the country, however, face a standard of living which, if never at the level of absolute desperation faced by all too many families of the third world, is a state of considerable poverty and deprivation.

This contrast between rich and poor is paralleled by differing standards and systems of health care. On the one hand it is possible, at a cost, to participate in a system of high-tech health provision backed up by comfortable customer orientated in-patient and after-care facilities. At the poorest end of American society provision is often sparsely distributed and, due to lack of funding, of a low quality in terms of technical aids or the environment for patient care.

Predictably, particularly vulnerable to deprivation and poor standards of health and health care are:

- the indigenous Indian population;
- the descendants of the slaves who, even after the civil war, were free only to accept the most menial tasks and employment; and
- Mexican and South American immigrants.

The differing rates of assimilation of such groups into the dominant white European culture have, to a large extent, determined the affluence of these groups and this in turn largely determines their access to both the prerequisites for health and to technologically advanced and effective health care. In general, therefore, indigenous Indians and black and Latin American immigrants have a lower standard of health and far worse health service than the affluent white middle class.

The governmental and political setting

The United States government system takes its shape from the principles of liberalism that encapsulate values of rights, self-help, and fear of arbitrary government. The nation is, consequently, one of the few regimes in the world that has always been a democracy and it can also validly claim that it is the mother of democracies in modern nation states.

The individualist radicalism of many of the early settlers generated the political theory, most popularly codified by the American federalists and Thomas Jefferson, that there should be as little government as possible. The state should not interfere with the religious or economic activities of an individual provided that person did not harm others. It was, however, accepted that some common rules and services were a necessity but these should be applied wherever possible at a local rather than national level. The concept of subsidiarity, that power should be passed down to the lowest group capable of efficiently supplying a service, now in current use by the European Union, was prefigured in the United States in the early nineteenth century by writers such as De Tocqueville who believed that community governments should supply most common services and that the federal government should have as small a role as possible.

In order to secure the freedom of the individual the governments that were established should, argued Madison and Jefferson, be based on democratic arrangements. In the small towns this may be a direct democracy but for the states and federal government this was impractical. Freedom of the individual from arbitrary decisions by these governments was best secured by democratic election of their legislators and chief executive and also a separation of powers between the executive, judicial and legislative sectors of government so that no one group or individual could dominate. Power in the United States was to be dispersed among many groups rather than concentrated in the hands of powerful co-ordinating units.

Pluralism was in part facilitated by the establishment of a federal system through the coming together of the original thirteen states under the Constitution of 1776. The number of states has now increased through the gradual expansion of the Union to fifty. The Constitution outlines the structure and powers of the federal government. Its powers are relatively few and concern the raising of an army and navy, control over foreign policy, the establishment of a common currency and regulation of interstate trade. Functions that are not reserved to the federal government by the Constitution are available to the state governments provided these do not offend the basic rights of citizens enshrined in the amendments to the Constitution popularly known as the Bill of Rights. The American states can, therefore, develop their own codes of criminal law, have different structures of local government and judicial systems and determine as they feel fit the provision of health care, among many other services.

The extent to which federal government can intrude into the activities of the states is always subject to regulation by the Supreme Court which rules on the correct interpretation of the Constitution. The nine Supreme Court judges are appointed by the President but cannot be dismissed except on grounds of improper or illegal behaviour. More radical presidents have been prevented from increasing federal control over the states by a conservative Supreme Court staffed by judges appointed by more cautious former presidents.

The federal government is divided into three sectors that comprise the legislature known as Congress, the executive dominated by the President and the Supreme Court. Each element balances the other. Congress, which passes legislation and acts as a check on the executive, is itself divided into the House of Representatives, elected every two years from approximately equal-sized constituencies, and the Senate comprising two members from each state who are elected for six-year terms of office. Any bill must pass through both houses and then requires the approval of the

President to become law, although the President's veto of a bill can be overridden by Congress if it reaffirms legislation by a two-thirds majority of both Houses.

The President is now perceived as the dominant politician within the United States and is elected every four years through a national ballot. The President is head of the government and also the commander-in-chief of the armed forces. As head of government the President selects, in theory, the entire federal bureaucracy, although in practice he selects the heads of the major departments of state who form the cabinet and these senior politicians along with the President will appoint and dismiss some 5,000 senior bureaucrats. The President receives much of his advice from personal advisers in the White House as well as from his secretaries of state in charge of the formal government departments.

In order to ensure that proposed legislation, such as a reform of the health service, becomes law, the President requires the support of a majority in Congress and can only be successful if he can persuade or induce sufficient members of Congress to accept his ideas. In many European countries such as Britain and Germany the head of the executive can usually be sure that their policies are accepted by the legislature since they are the effective leaders of the majority party in the legislature and can expect rank and file party members to accept their views. The United States President will be a member of either the dominant Republican or Democrat parties but will not be able to rely on the support of all his fellow party members in Congress, who owe their allegiance not to a national party organisation but to the organisation of their party at state level. Thus, in order to ensure that controversial legislation, such as a reform of the health service, is passed by Congress the President may often have to promise executive support to individual Congressmen/women to secure their help. This support may be in the form of help to expedite the passage of legislation being favoured by the Congressman/woman or the provision of federally sponsored investment or tax breaks to the Congressman/woman's state or constituency that will facilitate his or her re-election. The most effective presidents, in terms of domestic legislation, are not necessarily charismatic figures such as President Kennedy but skilled politicians such as Lyndon Johnson who know their Congressmen/women and the deals that they will accept.

Until the 1930s, the influence of the federal government was not particularly extensive in the lives of most United States citizens except in times of war. The depression of the 1930s, however, brought about a major change in the role of federal government which began to exercise its ability to raise vast resources through its powers of taxation to establish

Table 7.1 Percentage of GDP devoted to health care, 1960–91

Year	% of GDP devoted to health care
1960	5.3
1970	7.4
1986	11.0
1991	13.2

Source: United States Bureau of the Census 1994

schemes for alleviating poverty and stimulating industry by offering money to the states to allow them to implement government-sponsored economic and welfare programmes. This 'New Deal' strategy, established by President Franklin D. Roosevelt, formed the basis of a growing authority of federal government in the structuring of economic and social life within the states. It is now widely accepted that the federal government should play a leading role in encouraging the means to secure adequate health provision for the nation.

Economic performance

One of the most serious issues on the American economic agenda is the amount of public money devoted to health care. In 1991, expenditure on health was $752 billion, which represents $2,914 per year for each individual. Moreover, these costs have been steadily increasing. In 1986 expenditure on health had been $458 billion, or $1,837 a year for each American. Despite many schemes to prevent these rising costs nothing has so far succeeded in turning back the tide of an ever increasing proportion of the wealth of the United States being devoted to health care. Table 7.1 illustrates the scale of the problem.

THE DEVELOPMENT OF STATE INVOLVEMENT

The United States, seen from a European perspective, is often regarded as a nation reluctant to accept public involvement in the medical system. Indeed, many voices are raised against the dangers of what American conservatives term 'socialised medicine', as demonstrated by President Clinton's apparently unsuccessful struggle to adopt a system of national health insurance for the country.

Nevertheless, it is wrong to perceive health care in the United States as a system run primarily along market principles to generate a profit for free-wheeling medical entrepreneurs. Despite the apparently privatised appearance of the service, governments in their various forms accounted for 42 per cent of expenditure on health care in 1991 and a considerable proportion of medical expenses are met by public funds rather than by the individual consumer through, for example, the Medicare and Medicaid programmes for the elderly and for poor families.

Public involvement began, as in Europe and Australia, in the sphere of public health and in response to the urgent problems generated by a newly urbanised, industrialised nation. The formation of basic clean water supply and sanitation was primarily facilitated by local governments and in some cases private companies. By the twentieth century these facilities were regulated through the state by city and county governments or by state-controlled agencies, especially where major projects were involved or city governments were small and fragmented.

With respect to personal health care, in the earliest years of the United States almost all of this was provided by the application of folk remedies by the women of the family or by those regarded as wise in the lore of healing within village communities. The emergence of a profession of health care based on scientific principles occurred, as in Western Europe, during the eighteenth century and by the mid-nineteenth century the medical profession and the occupation of doctor or physician was recognised and respected. The powerful American Medical Association (AMA), representing United States doctors, came into being in the 1850s. The growth of the medical profession led to the development of private medical practices, usually paid for by patients when they sought the doctor's advice.

Many of the hospitals established in the United States derive from public rather than private initiatives, and were often founded by the larger local governments (especially in the cities and urban counties) and the states. Most of these institutions catered for the general public but usually required payment of fees by all but the poorest in society.

A few hospitals were operated at the federal level for the military or merchant marine. With the growth of federal involvement in social provision and the medical problems that resulted from military needs, the federal government began setting up hospitals for military veterans. However, the federal government was a very minor player in the growth of the hospital service.

In addition to this public provision many early hospitals were formed by voluntary, charitable associations, and in particular the Protestant churches. They soon gained support from the public sector and tended to be generously endowed and, by the beginning of the twentieth century, often received considerable public funds, from both state and local governments, in addition to what they raised through fees and investments made by their founders. In the later nineteenth century, as progressive waves of immigrants established different religious groups and cultures, there was an increase in hospital provision catering for specific interests with a particular growth in hospitals founded by Roman Catholic interests.

The formation of hospital services based on a purely commercial profit motive was a relatively late introduction and began to emerge more in the less developed southern states to cater for the wealthy and the middle class. These hospitals tended to be small and more likely to go out of business than the generally larger public and older voluntary institutions. However, since the 1960s there has been a rapid growth in privately operated profit-making health care as demands for health services have been stimulated by Medicare and Medicaid and the growth of private insurance systems. There is also an increasing tendency for smaller private hospitals to be merged or bought by larger organisations. The largest current private medical organisation is the Hospital Corporation of America, which in the mid-1980s owned some 400 hospitals (Kovnar 1986: 190).

The growth of the hospital system after the second world war was facilitated partly by direct provision of Federal Veterans Hospitals and by government aid for hospital building through the 1945 Hill-Burton Act. Regulations were subsequently made in 1974 to restrain the consequent rapid growth in health facilities and to achieve more efficient planning through the National Health Planning and Resources Development Act. The Act created health systems agencies throughout the country to review medical needs for their areas and advise on the provision of federal aid to new health care facilities.

Mental health hospitals began to be established in the late eighteenth century predominantly as asylums that isolated from society those deemed to be insane. By the beginning of the twentieth century most such institutions sought cures for their patients, sometimes by surgical means. Later in the century the development of psychiatry and drugs capable of regulating behaviour further revolutionised the treatment of mentally ill patients.

Until the mid-1950s, the treatment of the mentally ill was predominantly within institutions which were established in most states by the county administrations and were funded extensively by the state governments. There were also a smaller number of private mental health hospitals catering largely for wealthy fee-paying patients. Conditions in the county institutions were generally regarded as inadequate and unsympathetic as depicted in for example, the filmed novel *One Flew Over the Cuckoo's Nest*.

THE PRINCIPAL FEATURES OF SERVICE DELIVERY AND ADMINISTRATION

Primary health care

Although many patients have their fees paid through private or public insurance schemes, the American doctor is still predominantly an entrepreneur selling his/her skills within a marketplace.

During the last fifty years, doctors in the United States have moved away from the general practice that is customary in the UK, for example, where a doctor will consider any medical problem brought by a patient and refer difficult or unusual cases to consultants. The majority of American doctors now establish themselves as specialists dealing with a particular set of ailments. These doctors will not only provide professional help to the patient in their own surgeries but also attend their patients in hospitals. Many United States doctors, therefore, divide their time between giving advice in their own surgeries and in neighbouring hospitals to which they may refer the patients. Since specialisation can lead to higher fees than general practice, there is a financial incentive to further entrench this structure, often to the disadvantage of the patient.

The growth of specialisation has created a problem for many citizens who must, in effect, become their own doctor for the purposes of initial diagnosis of a complaint in order to decide which type of specialist they should visit. The system also results in few individuals being able to refer to a doctor who holds a complete record and understanding of their overall health and has a commitment to direct them to all appropriate forms of preventive health care.

Secondary care

The hospital structure, as it has evolved, cannot be referred to as a system but, as Starr (1982) observes, it displays a clear pattern. Purely profit-making health care facilities exist but they are in the minority and are largely specialised institutions catering for the very rich. The largest and wealthiest hospitals tend to be the older endowed institutions which cater for both rich and poor patients and deal principally with acute medical cases. In most cities the municipally funded hospitals are much poorer institutions, often starved of funds in deference to local concern over property tax revenues. These institutions tend to deal with long term chronic illnesses and provide a service for the less respectable poor, ethnic minorities, slum dwellers and vagrants, whom the more prestigious endowed institutions refuse to take.

Although there is a wide range of systems for ownership and control, hospitals are subject to regulation under licensing systems established by state legislation which usually defers to the standards set by professional associations.

The multiplicity of types of hospital ownership promotes a range of systems of hospital government that vary from teams of directors to boards of governors appointed by a public body such as a city council. Within the voluntary sector many hospital boards are self-perpetuating organisations that co-opt local medical or business interests into their circle.

Below the governing body of hospitals there has been a recognised traditional pattern of hospital organisation referred to as the dual authority structure. In most institutions the doctors are predominantly self-employed and contracted by the hospital to provide relevant medical services. The doctors regulate their pay and working conditions through arrangements established between the various hospital governments and the professional bodies. The remaining staff of the hospital – nurses, pharmacists, administrators and other ancillary staff – are generally employees of the hospital and often ultimately responsible to a president or chief executive who manages the non-medical components of the institution. In effect, power within a hospital is divided between the demands made by the board of governors, the senior administrators and the medical staff.

In recent years there has been some erosion of this pattern since a number of hospitals have developed structures in which medical staff are directly employed by the hospital, often within departments specialising in particular medical issues or as a team of medical staff contracted as a group to the hospital (Kovnar 1986: 202).

Mental health hospitals

Since the 1960s there has been a move away from separate state-operated mental institutions to systems that de-institutionalise patients and provide care within the community. In addition, many general hospitals have established facilities for dealing with the mentally ill on both an institutional and an out-patient basis. Care within the community has been facilitated by the efforts of the federal government to develop a community mental health centres programme to provide both in- and out-patient care in areas of the country where mental health provision is relatively poor. The service, whilst of value, nevertheless still remains rather badly financed.

The charge of underfunding can be levelled more generally at policies designed to de-institutionalise mental health care and provide more flexible and humanitarian help. In addition, by comparison with other chronic medical conditions, those with mental health problems have poor insurance cover. Over-zealous de-institutionalisation programmes have also, as in some European countries, pushed the more destitute and isolated mentally ill on to the streets to fend for themselves in a hostile environment of run-down slums and boarding houses.

Nursing homes

In addition to services for those with acute and mental health problems, a further major sector of the health care system concerns provisions for the elderly and chronically sick. There is a wide range of nursing and other care facilities for the elderly, in general provided in privately run nursing homes which often receive some of their income through patients' own funds and also help provided through Medicare and Medicaid.

Training the service deliverers

Professional clinical training is predominantly controlled by the professions themselves which, under the protection of government legislation to ratify competence to practise, set the standards and procedures for qualification. Doctors gain their qualifications through entry to medical schools which are usually based partly in universities and associated large hospitals. The schools are accredited by the Liaison Committee on Medical Association which is jointly composed of representatives of the AMA and the Association of American Medical Colleges representing the teaching institutions themselves.

In the 1970s it became apparent that there was an oversupply of trained doctors and in recent years there have been efforts to decrease the numbers of medical students and to restrict the entry of overseas trained doctors into the United States. There are, nevertheless, areas of the United States, particularly in the poor rural south, where the ratio of doctors to inhabitants is much less favourable than in prosperous city areas. The oversupply tends to lead to growing numbers offering specialist treatments in the larger cities and their suburbs.

Other medical professions are subject to similar patterns of training. Nursing, however, emerged as a profession much later than medicine and, until the late nineteenth century, nurses were untrained and their status was no better than that of domestic workers. Starr reports an observation that in the major hospital for New York 'at night no one attended the patients except the rats that roamed the floors' (1982: 155). During the last fifty years, of course, nursing has become recognised as a crucial profession. Nurses are registered if they have successfully completed appropriate courses, which range from one- or two-year courses at the lowest grades to degree and higher degree programmes for more senior and responsible positions.

Administrative arrangements

The cultural traditions of the United States and its political structure do not lend themselves to the establishment of a comprehensive public health care system. There is, in effect, no single system of health care in the United States but many different systems, most with both a public and a private component. Moreover, exactly what standard of health care is available to the citizen and at what price varies greatly from state to state and between urban and rural areas and is also dependent on the age, wealth and employment status of the individual.

Despite this fragmentation, there is extensive public involvement in health care in the United States, so it is not surprising that all levels of government play a part.

Local level

At the lowest tier of United States government, many larger local governments, especially cities and urban counties, having been among the earlier contributors to institutionalised health care, continue to provide hospitals, often for those with mental health problems and for the poorest members of their communities. Local government also retains some responsibility for the protection of the environment from pollution, which is secured through inspection and planning regulations.

State level

State governments provide hospitals for mental health, sanatoriums for chronic diseases and are involved in the regulation of doctors, dentists, and medical institutions. One of the most important responsibilities of states is their regulatory function, which they undertake in co-operation with the powerful professions. Dentistry, general practice and most specialised medical activities are subject to control to prevent fraudulent or dangerous practice. Regulation is achieved by licensing professionals to practise through statutory agreements between the states and the professional associations of the various health occupations that have over the years come to be accepted by the states as authoritative representatives of their practices. Thus, a state government normally legislates to license, for health care practice, individuals who have passed qualifications set by the appropriate professional body such as the AMA. Unless licensed, any individual who attempts to practise medicine can be liable, under criminal law, to charges such as assault. States are, therefore, important in establishing mechanisms for regulating standards and quality in the health services.

Some responsibility for the protection of the environment from pollution also lies with the states and, to this end, inspection and planning regulations exist at this level.

In order to fulfil their functions most states establish a department of health or an equivalent agency. These offices will be administered by a secretary or equivalent post appointed by the state governor or, in some states, directly elected.

Federal level

Responsibility for health care exists not only at local and state levels but also at the federal government level where health issues are co-ordinated by the United States Department of Health and Human Services (DHHS). This was created in its present form in 1977 by dividing the Department of Health, Education and Welfare into separate departments. The Secretary of the DHHS is a member of the President's cabinet and, like all secretaries of state appointed by the President is subject to the approval of Congress. The Department is concerned not only with health matters but with other forms of social security provision.

In relation to health it has two principal divisions. First, the Public Health Service administers a number of federal health programmes and agencies. For example, serious deficiencies at local and state government level with respect to the protection of the environment from pollution led to the creation of the Environmental Protection Agency. This often controversial body has powers of intervention to control, among other things, the pollution of rivers and the dumping of toxic waste. Similarly, through the Food and Drug Administration, the federal government is also in part responsible for securing hygiene standards and regulating unsafe food and the testing of medical drugs. The prevention of infectious diseases is largely a federal responsibility through funded programmes for vaccination administered by hospitals.

Second, the Health Financing Administration is responsible for the principal structures for funding health provision to the elderly and poor (Medicaid and Medicare).

In addition to the agencies that are responsible to the DHHS there are several other federal departments with an interest in health provision: the Defence Department administers military hospitals, and the Department of Labour is concerned with occupational health issues.

The federal government sponsors a vast number of *ad hoc* agencies that have an impact on health care. These include the Veterans Administration, which operates the largest centrally controlled health system in the United States for the benefit of former military personnel.

FINANCING ARRANGEMENTS

Some of the most serious controversies in United States health care derive from problems connected with the financing arrangements. Systems for paying for health services are both inequitable and incapable of restraining increases in costs. In 1986 expenditure on health was $458 billion, but by 1991 the figure was $752 billion.

Although costs of health care have traditionally always been expected to be met largely by the consumer in relation to the use made of the service, the many governments of the United States are also a major source of funding. In 1986 55 per cent of costs were met by individual consumers and 42 per cent by governments, with the remaining 3 per cent being met by philanthropic charities. Since the 1970s there has been a gradual increase in government spending, whilst the sums donated by charities has declined (United States Bureau of the Census 1994).

The unpredictability of illness creates serious problems for United States citizens. A healthy person can expect few demands on personal income to meet medical costs but once an individual becomes seriously ill costs can be enormously expensive. The bill for even a minor operation may be several thousands of dollars and without any form of financial help, skilled medical care to alleviate a chronic long term illness can be prohibitively expensive.

For most United States citizens the costs of health care are met by some form of private medical insurance cover. There are a number of private insurance corporations competitively offering health insurance schemes tailored to suit differing needs and risks. In addition, during the 1930s depression, non-profit making insurance services, such as Blue Cross and Blue Shield, encouraged respectively by the Association of American Hospitals and the AMA, were established to supply insurance schemes for hospital and physicians' fees at a time when increasing poverty was forcing many citizens to cut back on their private insurance schemes.

The extent of cover provided by private and non-profit-making insurance varies but normally includes hospital charges and often fees for general practice services. Frequently, schemes will not cover all necessities and many patients have to meet a proportion of their health costs. The costs of insurance schemes are considerable and form a significant item in the budget of many United States families. Most individuals in salaried work, however, expect to receive, as part of their terms of employment, free or subsidised health insurance cover from their employer for themselves and their families.

The cover provided by employer-operated schemes is, however, of limited extent and leaves most of the more vulnerable elements of the population in need of help. Until the 1960s the poor unemployed usually had no health cover whilst the elderly retired population often had no recourse to comprehensive health insurance and yet are the group most likely to be in need of substantial medical help.

During the last thirty years a number of more novel systems of health insurance have been established. A scheme pioneered on the west coast of America by the Kaiser-Permanite group is based on payment by subscribers to a specific group of medical practitioners, rather than to a fund, that provides health care at any hospital. This idea was further developed under the Nixon administration to create a considerable change in traditional health care operations by the formation of Health Maintenance Organisations (HMOs). The federal government provided funds to facilitate the formation of medical groups which provided comprehensive general practice and basic hospital services, not through payment of fees for specific services but through a pre-paid system in which members of the subscribing public paid a regular fee to the HMO and received health care from the organisation when needed.

The government preferred such a scheme as it was thought that this method of pre-payment would induce doctors and health administrators to place greater reliance on preventive health and cost reduction rather than to seek expensive interventionist methods of health care that brought in high fees for dealing with specific problems. In practice, it appears that the development of HMOs has increased the tendency of United States medicine to become part of the world of big corporate business as profit-making companies with high capital are best able to establish comprehensive HMO schemes.

Subsidising the elderly and poor

The difficulties faced by the elderly and the unemployed led to the development of the Medicaid and Medicare to provide subsidised health cover for these vulnerable groups. Medicare, which became operational in 1966, provides benefits for citizens over the age of 65 who are willing to pay a much subsidised health care premium. The scheme covers payment for most, but not all, hospital and home care costs incurred by a patient, although there are time limits under which payment is received and for long illnesses a patient may find that cover is not available. For an additional payment the elderly can be covered at a much subsidised rate for the costs of general practice doctors. The Medicare scheme is a federal programme, funded by the federal government out of general taxation.

Medicaid became operational in 1967 to provide medical care to the poor who were eligible and in receipt of welfare benefits. The scheme pays in full most types of medical fees for the elderly poor; families where the parents are unemployed or unable to work due to illness; single parent families; and people with disabilities. The scheme is operated jointly by the federal and state governments with each contributing to its funding.

In effect, Medicaid was an arrangement to graft a health insurance scheme on to the previously existing social security systems for unemployment and destitution operated by each state. Eligibility for Medicaid is determined in line with the social security arrangements established by each individual state and can differ from one part of the country to another. In general, however, certain classes of individual are not covered by the scheme even if they are living below the poverty line and some of these poor individuals are not covered by any other health insurance system.

Those not covered by health insurance or the government-sponsored aid scheme must use, should a facility be available, municipal or voluntary hospitals. These provide a free health care service which, as observed earlier, is often of inferior quality to that provided by health services based on payment.

In addition to these most widely used forms of health cover a few groups can gain aid from the federal government, such as war veterans, serving members of the armed forces and certain people with problems associated with drug abuse. There is also a federal health programme available for indigenous Indian communities and schemes for compensating individuals suffering from industrial injuries or diseases.

CONTEMPORARY ISSUES IN HEALTH POLICY

Classic capitalist economics suggests that cost containment and value for money is achieved by open market competition when many rival suppliers are bidding for the custom of independent consumers. In the United

States, despite the uncontrolled competitive nature of the health care systems, there appears, as indicated above, to be a serious breakdown in this theory as the United States has far higher medical costs per person than other developed nations and yet is no more capable of delivering a comprehensive health service.

The methods of payment for health care, based largely on private, employer or government-funded health insurance schemes, has helped fuel a system that has led to spiralling health costs. Neither the health providers nor the insurers need be particularly interested in lowering these costs. Higher costs lead to better payment for doctors and other clinical staff and greater reliance on expensive equipment and surgical rather than preventive health care. Insurance companies are not unhappy at a system that entails high costs since they can ensure that employers and the government will adjust insurance payments to meet the increased payments and thus increase the overall turnover of the insurance business. Since the 1970s the entry of large corporate business interests into the supply of medical care has also increased the profit-making demands on the health system.

The absence of a medical system directly funded by either state or federal governments ensures that there are far too few means within the public sector to secure controls over health policy and the direction of health expenditure. Kronenfeld observes that

> This country does not have controls on the amount of resources going into health care, unlike most other countries in the world. No one entity controls costs, in comparison to Britain or Canada, where politicians play a role in determining funding levels for health care as for all other types of programme.
>
> (1993: 120)

The Clinton proposals for health reform

The costs of health care in the United States and inequities in its provision have for several decades fuelled strong arguments for a reform of the system to replicate European structures that appear to operate far more efficiently. President Clinton, in part, secured his election as President on a promise to comprehensively restructure health care in the United States to alleviate its many problems.

In the spring of 1994 the President, whose wife Hillary had been given the task of leading the campaign for health reforms, announced proposals to establish a system of compulsory but comprehensive health insurance.

The proposal was to create regionally based health alliances to be administered by a national health board which would be empowered to buy health
services for anyone in the population from hospitals and doctors at a price
subject to negotiation, although large businesses could also buy health
services for their employees. States would ensure that coverage of their
territories was comprehensive.

Payment for the service would be through an annual payment for the
individual or at a higher rate for a family. Those in employment would
have 80 per cent of this cost contributed by their employer and would
have to meet the remainder from their own income. Those not employed
or self-employed would have to contribute the payment themselves but,
for the poor, there would be mechanisms to ensure that the government
paid for their health care.

The structure proposed by Clinton was not dissimilar to European
models of health insurance but was, nevertheless, a radical departure from
the unsystematised structure of health provision in the United States. The
chances of the proposals becoming law are fast receding as the President's
proposals for domestic reform are meeting increasing opposition from the
Republican Party backed by medical interests such as the AMA and health
insurance companies.

Pluralism and reform

It is frequently argued that the democratic structure of the United States
political systems, based on many checks and balances to prevent arbitrary
government, has become a means to secure negative unreformist politics.
It is suggested that many necessary reforms to the United States social
system are thwarted because of the power of special interest groups which
campaign on their own behalf. Thus, the gun lobby in the United States,
based on the interests of armaments manufacturers, can muster sufficient
support among right-wing Congressmen/women to hamper the passage
of legislation through Congress to prevent the free use of lethal weapons,
despite the fact that the American public at large supports such legislation.

Similarly such interests are at work preventing the emergence of a more
cost efficient and comprehensive system of health care. There are many
routes through which wealthy vested interests such as the AMA, the insurance companies or businesses directly supplying goods and service to the
health industry can check the progress of legislation that would modernise
the United States system to provide cheaper and more equitable health
care. As wealthy groups, they pay for the services of skilled lawyers and
lobbyists to persuade legislators to support their interests. They may also

fund the political campaigns of Congressmen/women. The AMA is a major contributor to political funding (Banta 1986: 378).

The failure of the Clinton proposals for health reform will undoubtedly be regarded as evidence that the United States political system is predominantly a negative instrument, favouring the narrower interests of wealthy corporations and professions.

REFERENCES AND FURTHER READING

Banta, H. D. (1986) 'The federal legislative process and health care', in S. Jonas (ed.) *Health Care Delivery in the United States*, 3rd edn, New York: Springer.

Kovnar, A. R. (1986) 'Hospitals', in S. Jonas (ed.) *Health Care Delivery in the United States*, 3rd edn, New York: Springer.

Kronenfeld, J. J. (1993) *Controversial Issues in Health Care Policy*, Newbury Park, CA: Sage Publications.

McKinlay, J. B., McKinlay, S. M., Jennings, S. and Grant, K. (1983) 'Mortality, morbidity and the inverse care law', in A. L. Greer and S. Greer (eds) *Health Care in Urban America*, Beverley Hills: Sage Publications.

Office of Economic Co-operation and Development (1987) *Financing and Delivering Health Care*, Paris: OECD.

Paton, C. R. (1990) *US Health Politics*, Aldershot: Avebury.

Starr, P. (1982) *The Social Transformation of American Medicine*, New York: Basic Books.

Thompson, F. J. (1981) *Health Policy and the Bureaucracy*, Cambridge, MA: MIT Press.

United States Federal Government (1986) *Digest of United States Statistics*, Washington.

United States Bureau of the Census (1986, 1994) *Statistical Abstract of the United States*, Washington, DC: The Reference Press.

Chapter 8

Conclusion

Ann Wall

In the foregoing chapters, the authors have sought to provide an accessible, systematic account of how six countries organise, deliver and finance their health care systems and of the socio-political settings within which the systems operate. Implicit in this approach is the assumption that the systems differ; that these and, indeed, other countries have tackled the task of providing health care services in markedly different ways. In so far as health care systems are shaped by particular political systems, national traditions and cultural heritages and reflect the history, ideology and values of a society, this is true. One of the purposes of this chapter is to identify differences.

In order to do this, reference will be made to a simple taxonomy of health care systems, based on one devised by the OECD in 1987, which categorises systems according to their coverage, main source of funding, ownership of health care services and facilities and the status of health care. This produces three models of health care systems which are shown in Table 8.1.

The first is that described as the Beveridge or NHS model. It involves

Table 8.1 Models of health care systems

Model	Coverage	Funding	Control	Status
Beveridge	universal	taxation	public	social service
Bismarck	universal	social insurance	mixed	social right
Modified market	partial	private insurance	private	insurable risk

Source: based on OECD (1987: 24)

universal coverage, tax funding, national ownership and control of services and facilities, with the status of health care being that of a social service. Sweden fits this model as do the UK and Italy, although recent reforms in these countries have resulted in a movement away from some of the principles.

The Bismarckian model is based on compulsory, universal, social insurance, usually within the context of other social security measures. It is financed by contributions from employers and individuals through government-regulated, non-profit-making insurance funds. These funds are essentially purchasing organisations rather than providers, acting for their members by arranging contracts for services from self-employed physicians and from independent hospitals as well as publicly owned facilities. It is viewed as a way of ensuring access to care without too much government interference with the autonomy of providers, especially doctors. In this model, ownership of services and facilities may be public or private, but they are regulated by the government. In societies based on the Bismarckian model, health care has the status of a social right. The Dutch health care system has many features of the Bismarckian model. Interestingly, in the UK, the reforms in the 1980s pursued the idea of separating purchasers and providers but rejected the notion of insurance, either public or private, as a mechanism for achieving this.

The third model is the modified market or consumer sovereignty model. In this case, health is viewed as a commodity and ill health as an insurable risk. Emphasis is placed on private insurance purchased either by the individual or by the employer, and on private ownership of services and facilities. However, the 'market' is 'modified' by the government in the sense that the behaviour of service providers is controlled and direct provision is made for those who cannot provide for themselves. This model best describes the systems found in the USA and Australia.

Of course, these models are essentially 'ideal types'. In reality, no system is completely universal: most use more than one source of funding and exhibit both public and private elements of control. It is the particular balance which is struck on these characteristics in any one country which gives the system its character.

Whilst it is true that there are substantial and significant differences between the health care systems, what also becomes clear from the studies is that there is a high degree of similarity between them and that they share a number of common features which would also be found in the health care systems of other liberal democracies. Arguably, this can be accounted for by reference to the nature of health and health care in modern societies and to the pressures to which this gives rise. These pressures include an inauspicious socio-demographic context; the necessity for a high degree of state involvement in health care; escalating costs and limited options for raising the required resources; the difficulties associated with cost containment and the consequent need to ration health care and to reassess traditional approaches to service provision. A further purpose of this concluding chapter is to comment on these pressures and it is to this that attention is now turned.

SOCIO-DEMOGRAPHIC CONTEXT

In examining the context of health care in their chosen countries, each of the authors drew attention to demographic and epidemiological changes which have increased both the numbers requiring treatment and the length of time such treatment takes. In addition, social factors relating to poverty, inequality and other divisions, all of which have worsened during the last fifteen years, have added to the challenges facing governments. This is particularly the case in the USA, which is a nation starkly divided along social, religious and racial lines. In Italy, uncontrolled immigration and the lowest birth rate in Europe have made the demographic context especially pertinent.

Urbanisation, to which several authors refer, also has an impact on the nature of health need, and can give rise to social unrest. The changing role of women has had an impact on the availability of informal carers in the community, women's role in the home and their child-bearing behaviour. These changes have been particularly marked in Italy and the Netherlands.

Of equal, if not greater, significance is economic performance, which is so important a determinant of the amount of money made available for health care. The period from the end of the second world war to the mid-1970s was one of growth. Western economies performed well and expenditure on health care increased. In Chapter 3 reference was made to Italy's economic miracle in the post-war years, based on cheap unorganised labour from the south of the country. In retrospect, the period between the second world war and the late 1980s was something of a golden age, when the chief issue was how to plan and spend wisely.

The oil crisis in 1973 signalled the end of this era and the onset of a period of cost constraint. The economic implications of the crisis meant a levelling off of economic growth and consequent disquiet about public sector funding in general and the funding of large programmes, such as health care, in particular. The funding of health care in all the countries has been a much more controversial subject over the last twenty years or so.

In short, the socio-demographic environment has, at one and the same time, increased the demands made on health care systems and reduced the resources available to meet them.

THE NECESSITY FOR STATE INVOLVEMENT IN HEALTH CARE

It is clear that in all the countries considered there are powerful pressures for state regulation and control. Even in the USA and Australia, which have relied heavily on private provision, governments have played a large part in health care, controlling the activities of private providers and making considerable direct provision.

One of the main reasons for this is that individuals cannot look after all aspects of their own health. They may not have the financial means and knowledge to do so and rarely are they in a position to exercise full control over those aspects of their lives known to affect health such as where they work and live, the air they breathe and the food they eat. Moreover, it is in the interests not only of individuals themselves, but also of the community at large, to maintain the health of all its members. In other words, health care carries external benefits. Therefore, it falls to governments to attempt to ensure that all citizens have access to a reasonable standard of care. This was made explicit by the post-war Constitution in Italy, Article 32 of which stated that, 'The Republic provides health safeguards as a basic right of the individual and in the interests of the community' (as quoted on p. 61, above).

Some governments have gone further and adopted the principle of *equal* access to health care. This was one of the founding values of the British NHS in 1948 and of the Italian NHS in 1978. The principle of equity was incorporated into the Australian health care system and, in the Netherlands, social justice was a guiding principle for health care policy-makers from the inter-war years. Even in the USA, some of the current disquiet regarding the health care system centres on its inequities.

Another reason for the high level of government involvement is that many health services lack exclusivity, that is, they can be provided only for the whole population. This applies particularly to services relating to public health and environmental control. Interestingly, all the authors make the point that government involvement began in the nineteenth century in the sphere of public health. For example, Italy's first health care initiative was taken in the area of public health in 1865 and in the Netherlands and the UK it was the cholera epidemics of the 1830s and 1860s and other problems rooted in poverty and poor sanitation which prompted governments to take action.

As well as the need to secure external benefits, a further pressure for state involvement is the need to plan the use of different services and ensure that resources are allocated in an efficient way. This is because health care costs are unevenly spread. On the one hand, primary health care services are used by most people on a regular basis and they are relatively cheap. The hospital sector, on the other hand, is much more expensive and is used by a comparatively small number of people. Thus, although there are some national variations, in all cases the bulk of health care spending is on hospital services. For example, in Italy, hospitals absorb 60 per cent of resources and in the UK, 70 per cent. Moreover, most money is spent on those who are desperately ill and on those in the last stages of life. Much of the motivation for American government involvement in health care from 1974 was to restrain the growth of hospitals and achieve more efficient use of health care facilities.

A final point is that the consumer is seldom able to pay directly for health care because costs are likely to be high, and, more important, unpredictable. As Table 8.1 (p. 183) illustrates, some system of collective funding, either through taxation or insurance, has to be organised. This pertains even in the USA where 'a considerable proportion of medical expenses are met by public funds' (p. 170, above).

The most striking evidence of government involvement is the level of public expenditure on health care. Of the countries described in this book, only in the USA is the public share of expenditure below 50 per cent. Indeed, in the other countries, the public share is above 70 per cent, signalling the significant financial interest which governments have in health care.

In short, in order to promote and maintain the health of the population and to ensure that health services are accessible, efficient and adequately funded, a comparatively high level of government involvement is required. Moreover, in all the countries considered here, this involvement increased during the twentieth century, especially in the period between the second world war and the late 1980s. This trend had major implications for public expenditure.

ESCALATING COSTS AND LIMITED SOURCES OF FUNDING

As the data in Table 8.2 indicate, by and large, levels of public spending rose steadily until the 1980s.

The growth in the financial commitment of governments reflected both increased public sector involvement and an overall increase in the

Table 8.2 Public expenditure as a percentage of total health expenditure, 1960–85

	1960	1970	1975	1980	1985
Australia	48	57	73	63	72
Italy	83	86	86	81	77
Netherlands	33	84	73	75	75
Sweden	73	86	90	93	90
UK	85	87	91	90	86
USA	25	37	41	42	41

Source: based on OHE (1995)

Table 8.3 Expenditure on health care as a proportion of GDP, 1960–92

	1960	1970	1980	1987	1992
Australia	4.6	5.0	6.5	7.1	8.2
Italy	3.3	4.8	6.8	6.9	8.1
Netherlands	3.9	6.0	8.2	8.5	8.9
Sweden	4.7	7.2	9.5	9.0	7.9
UK	3.9	4.5	5.8	6.1	7.5
USA	5.2	7.4	9.2	11.2	13.0

Source: OHE (1995)

amount spent on health care. The data in Table 8.3 indicate that as national income rose, so did the proportion of GDP devoted to health care.

The rising cost of health care in part represented a response to now familiar trends such as: technological progress which has generated new and ever more expensive treatments, techniques and drugs; and to the changing demographic and epidemiological environment, discussed above.

However, this is not the full explanation. Pressure to spend more on health care also had to do with the nature of the relationship between the supply of resources for health care and demands upon them, which, in modern society, is complex. On the supply side, as Table 8.1 indicates, there is a limited number of ways in which sufficient funds for health care purposes can be raised, that is, private or social insurance and taxation. It is through these means that financial resources are made available to generate the human and technical resources necessary for the delivery of health care. However, these resources, whilst part of the supply chain, also generate demand. This is because the doctor is often the patient's agent and adviser and plays a gatekeeping role with respect to allowing access to other parts of the health care system.

All the authors made reference to these roles and to the considerable clinical freedom which doctors are able to exercise in carrying them out. This is borne out by the fact that variations in surgical intervention rates cannot be explained wholly in terms of epidemiology, but must be due also to variations in the level of supply (if you have more surgeons you will get more surgery, and vice versa) and different clinical styles. Paradoxically, the impact of resources on demand is not to meet it, but rather to stimulate it.

On the demand side, as discussed above, few people are able to pay directly for their health care, so price, the natural brake on demand in the marketplace, tends not to operate. It is need for health care and the ability and willingness of individuals to take action to make their needs known (for example, making an appointment to see a doctor) which is pertinent, and these appear to have no natural limits.

Taken together, these factors contributed to soaring health care costs in the years following the war.

In summary, governments are obliged to involve themselves in health care and to spend increasing amounts of public money. Yet the demand for resources appears insatiable. Consequently, at the most general level, the dominant, common problem facing those responsible for health care in the countries considered here is how to make health care systems less costly.

COST CONTAINMENT

The staggering rise in the cost of health care in the period between the second world war and the 1980s created alarm within governments. Added to this was a growing desire to slow or reverse the upward trend in public expenditure generally and to assert control over public spending on health, in particular. The data in Table 8.4 demonstrate that, with the exception of the USA, public expenditure as a percentage of total health expenditure was less in 1995 than it had been in 1985.

Attention is drawn in each of the chapters to the preoccupation of governments with the cost of health care. In Italy, the primary function of the National Health Fund, created as part of the reforms in 1978, was to control health spending. Similarly, Dutch governments, since the early 1980s, attempted to 'stabilise the real cost . . . of health care' (p. 87, above); and in America the costs of health care 'fuelled strong arguments for a

Table 8.4 Public expenditure as a percentage of total health expenditure, 1985 and 1995

	1985	*1995*
Australia	72	69
Italy	77	76
Netherlands	75	73
Sweden	90	88
UK	86	85
USA	41	49

Source: based on OHE (1995)

reform of the system' (p. 180). In Sweden: 'From central government's point of view there are serious difficulties associated with financing' (p. 122). Similar views were expressed in Australia and the UK. Indeed, by the 1980s the mood was, universally, one of concern over levels of spending.

Broadly, there are three possible approaches to containing costs: limiting the funding available for health care; restricting demand on those funds by controlling the activities of doctors and other service providers; and rationing. All three have been adopted in the countries examined here.

Limiting funding

With the exception of the USA, where the inability of governments to control the amount of resources going into health care has been a continuous source of frustration, all the health care systems have been subject to limitations on their funding. This has been achieved through a variety of mechanisms including the imposition of budgets such as fundholding GPs in Italy, the UK and Sweden; cash limits; building controls; wage and salary controls; attempts to hold down the price of drugs, particularly in Italy; and restricting medical technology, particularly in the Netherlands.

Controlling the activities of doctors and other service providers

In effect, the purpose of many of these budgetary measures is to control the behaviour of doctors, with respect to referral, prescribing, and other clinical activities, and this, not surprisingly, has proved to be controversial. Subjecting doctors to financial discipline and introducing financial considerations into medical practice strike at the heart of professional autonomy and are resisted on the grounds of the necessity for professional freedom to make sound clinical judgements. Such a view has considerable public support.

Moreover, such measures are often difficult to devise and implement and perverse incentives frequently operate. For example, in many systems doctors earn more if they do more, so in Australia and the USA there may be an incentive to keep people in hospital. In contrast, in the UK the incentive may well be to get people out.

Governments are further constrained in their attempts to control professional service providers by the fact that health care systems are highly dependent on them. For example, the largest item in the Italian health service budget, just under 40 per cent, is that devoted to personnel whilst in Sweden, 10 per cent of the labour force is involved in health care, demonstrating that health care is, *par excellence*, a labour-intensive service. This feature has been exacerbated by demographic and social trends which have meant increasing problems with recruiting and retaining staff. Indeed, staffing may ultimately prove a more serious problem than lack of money.

The activities of clinical service providers have been underpinned by the powerful pharmaceutical companies promoting expensive drugs and lobbying against the use of cheaper equivalents. This is of particular relevance in Italy which is one of the largest spenders per capita on pharmaceutical products in Europe. Pressure to maintain high levels of spending on drugs has added considerably to the problems of governments seeking to contain health care costs.

Nevertheless, all the governments concerned have flexed their muscles with respect to the clinical professionals and there is now some evidence that their freedom is being curtailed. Payment to doctors and other service providers is controlled and, in the UK, Italy and the Netherlands, management procedures to scrutinise professional practice and improve efficiency have been imposed. In the USA, some measure of control has been achieved by doctors being more frequently employed by the hospital in which they work rather than being self-employed. In short, clinical freedom is no longer quite the sacred cow of earlier decades.

In the context of burgeoning demand and explicit efforts on the part of government to contain costs, it is hardly surprising that investment in health care is rarely considered adequate and charges of underfunding are frequently made. In Italy, for example, the money allocated to the National Health Fund was always well below what the regions and local health authorities needed to perform their services. Similar charges have been made in Australia and in the UK.

In practice, efforts to control costs have actually meant curtailing the rate of increase rather than cutting back in real terms and, even in this sense, have met with varying degrees of success, with the USA being the least successful. Consequently, all governments have relied heavily on the third approach to cost containment, that is, rationing or inhibiting the demands made by service users.

Rationing health care

Rationing has generally been less difficult to impose because, by and large, it has operated in an informal, inexplicit way, and it is directed at service users, who are far less powerful than the medical profession. Mechanisms to inhibit demand are evident in all the countries studied. They include imposing restrictions on eligibility, delay, deterrence and deflection.

Restrictions on eligibility

Imposing restrictions on eligibility, or 'de-entitlement', is a recent feature of the British health care system. Age, residence, and lifestyle conditions have been imposed on patients seeking certain types of treatment. It was the feasibility of rationing health care in an NHS system which drew the Italian right towards such a model as the basis for reforming the Italian system in the late 1970s.

Delay

Delay is, perhaps, the main rationing mechanism used, and, waiting is a common feature of NHS systems like the UK and Sweden and also of the public part of the Australian system. The management of waiting lists has proved one of the most common and challenging problems in these countries. Historically not such a problem in social insurance systems, waiting is now increasingly common in the Dutch system. Predictably, it is virtually unknown in fee-for-service systems such as the USA.

Deterrence

Deterrence encompasses anything which puts an individual off using health services. Fear can act as a deterrent as can charging at the point of use. Such charges have been applied increasingly in Italy and the UK. Unfriendly staff, unwelcoming buildings, waiting and the anticipation of waiting can all deter potential service users.

Deflection

The final way in which demand for health care services is restricted is by deflecting the patient to the private sector or another part of the public sector. This, clearly, places pressure on other services which bear the brunt of limited resources for health care, as has been evident in the UK where some of the demand for health care, especially from those requiring long term support, has been deflected to local authority social services. In Italy the rate of hospitalisation has been reduced by improving primary health care and expanding social services so that patients, particularly psychiatric ones, can be supported in the community. Similarly, in Australia

> the social costs associated with the elderly and people with physical or mental disabilities tended to be shifted to the welfare sector, nursing homes, the voluntary sector, hostels and even prisons; and the personal costs tended to be borne by individuals and their families.
>
> (p. 44, above)

In the private sector, deflection may act as a spur. Again, in the UK, which has a long tradition of public provision of health care, the stimulation of the private sector in this way has been both visible and controversial. In Italy

> there can be no doubt that private providers have had something of a vested interest in ensuring that the public sector did not function as efficiently as it might. Patients dissatisfied with the quality of services provided by the public sector would turn to the private sector.
>
> (p. 73, above)

In the USA and Australia, however, this has been a less significant approach because of the already heavy reliance on private provision.

It is of course important to stress that, at least until recently, these devices have not been used explicitly for rationing purposes. However, as the tension between supply of resources and the demands made on them becomes more critical, there is evidence that rationing will become more explicit and formal. Some of this evidence, such as the Oregon experiment (in which the public were invited to rank various types of health care in priority order) and voluntary euthanasia legislation in the USA, has had a high international profile and been subject to intense debate.

At a less sensational level, most spending strategies now rest much more explicitly on the assumption that informed and intelligent choices have to be made about what can realistically be done, rather than taking on board responsibility for everything which is technically possible. For example, not all new therapies are equally effective and some old ones have been superseded. In Sweden, 'rational calculation' has underpinned much of the evaluation of health care since 1978. Similarly, in the Netherlands, the Dunning Report suggested four criteria which should be used to determine whether or not specific health care activities should be included in the 'package of "basic health services"' (p. 101, above).

Moreover, some patients are more likely than others to benefit from certain treatments and some groups and individuals are more vulnerable than others. Attention is, therefore, increasingly being given to finding ways of ensuring that resources are directed in an appropriate way. Ironically, this could produce a kind of political triage, sifting through casualties to determine the order of severity, and this is likely to be one of the most compelling issues in the future.

Policies designed to limit funding and restrict demand inevitably run the risk of undermining the health care systems and ultimately the health status of the communities they serve. Such charges have frequently been levelled by critics. All governments have been at pains to argue that cost containment goes hand in hand with attempts to secure more effective use of available resources. This argument has been used to justify more overt rationing devices and efficiency savings. It has also underpinned a more radical reassessment of accepted approaches to health care.

REASSESSING TRADITIONAL APPROACHES TO SERVICE PROVISION

The health care systems described in this book rest on a medical interpretation of health and illness and consequently give a high profile to hospital-based, curative therapies and professional service providers. Relatively little emphasis is placed on the promotion of health and prevention of illness. Primary health care tends to be underdeveloped even in the UK, where the GP deals with 90 per cent of all illness episodes, and most patients are referred too quickly to expensive hospitals and specialists. Significantly, the motivation for reform of the Italian health care system in the 1960s was the 'lack of an adequate system of primary health care to regulate demand for hospital care' (p. 63, above).

The steady growth in spending throughout the twentieth century reflects both the costly nature of such an approach and the assumption, albeit implicit, that more investment in services of this kind would produce commensurate improvements in health status. However, this was not necessarily the case.

Although assessment of the effects of health care interventions, in terms of treatment and advice, has been impeded by lack of information on the costs, benefits and outcomes, more systematic evaluation of the link between intervention and outcome suggests that it is, at best, variable. Health care may or may not produce health. This appears to hold true at both the individual and the societal level. At the level of the individual, whether patients recover or deteriorate may have nothing to do with the treatment they receive. At the societal level, there is little connection between how much is spent on health care and the health status of the population.

It is now widely accepted that improvements in health often stem, not from the health care system itself, but from changes taking place outside its narrow confines. In other words, doubts are cast upon the continued appropriateness of accepted approaches to health care. Such revelations are fortuitous for governments keen to spend less on health care services. They are used as part of the rationale for seeking ways to shift the emphasis away from expensive hospitals and personal health services to community-based public health strategies designed to promote health and prevent illness, which are believed to be cheaper.

Some measure of success has been achieved in this respect. The steps taken by the Italian government since the 1980s to improve primary health care and social services and thereby reduce rates of hospitalisation have generally been adjudged effective. In the USA the growth of health maintenance organisations in the 1970s, designed to give incentives to doctors to undertake more preventive work, signalled an intention to shift the emphasis.

Policies of de-institutionalisation of patients with mental health problems in America and the community care policy in the UK further testify to a change of direction. However, these strategies have been subject to considerable criticism largely on the basis that underfunding has meant that patients have been neglected in community settings.

Regardless of whether or not they are deemed to be effective, such changes are tangential; commitment to hospital-based curative services remains at the heart of health care systems. In the USA, for example, there has actually been a decline in the number of GPs over the last fifty years, with the majority of doctors now establishing themselves as specialists.

VALUES AND HEALTH CARE SYSTEMS

So far, in this chapter, the emphasis has been on those things which the countries have in common:

Table 8.5 Per capita health spending (public and private combined) (£)

Australia	Italy	Netherlands	Sweden	UK	USA
800	1,150	1,100	1,300	750	1,800

Source: OHE (1995)

- demographic, epidemiological, social and economic trends;
- pressures for state involvement;
- escalating costs and limited sources of funding;
- difficulties associated with cost containment and rationing; and
- moves to radically reassess medically oriented approaches to health care.

It is tempting to stress the similarities and to explain the actions of governments as a result of circumstances over which they have little or no control. To do this, however, is to lose sight of the point at which this chapter started: that there are certain very important differences between the systems. For example, there can be little doubt that all the health care systems have absorbed increasing amounts of money in the years since the second world war. However, variations in the level of funding remain to be explained. As the data in Table 8.5 indicate, measured in per capita terms, in 1995 spending ranged from £1,800 in the USA to £750 in the UK.

Although such comparisons have to be treated with caution because of variations in the accuracy of national reporting, comprehensiveness and comparability of the underlying data, and vagaries of international exchange rates, they draw attention to significant differences in spending levels. Similar variations are apparent when health expenditure is measured against GDP, as the data in Table 8.4 indicate. In other words, the *trends* are similar in all the countries but the differences in *levels* of expenditure are quite significant.

As well as variations in the amount spent, other differences relate to the way in which funds are generated and the manner in which different governments have responded to the need to control costs and ration health care.

In making decisions in these areas, those responsible do so within a broad, often implicit frame of values which determines the content and tenor of such decisions. Indeed, the substance of the decisions reveals as much about the ideology and moral stance of those concerned as it does about their expertise in health care matters; and as much about the history and cultural traditions of the societies, as it does about the practical problems involved in providing health care in a modern society.

In discussing cultural traditions and the governmental and political settings, authors highlighted those aspects of their countries which are most pertinent, and it is here that the key differences may be identified. In examining these differences, reference will be made to the taxonomy of health care systems discussed earlier (Table 8.1). By focusing on differences in coverage, funding, control and status of health care, the taxonomy demonstrates that there are distinct standpoints on a number of central matters and that contrasting sets of values underpin the decisions taken on these matters.

The NHS model, based on universal coverage, tax funding, public control and health care as a social service, implies that principles such as equality, social justice, effectiveness and citizenship have a high profile. The UK NHS, created in the post-war climate of euphoria and designed to slay the Beveridgian giant of sickness, was founded explicitly on such principles (p. 140, above). It is the threat to these principles, which recent reforms represent, that has generated such controversy in the UK. 'It is clear that the period of New Right government broke with the post-war social democratic consensus and raised debate to white heat level' (p. 160).

By contrast, Sweden, held up as an example of what a welfare state could and should look like (see p. 104), remains committed to social democratic values despite having to trim social expenditure in the 1980s.

The Bismarckian model with its universal coverage, social insurance funding, mixture of public and private control and notion of health as a social right, rests on an assumption that ill health is a personal risk with public implications and, therefore, requires a strong governmental hand.

Italy's health care system corresponded to the Bismarckian model from the period between the two world wars until 1978. Spence argues that such an approach fitted the Italian political culture which had been shaped by lack of trust in political institutions and a fear of Fascism with a consequent desire to limit the authority of the state and promote a strong voluntary sector. Many voluntary bodies were religious in nature and the role of the Church in this respect was to delay welfare legislation. Reforms to the system in 1978 centralised power and changed the way in which services were funded. This represented a decisive move in the direction of the NHS model. However, both supporters and critics agree that the Italian NHS has fallen short of the ideal and the system is, once again, in a state of flux. Such failure can be attributed to a tradition of administrative inefficiency and corruption and to the fragmented (communal) political system.

The essentially Bismarckian health care system in the Netherlands is founded on the values of private initiative, independence, self-help and a respect for the autonomy of the agencies and professions involved in the health care system (pp. 78–9, above). These have pushed in the direction of self-regulation by the agencies and independent contractor status for the doctors, rather than control by the state. At the same time, a cautious side to the Dutch nature has ensured that change in the health care system has been incremental. Moreover, a strong sense of obligation has generated acceptance of responsibility on the part of individuals to pay for health care. Thus obligation for, rather than rights to, health care, has taken centre stage in the Netherlands.

These values have been tempered by a commitment to social justice and a sense of solidarity and mutual dependence which have ensured a strong role for the Dutch government in securing adequate health care for the whole population (pp. 78–80, above). Thus, although essentially Bismarckian, the funding incorporates elements of private insurance and taxation as well as social insurance (see p. 94, above). The Netherlands might be best seen as a reluctant Bismarckian, in which private insurers have been obliged to behave in a socially acceptable way and no one is denied access to health care on the grounds of poverty.

The modified market model views health as a commodity to be purchased in the form and to the extent that the individual chooses; and ill health as an insurable risk. Commercial values are afforded a high priority in systems based on this model; that is, markets are more efficient than bureaucracies; offer more choice to users; and facilitate competition which will encourage a plurality of providers.

The USA is, *par excellence*, a free enterprise culture founded on individualist liberalism and a belief in 'as little government as possible' (p. 166, above). There is a powerful democratic tradition in America with a strong concept of subsidiarity and dispersal of power. This value framework has coloured the American approach to health care and has given rise to a situation in which there is no single health care system; the private sector plays a large part; clinicians operate as self-employed independent entrepreneurs; and rationing decisions tend to be made by reference to referenda and legislation. Most citizens either take out private health insurance cover or are so covered as part of their terms of employment yet still have to meet a proportion of their health care costs themselves. In other words, health care in the USA fits squarely in the modified market model.

By contrast, Australia, although a modified market system, with a heavy reliance on private sector insurance funding, has a far greater degree of public control and universal coverage than the USA. This reflects Australia's somewhat paradoxical cultural traditions in which a strong individualist underpinning is tempered by a commitment to the values of equity, access, equality and participation (pp. 17–18).

In summary, the ideological framework in which health care decisions are made affects substantially the nature of the decisions and, in effect, the type of health care system that exists. All the health care systems discussed here are in a state of flux, either just having been or about to be reformed. It would appear that whatever the approach adopted and value system embraced, there is no one right way to provide health care services in a modern complex society.

REFERENCES AND FURTHER READING

Economist (1988) 'Sick Health Services. Europeans seek the right treatment', *Economist*, 16 July.

Ginsberg, N. (1991) *Divisions of Welfare: A Critical Introduction to Comparative Social Policy*, London: Sage Publications.

Heidenheimer, A. J., Heclo, H. and Teich Adams, C. (1990) *Comparative Public Policy: The Politics of Social Choice in America, Europe and Japan*, 3rd edn, New York: St Martin's Press.

Mishra, R. (1990) *The Welfare State in Capitalist Society: Policies of Retrenchment and Maintenance in Europe, North America and Australia*, New York: Harvester Wheatsheaf.

OECD (1987) *Financing and Delivering Health Care. A Comparative Analysis of OECD Countries*, Paris: OECD.

OECD (1992) *The Reform of Health Care: A Comparative Analysis of Seven OECD Countries*, Paris: OECD.

OHE (1995) *Compendium of Health Statistics*, 9th edn, London: Office of Health Economics.

Raffel, M. W. (ed.) (1984) *Comparative Health Systems: Descriptive Analyses of Fourteen National Health Systems*, University Park and London: Pennsylvania State University Press.

Index

Note: Since each country is largely covered within a particular chapter of the text, index entries under countries are mainly restricted to institutions, acts of parliament, official bodies, etc. Alphabetical arrangement is word-by-word.

aboriginal population 14, 16–17, 18
accountability
  weakness: Italy 66–7; UK 144, 148, 154–5
administration and management 7–9
  Australia 32–8
  Italy 65–9; reform 62–4, 71–4
  Netherlands 91–3
  Sweden 112–13, 115–18
  UK 140–2; New Right reforms 144–51, 155–6; reforms (pre-1979) 142–4
  USA 173, 175–7; reform 180–1
  see also maladministration
advisory bodies
  Netherlands 83–4, 85, 93–4
  UK 143
ageing population
  Australia 14
  implications 3
  Italy 47, 49
  Netherlands 77
  Sweden 105, 126
  UK 128–9
AIDS 16, 105–6
Australia
  Australian Assistance Plan 25, 26
  Australian Medical Association 22
  Community Health Programme 25–6

Department of Health Housing and Community Services 35–7
Department of Veterans' Affairs Repatriation Commission 38
health care development 24–6
health care funding 26, 38–43, 198–9
Health Insurance Commission 38
health service delivery and administration 27–38
Institute of Health and Welfare 37
Labour government 25–6
Labour Party 21, 23
Liberal government 25
Medibank 25, 26
Medicare 35, 38–9, 41
National Health and Medical Research Council 37
see also under specific topics

Berlusconi, Silvio 48
Bevan, Aneurin 141, 154
Beveridge (NHS) model 183–4, 197
biomedical health care model 4, 44, 194
birth rates
  Australia 13
  Italy 49
  UK 128, 129
Bismarckian model 183, 184, 197–8

capitalism 160, 165

Castle, Barbara 158
central government
    health care responsibilities: Australia
        25–6, 31, 33–8; Italy 67–8;
        Netherlands 92–4; Sweden
        116–18; UK 142, 146, 156, 159;
        USA 170, 176–7
    USA: role 167–9
centralisation
    Italy 58
    UK 142, 156
child health care
    Netherlands 83
    UK 139, 140
Church
    cross societies 89–90, 98
    health and welfare role: Italy 53;
        Netherlands 89–90; Sweden 110;
        USA 170–1
class structure see social
Clinton, Bill
    health reforms 163, 169, 180–2
coalition government
    Italy 48, 57, 63
    Netherlands 80–1
    Sweden 104, 107–8
collectivism 4, 111, 134 186, 197
communal government (Italy) 57–8
    health care responsibilities 59, 65–6
community care
    UK 149–50, 155, 160, 195
    USA 173–4
community health care
    UK 139–40, 141, 149–50
community health councils (UK) 144
competition
    health care based on: USA 179–80,
        198
    in hospital service: Italy 72; UK
        148–9
    proposals for: Netherlands 100–1
    resource allocation through: UK
        147–9, 156
    see also market
competitive tendering 146
consensus politics 134
consociationalism 81
constitution
    Italy 56, 57, 61

Sweden 106
    UK 132–3
    USA 167
corporatism
    Australia 21
    Netherlands 81
    Sweden 106
    UK 133–4, 143, 160
corruption
    Italy 47–8, 52, 56–7, 67
costs, health care
    control 185–6, 189–94; Australia 43;
        Italy 47, 70–1, 189; Netherlands
        86, 87; UK 146, 152–3
    increase 47, 157, 180, 187–9
    Italy 47
    Netherlands 85, 88, 189
    Sweden 121, 190
    UK 157, 187
    uneven spread 187
    USA 177–8, 180, 187, 189–90, 192
    see also health expenditure
cross societies 89–90, 98
cultural traditions 4–5, 197–9
    Australia 17–18, 199
    Italy 51–3
    Netherlands 78–9
    Sweden 105–6
    UK 130–1
    USA 165

death, causes of 3
    Australia 15–16
    Italy 50–1
    Netherlands 78
    USA 164
death rates
    Italy 55
    see also infant mortality
democracy
    lack of: Italy 66–7; UK 144, 145, 148,
        154–5; see also corruption
    tradition of: Australia 20–1
demographic structure 2–3, 185
    Aboriginal population 14
    Australia 12–14
    Italy 49–50
    Netherlands 77
    Sweden 105

UK 127–9
USA 163–4
dental care
  Australia 26
  Sweden 120
dependency ratio 2–3
  Australia 14
  Netherlands 77
  Sweden 122
  UK 129
disabled population, care of
  Australia 44
diseases *see* death, causes of;
  epidemiological trends
doctors
  Australia 22, 45
  clinical freedom 45, 91, 155–6, 189,
    191
  financial constraints on 190–1
  health policy role and power 22, 141,
    143–4, 155, 159, 160
  Netherlands 82–3, 84, 91, 92, 98
  payment: Australia 41, 42;
    Netherlands 95, 98; Sweden 119;
    UK 138, 149, 150, 153; USA 172,
    173
  regulation 82–3, 84, 175–6
  Sweden 115
  training 27, 82–3, 115, 174
  UK 141, 143–4, 155, 159, 160
  USA 170, 172, 173, 174, 175–6,
    195
  see also general practitioners; hospital
    doctors

economic growth 185
  Australia 16, 21, 23
  health impact 6, 16
  Italy 58–9, 185
  Netherlands 81
  social costs 21
  Sweden 108–9
  UK 134–5
economic recession 185
  Sweden 104
  UK 135
  USA 168–9
education
  and health: Italy 55–6

  see also health education
elderly, care of 193
  Australia 44
  costs and funding 44, 128–9, 179
  Italy 71
  Sweden 124, 125–6
  USA 174, 179
electoral system, British 133
elitism 130–1, 133
employees
  health care services: Sweden 112
  health insurance: Italy 60, 62;
    Netherlands 97; USA 178
  see also unemployment
epidemiological transition 3
epidemiological trends 3, 185
  Australia 15–17
  Italy 50–1
  Netherlands 77–8
  Sweden 105, 123
  UK 129–30
  USA 164–5
equality 106
  see also inequality

family
  health care role: Sweden 126; UK
    135–6, 160
  health measures centred on: Italy 61
  importance: Italy 53
federal government (USA) 167–9
  health care responsibilities 170,
    176–7
fees and charges
  Australia 41–3
  Italy 70–1
  Netherlands 95, 98
  Sweden 119–20
  UK 138
  USA 172
fertility rates
  Australia 13, 14
  Sweden 105
Fraser, Malcolm 26
funding 9–10, 183–4, 185–6
  Australia 26, 38–43, 198–9
  ideological influences on 195–9
  insufficient 191
  Italy 69–72, 191, 197

limitations on 190
Netherlands 85–6, 87, 94–9, 199
through public expenditure *see*
    public expenditure
Sweden 109, 118–20, 122, 125, 197
UK 142, 151–4, 156, 157–8
USA 176–80, 198; hospitals 171,
    172, 173–4; reform proposals
    180–1
see also costs; fees and charges; health
    expenditure; health insurance;
    taxation

gender, health and *see under* women
general practitioners
    Australia 27, 28, 41
    Italy 64, 72
    Netherlands 89, 98
    payment 41, 98, 119, 138, 149, 153,
        157
    Sweden 112, 119, 124
    UK 138–9, 141, 149, 153, 157
    see also hospital doctors
government
    advisory bodies: Netherlands 83–4,
        85, 92–4; UK 143
    fragility: Italy 48
    health care agencies and
        departments: Australia 33, 34,
        35–8; Italy 67, *68*, 69, 70; Sweden
        116–18, 122–3, 124; UK 146, 159;
        USA 176–7; *see also under specific
        countries*
    health care role, development of 5;
        Australia 24–6; Italy 59–64; need
        for 186–7; Netherlands 82–8;
        Sweden 109–11; UK 137–44;
        USA 169–71
    health insurance for employees:
        Netherlands 97
    minimal: USA 166
    organisational structure: Australia
        19–20; Italy 57–8; Netherlands
        80–1; Sweden 106–7; UK 133;
        USA 167–8
    regulatory role *see* regulation
    Sweden: changes 104
    see also central government;
        health policy; local government;
    policy-making; regional
        government; state government
Griffiths, Sir Roy 145–6, 149, 156
guilds, welfare through 110

Hawke, Bob 21, 26
health
    external benefits 186
    improvements 1; health care not
        closely linked to 44, 195
    indicators *see* epidemiological trends;
        infant mortality; life expectancy
    inequalities: Sweden 123; UK
        159–60; USA 165–6
    medical interpretation 43–4, 194
    socio-economic factors affecting 5,
        6; Italy 54–5; Sweden 106; UK
        159–60
health authorities
    Australia 24, 32–3, 34
    Italy 64, 65, 66–8; administrative
        reform 71–3; democracy 66–8;
        financing 70; maladministration
        and corruption 48, 67, 73
    Sweden 112–13
    UK 142–3, 144; funding 152–3; and
        GPs 149; hospital independence
        from 148–9; local diversity 151;
        patronage 155; post-1979 reforms
        145, 147–8, 154
    see also hospital authorities
health care
    accessibility 5, 11, 166, 186
    biomedical model 4, 44
    as circular process 8
    comparative literature on xii
    costs *see* costs
    demand for: reduction 45, 192–4
    demand/supply imbalance 1, 188–9;
        Australia 43, 45; Sweden 108–9;
        UK 157; *see also* costs
    development: Australia 24–6; factors
        affecting 7; Italy 59–64;
        Netherlands 78–9, 82–8; Sweden
        109–11; UK 137–44; USA
        169–71
    eligibility restrictions 192
    expenditure *see* health expenditure
    fees and charges *see* fees and charges

financing *see* funding
free: Australia 42; USA 179
inequality: UK 159–60; USA 166
narrow definition 43–4
organisation and administration *see*
    administration and management;
    organisational structure
problems and conflicts 1, 10–11,
    187–94; Australia 43–5; Italy
    71–4; Netherlands 99–102;
    Sweden 122–6; UK 154–61;
    USA 179–82
quality: Netherlands 76, 80
rationing 192–4; Australia 45;
    Netherlands 101–2, 194; *see also*
    costs; resource allocation
service delivery *see* organisational
    structure
workforce 31–2, 67, 82, 91, 92,
    114–15, 191
health care providers *see* doctors; nurses
health care systems
models 183–4
ideological framework 196–9
similarities 184–5
health education
Australia 44
Netherlands 89
UK 159
health expenditure
Australia 23–4, 38, 188, 190, 196
control 189–94; Australia 43; Italy
    47, 70–1; Netherlands 86, 87; UK
    149, 152
ideological framework 196–9
increase 157–8, 187–8, 189–90
Italy 47, 69, 70–1, 188, 190, 196
Netherlands 82, 86, 87, 88, 188, 190,
    196
planning 87, 151–3
public *see* public expenditure
Sweden 109, 120–1, 196
UK 149, 151–3, 157–8, 196
uneven distribution 187
USA 163, 169, 170, 177, 188, 190,
    196
see also costs; funding
health inspectors
Netherlands 83, 92–3

health insurance 10
Australia 25, 26, 38–40, 41
under Bismarckian model 184
Italy 60, 61–2, 72
Netherlands 79, 84–6, 94, 95–9;
    reform proposals 100–1
private *see* private health insurance
Sweden 118–19
UK 138–9, 150, 158
USA 171, 177–9, 180; reform
    180–1
health policy
Australia 17–18, 20, 21, 22, 25–6
Netherlands 86–8
Sweden 116, 123–6
see also policy-making
health service ownership 183–4
home care services
Sweden 112
hospital authorities
UK 141, 142
hospital beds
Sweden 109, 113, 114; for long-stay
    elderly 125, 126
hospital doctors
Australia 29, 30, 42
Netherlands 98
payment 42, 98, 153, 173
UK 136, 150, 153
USA 173
hospital service
Australia 28–31, 33, 35
funding and charges 40, 41; Australia
    40, 41; Netherlands 86, 87, 94–5,
    98–9; Sweden 119–20; UK 157;
    USA 171, 172, 173–4, 187
Italy 64–5, 187; reform 62–3, 72–3
Netherlands 90–1; funding and costs
    86, 87, 94–6, 98–9; planning 93
private *see* private hospitals
proportion of health expenditure on
    187
psychiatric *see* psychiatric hospitals
Sweden 112–14; development 110;
    fees and charges 119–20; reform
    proposals 124–5; waiting lists 122,
    124
UK: administration and
    management 142–3, 144, 145–6;

evolution 137–8; private patients
158; self-governing trust status
148–9, 154; underfunding 157
USA: development 170–1; funding
171, 172, 173–4, 187;
organisational structure 172–3
hospitalisation
duration: Sweden 113, 114
rate 194; Italy 65, 193, 195

ideology *see* New Right; values
illness
prevention *see* preventive health
programmes; public health
responses to: and culture 4
immigration
Australia 13
Italy 49
USA 163–4, 165, 166
income
health expenditure as proportion of:
Australia 41–2
health insurance premiums based on:
Netherlands 79, 96
medical personnel *see under* doctors
income distribution 6
incrementalism 78–9, 101
individualism 4
Australia 17
Italy 52, 53
USA 165
industrialisation
Sweden 109–10
inequality
Australia 18–19
and health 6, 185
health and health care: Sweden 123;
UK 159–60; USA 165–6, 186
UK 132
USA 164, 165–6, 185
infant mortality
Australia 15, 16
Italy 50
Netherlands 77, 78
Sweden 105
USA 164
insurance *see* health insurance
interest groups
Australia 22

Netherlands 93, 94
UK 127, 133–4, 136, 140–1, 143–4,
160
USA 181–2
Italy
Christian Democratic Party 48, 53,
57, 62
Communist Party 57
D'Aragona Commission 61, 186
Fascist regime 60–1
Fondo Sanitario Nazionale 70
Forza Italia 48
health care development 59–64
health care funding 69–72 191, 197
Health Service Act (1978) 64, 67
health service delivery and
administration 64–9
Higher Institute for Health and
Safety at Work 68
Istituto Nazionale per l'Asicurazione
contro Malattie 60–1
Istituto Superiore di Sanita 68
Ministry of Health 68
National Health Council 68
National Health Plan 67–8, 70
National Health Service: creation 57,
63, 65–6, 197; maladministration
and corruption 47–8
Opera Nazionale Maternita ed
Infanzie 61

Keynesianism 134, 135

labour market
Italy 58–9; and birth rate 49–50
legislation
Italy 59, 62–3, 64, 67
Netherlands 82–3, 84–6
Sweden 111, 116
UK 137, 138, 139–40
USA 168, 171
*see also specific Acts, etc. under individual
countries*
life expectancy
Australia 15, 16
and income distribution 6
Italy 47, 49, 54–5
Netherlands 77, 78
Sweden 105

USA 164
see also infant mortality
lifestyle, health and 4, 44
  Italy 55
  Sweden 105, 123
  UK 159
local government
  Australia 20
  health care responsibilities: Australia
    32; Italy 59, 65–6; Netherlands
    88–9; Sweden 107, 110–11, 113,
    115–16, 125–6; UK 137, 139–40,
    141, 149, 155; USA 170, 175
  Italy 57–8
  Netherlands 81
  Sweden 106–7; taxes 118, *119*

maladministration
  Italy 47–8, 67, 73
managerialism
  UK 145–6, 155–6
market
  health care based on 184, 198–9;
    Italy 74; Swedish proposals 124–5;
    UK 147–51, 156
  see also competition; private hospitals;
    private patients, *etc.*
medical profession *see* doctors; nurses;
    professional associations
Medicare
  Australia 35, 38–9, 41
  USA 170, 171, 179
mental health
  Netherlands 77
mental health care
  Australia 30
  Italy 65
  Netherlands 91
  Sweden 113, 121
  USA 171, 173–4, 195
  see also psychiatric hospitals
midwives
  Netherlands 90
migration
  Australia 13
  Italy 54
  see also immigration
modified market model 183, 184,
  198–9

NHS model 183–4, 197
National Health Service *see under* Italy;
    United Kingdom
Netherlands
  Central Agency for Health Care
    Tariffs 95
  Central Council for Public Health
    85
  cross societies 89–90, 98
  Dekker and Dunning commissions
    87–8, 99–102, 194
  Exceptional Medical Expenses
    (Compensation) Act (1968) 86,
    98
  Health Acts 83, 85
  health care development 78–9, 82–8
  health care funding 85–6, 87, 94–9,
    199
  Health Council 83–4, 85, 93
  Health Insurance Act (1966) 96
  Health Minister: bodies advising
    92–5
  Health Ministry 81, 87, 92
  health service delivery and
    administration 88–95
  Hospital Tariffs Act (1965) 86
  Hospitals Council 93
  National Advisory Council for
    Public Health 93
  provincial health councils 91–2
  Public Health Supervisory Service
    92–3
  sickness funds 84–5, 94–6
  Sickness Funds Act (1964) 85–6
  Sickness Funds Decree (1941) 84–5
  Sickness (Health Insurance) Fund
    Council 94
  Sickness Insurance Act (1930) 84
New Right
  Australia 21
  UK 131, 135; NHS reforms 144–51,
    154–8, 160
Northern Ireland, health reform in 143
nurses
  Australia 22, 31–2
  Netherlands 92
  Sweden 114–15
  training 22, 174–5
  USA 174–5

nursing homes
  Australia 30, 41
  Italy 71
  USA 174

occupation, health and
  Italy 55–6
ombudsman system
  Sweden 108
  UK 155
organisational structure 7–9
  Australia 27–32
  Italy 64–5
  Netherlands 88–93
  Sweden 112–13
  UK 142–3, 144–51, 159
  USA 172–4
  see also administration and
    management

parliament
  Australia 19–20
  Netherlands 80
  Sweden 106, 107
  USA 167–8
participation, democratic
  Sweden 108
partitocrazia 56, 66–7
patients
  fees and charges see fees and
    charges
  high expectations: Netherlands 80
  private see private patients
  rights see rights
patronage
  UK 155
  see also corruption
pharmaceutical costs
  Italy 70–1, 191
pharmacists
  payment: UK 153
pillarisation 80
pluralism 167
policy-making 5–6
  Australia 20, 21–2
  coalition government: Italy 57
  financial constraints 9–10
  interest-group involvement:
    Australia 22; Netherlands 93–4;
  UK 127, 133–4, 136, 140–1,
    143–4, 160; USA 181–2
  Netherlands 81, 87, 92–5, 101
  Sweden 106
  see also health policy
political parties
  Australia 21
  Italy 53; coalitions 48; corruption
    47–8; power 56–7, 62, 66–8
  Netherlands 80
  Sweden 106, 107
  UK 133
  USA 168
  see also particular parties under
    individual countries
political structure 5–6
  Australia 19–22
  Italy 56–8, 197
  Netherlands 80–1
  Sweden 106–8
  UK 132–4, 160
  USA 166–9
politicians, corrupt
  Italy 48, 56–7
population
  density: Netherlands 77
  elderly see ageing population; elderly,
    care of
  distribution 3; Australia 12
  growth: Australia 12–13; Italy 54;
    UK 128; USA 163
  structure see demographic structure
poverty
  and health: UK 129–30, 140
  and health care: USA 166, 179
  increase: Australia 18
  see also inequality
pressure groups see interest groups
preventive health programmes
  Australia 44
  insufficient emphasis on 194
  Sweden 112
  UK 139, 159
  USA 178, 195
  see also public health
primary health care
  Australia 27–8
  Italy 64, 195
  Netherlands 88–90

Sweden 112
UK 138–40, 141
underdeveloped 194
USA 172
see also general practitioners
private health insurance 184
    Australia 39–40
    Netherlands 96–7
    UK 150
    USA 171, 177–8, 180
private hospitals
    Australia 29, 30, 33, 41, 42
    Italy 65, 72–4
    Netherlands 99
    UK 150
    USA 171
private patients
    Australia 29, 30, 41
    UK 136–7, 158, 193
private sector, health care based on
    Netherlands 76
    USA 163
privatisation 193
    UK 146, 150, 158
professional associations
    Australia 22
    UK 139, 155
    USA 170, 174, 176, 181, 182
provincial government (Italy) 58
    health care responsibilities 59
psychiatric hospitals
    Italy 65
    Sweden 113
    USA 171
    see also mental health care
public debt, Italian 47
public expenditure
    health care funding through 187–8,
        189, 190, 198; Australia 23–4, 26,
        38, 40–1, 42; Italy 69–71;
        Netherlands 87, 95–6, 98; Sweden
        109, 118–19, 120; UK 142, 151–4,
        157–8; USA 171, 172, 176, 177,
        178–9
    on welfare *see* welfare state
public health
    Australia 24
    Italy 59, 186
    need for government action 186

Netherlands 83, 88–9, 92–3, 186
Sweden 112
UK 137, 186
USA 164–5, 170, 176
public hospitals
    Australia 28–9, 30
    Italy 65, 72, 72–4

race
    and life expectancy: USA 164
racism
    UK 132
redistribution, belief in
    Italy 52
regional government (Italy)
    health care responsibilities 62–3, 68,
        71–2
regulation
    Australia 30
    Netherlands 76, 78, 82–3, 198
    USA 163, 175–6
religion
    Italy 53
    UK 132
    see also Church
repatriation hospitals 29, 35
resource allocation 187
    Sweden 123, 194
    UK 146, 147–9; through internal
        market 147–9, 156
responsibilities, Dutch emphasis on 79
rights
    to health care: Italy 61, 186
    lack of: UK 133
    and obligations: Netherlands 79, 198
    patients 116, 124, 155; Sweden 116,
        124; UK 155
    USA 167
Roosevelt, Franklin D. 169

sanitation reforms
    UK 137
Scotland, health reforms in 143, 145
second world war
    and community health care: UK
        139–40
    health debate during: UK 140
    and hospital administration: UK 138
secondary care *see* hospitals

self–regulation 78
separation of powers 167
sexism 132
sickness funds 84–5, 85–6, 96
social class
    and health: Italy 54–5; Sweden 106;
        UK 159–60
    importance: UK 130, 131
social insurance
    Italy 59–61
    see also health insurance
social policy
    Australia 17
social services, heath care demand
        deflected to 193
social structure 5, 185
    Australia 18–19
    Italy 54–6
    Netherlands 80
    Sweden 106
    UK 131–2
    USA 165–6
socialism, economic growth and 134
standard of living
    Australia 18
    Sweden 106
    USA 165
state see government
state government
    health care responsibilities: Australia
        32–3, 40–1; USA 175–6
    USA: role 167
subcultures, Italy characterised by 52
subsidiarity concept 166
suicide
    Australia 15–16
    Italy 55
Sweden
    health care development 109–11
    health care funding 109, 118–20,
        122, 125, 197
    Health and Medical Services Act
        (1983) 116, 123
    Health Ministry 116–17, 124
    health service delivery and
        administration 112–18
    National Board of Health and
        Welfare 117, 122, 123
    ombudsmen 108

Social Democratic Party 106, 107,
    111
Social Services Act (1982) 111
Swedish Planning and
    Rationalisation Institute of Health
    and Social Services 117
welfare state 104, 107, 108–11, 197

tangentopoli see corruption
taxation
    Australia 17
    health care funding through 10;
        Australia 38, 39, 40–1; Italy 70;
        Netherlands 95–6, 98, 102;
        Sweden 118, 119; UK 151, 158
    Italy: centralisation 58; inequality
        52–3
    Sweden: high level accepted 109
technological developments
    and health: Australia 16
Thatcher, Margaret 131, 134, 144, 150,
    153–4
toleration 79
trust, lack of 52, 53

underclass 131–2
unemployment
    Australia 23
    and health care: USA 179
    and suicide: Italy 55
    UK 132
United Kingdom
    Beveridge Report 140
    British Medical Association 139, 155
    Care in the Community policy
        149–50, 155, 160
    Conservative government: welfare
        state cuts 135, 144, 160
    Conservative Party 131, 133
    empire 130, 131
    health care development 137–44
    health care funding 142, 151–4, 156,
        157–8
    Health Education
        Council/Authority 159
    health service delivery and
        administration 141–51
    Health Services Supervisory Board
        146

Labour Party 131, 133, 135
Merrison Report 158
NHS Management Executive 146
National Health Service: alternatives
    to 135–7, 158; consensus on 134,
    197; creation 140–1; democratic
    weakness 154–5; as model for
    Italian reform 63; politicisation
    127, 135, 160–1; reforms (post-
    1979/New Right) 144–51,
    155–6, 160; reforms (pre-1979)
    142–4; *see also under specific aspects,*
    e.g. administration
National Insurance Act (1911) 148
Resources Allocation Working Party
    152–3
unity 130–1
United States
    American Medical Association 170,
        174, 176, 181, 182
    Bill of Rights 167
    Congress 167–8
    Department of Health and Human
        Services 176
    Environmental Protection Agency
        176
    Food and Drug Administration 176
    fragmented health care system 175
    health care development 169–71
    health care funding 171, 172, 173–4,
        176–80, 180–1, 198
    Health Financing Administration
        176
    health maintenance organisations
        178, 195
    health service delivery and
        administration 172–7; reform
        proposals 163, 180–2
    Hospital Corporation of America
        171
    Medicaid 170, 171, 179
    Medicare 170, 171, 179
    National Health Planning and
        Resources Development Act
        (1974) 171
    New Deal 169
    president: role and power 167, 168

Public Health Service 176
Supreme Court 167
urbanisation 185
    Australia 13
    Italy 54
    Netherlands 80

vaccination
    Netherlands 83
    UK 139, 140
values
    Australia 17
    and funding 4–5, 9, 11, 195–9
    Netherlands 76, 78–9, 198
    Sweden 111, 197
    UK 127
    USA 165, 166, 198
    see also particular values
voluntary organisations
    Australia 24–5
    Italy 53, 64, 197
    UK 136, 137–8, 150
    USA 170–1

waiting lists 192
    Sweden 122, 124
Wales, health reforms in 143
welfare
    Italy: beliefs about 52; Church
        role 53; dissatisfaction with
        54
welfare benefits
    Sweden 118–19
    USA: Medicaid linked to 179
welfare state
    Sweden: development 109–11;
        exemplary 104, 107, 197;
        financial constraints 108–9
    UK: cuts 135, 144, 160
Whitlam, Gough 25, 26
women
    changing role 185; Italy 53
    employment: Italy 59
    health: UK 140
    health care role: UK 136, 160
working class
    Australia 20–1